Key Terms in Semantics

Key Terms series

The *Key Terms* series offers undergraduate students clear, concise and accessible introductions to core topics. Each book includes a comprehensive overview of the key terms, concepts, thinkers and texts in the area covered and ends with a guide to further resources.

Titles available in the series:
Key Terms in Linguistics
Howard Jackson

Key Terms in Pragmatics
Nicholas Allott

Key Terms in Second Language Acquisition
Bill VanPatten and Alessandro G. Benati

Key Terms in Semiotics
Bronwen Martin and Felizitas Ringham

Key Terms in Syntax and Syntactic Theory
Silvia Luraghi and Claudia Parodi

Key Terms in Systemic Functional Linguistics
Christian M.I.M. Matthiessen, Kazuhiro Teruya and Marvin Lam

Key Terms in Translation Studies
Giuseppe Palumbo

Forthcoming titles:

Key Terms in Discourse Analysis
Paul Baker and Sibonile Ellece

Key Terms in Stylistics
Nina Nørgaard, Rocío Montoro and Beatrix Busse

Key Terms in Semantics

M. Lynne Murphy and Anu Koskela

continuum

Continuum International Publishing Group

The Tower Building   80 Maiden Lane

11 York Road   Suite 704

London SE1 7NX   New York, NY 10038

© M. Lynne Murphy and Anu Koskela 2010

British Library Cataloguing-in-Publication Data

A catalogue record for this book is available from the British Library.

ISBN: 978-1-8470-6276-5 (hardback)
      978-1-8470-6277-2 (paperback)

Library of Congress Cataloging-in-Publication Data

A catalog record for this book is available from the Library of Congress.

Typeset by Newgen Imaging Systems Pvt Ltd, Chennai, India

Printed and bound in Great Britain by CPI Antony Rowe, Chippenham, Wiltshire

Contents

Typographic conventions

In semantics and linguistics in general, it is customary to use special formatting to indicate references to the objects of inquiry: words themselves, their meanings, concepts, categories, semantic features, and so on. It is, for example, important to mark cases where a word or expression is used metalinguistically, that is, to refer to itself – there is, after all, a vast difference between writing about the meaning of life and the meaning of *life* (i.e. the word *life*), and the semanticist is (in her day job at least) more likely to be concerned with the latter. There are also general conventions for marking ungrammatical or anomalous uses of language, which we have adopted here. For the purposes of this book, we have also used special typographic conventions to mark important terms as they are introduced and defined, and to indicate cross-references to the entries for other key terms or key thinkers.

Italics is used to mark metalinguistic uses: In the sentence *My dog has fleas*, the word *fleas* is in the plural.

Single quotation marks around a word or phrase (' ') mark meanings of words/phrases: *Spill the beans* means 'reveal the information'.

SMALL CAPITALS are used to mark semantic features (e.g. [MALE]), semantic roles (e.g. AGENT) or references to concepts and categories: The boundaries of the category SPORT are fuzzy – does chess count as a sport?

An asterisk (*) marks linguistic expressions that are ungrammatical, that is, ill-formed according to the rules of the language (e.g. *I home going).

A hash (#) marks linguistic expressions that are semantically ill-formed or anomalous (e.g. #male mother).

A question mark (?) marks expressions whose grammatical or semantic acceptability is questionable or borderline.

All of the above are conventions that are commonly used in semantics. In addition, we use the following typographical conventions in order to highlight certain types of information in this book.

Bold font marks important terms as they are introduced within an entry for a key term or a key thinker (e.g. 'Closed-class words are also called **function words** or **grammatical words**.').

BOLD SMALL CAPITALS mark cross-references to other entries in the key terms or key thinkers section, where you can read more about that term or thinker. For example, '**Natural Semantic Metalanguage (NSM)** is a COMPONENTIAL semantic theory that has been developed by **ANNA WIERZBICKA** and colleagues since the 1970s' indicates that you can read more about componential theories under the key term COMPONENTIAL and about **ANNA WIERZBICKA** in the key thinkers section.

Introduction

Meanings are 'slippery customers'. Take the word *eat*, for example. It seems simple enough – we do it several times a day. But start examining it in real English contexts (here in its past tense *ate*), and we see that it can be used in many different ways.

(1) I ate a biscuit.
(2) I ate already.
(3) I had a car, but it ate too much fuel.
(4) I ate the cost of the defective software.

In (1) *ate* describes an action that 'I' did to a biscuit, which involves putting it in my mouth, probably chewing it, and swallowing it. In (2) what I ate is not mentioned, but we assume that it is something of meal-like proportions – if someone asked *Did you eat yet?*, you wouldn't answer (2) if you'd only had a biscuit. So is 'meal' part of the meaning of *eat* here? In (3) and (4) the ingesting is metaphorical – in (4) it doesn't even refer to a physical action. So what is the meaning of *eat*? Does it have just one? Does it have as many as four, or are some of these interpretations due to the same 'core' meaning for *eat*? In other words, is having different uses or interpretations the same as having different meanings?

Let's take another example – the use of *not*. Seems like a very simple word – it takes whatever you add it to and makes it mean the opposite. But what is it added to in sentence (5)?

(5) You may not go to the party.

You have probably automatically interpreted this as meaning 'you do not have permission to go to the party', but it might also be interpreted as 'you have permission to not go to the party.' (Imagine if you really didn't want to go to a party, but your parent or partner wanted you to. They might relent and say (5) if you make your case against the party strongly enough.)

The fact of the matter is that most sentences and even words in English or any other language can be interpreted in many ways. It's also the case that meaning – unlike more 'concrete' aspects of language like grammar or pronunciation – is as abstract a thing as there can be. The combination of the inherent ambiguity in language and the abstractness of meaning forces serious students of meaning to rely on very precise but abstract vocabulary for the description of meaning and of theories of how meaning works. This book is to give students a guide to such vocabulary and to some of the thinkers who invented it.

Meaning can mean many different things, and this book is focused on a subset of the traditions that are concerned with meaning and a subset of the phenomena that are considered to be meaning. Our focus here is on **linguistic semantics**, the branch of the science of linguistics that approaches the meaning of linguistic expressions with reference to the structures of language that either reveal (or possibly constrain) the range of possible linguistic meanings and the architecture through which meaning is constructed or represented. Although scholars have pondered the semantic aspects of language for millennia, the Anglo-American tradition of linguistic semantics can be considered to be less than a century old.

For most of history, philosophers have been responsible for thinking about the relationships between language, meaning and reality. In the first half of the twentieth century, **analytic philosophy** characterized the discipline in the English-speaking world. An analytic philosophical approach uses the tools of formal logic in order to clarify propositions. Philosophy of language became one of the main areas of concern among analytic philosophers, such as Bertrand Russell and W. V. O. Quine. During the first half of the twentieth century, problems of meaning were left to the philosophers, as some linguistic scholars at this time went so far as to claim that meaning is not a subject for linguistic study, but rather that it is a matter for psychology and philosophy. These attitudes shifted through the influence of European scholars, particularly Ferdinand de Saussure, through the realization that some grammatical problems needed to be framed in semantic terms, and also as linguistic redefined themselves (following Noam Chomsky) as pursuing a psychological science. Still, philosophy and linguistics are sometimes indistinguishable in semantics in that many of the theories of meaning applied by linguists were invented by philosophers, such as Jerrold Katz and Jerry Fodor and Richard Montague.

Thus, while this book focuses on the ideas that are used in linguistic semantics, a fair number of the terms and thinkers discussed are from the philosophical tradition. Rather than trying to cover *all* of philosophy of language in addition to linguistic semantics, we discuss the philosophical concepts that are most likely to crop up in linguistics reading.

The study of meaning can also be framed in the terms of other, related fields: pragmatics, semiotics and grammatical theory. Pragmatics is the study of language interpretation in context – as opposed to the traditional definition of semantics as the meaning that is communicated by the linguistic expressions themselves (without reference to the context). This definition is made problematic by the fact that some recent semantic theories (especially cognitive linguistics theories) do not distinguish between linguistic meaning and meaning-in-use. Nevertheless, we restrict our discussion of proper pragmatics terminology to a few key terms that are best considered in contrast with semantic terms, and refer students to the companion volume *Key terms in pragmatics* by Nicholas Allott for more specific discussion of pragmatic terms and thinkers.

Semiotics is the study of signs, which are by definition meaningful, but which are not necessarily linguistic. So, for example, one could carry out a semiotic analysis of the symbols used to mark male and female toilets (some of which would be verbal, some pictorial). Linguistic semantics, on the other hand, always considers meaning with reference to particular linguistic forms and structures. We limit our discussion of semiotic terminology to that which is used significantly with linguistic semantics. Another volume in this series, *Key terms in semiotics* by Bronwen Martin and Felizitas Ringham, more thoroughly covers that field.

Finally, the study of grammar (syntax and morphology), especially functional approaches to grammar, can also overlap with semantics to some degree. This book includes a number of grammatical terms (like *adjective* and *number*) but does so with a focus on the semantic qualities that typify such grammatical categories. For more on grammatical theory, we recommend *Key terms in syntax and syntactic theory* edited by Silvia Luraghi and Claudia Parodi.

Semantic approaches can be divided into two main types. **Denotational** approaches attempt descriptions of the relation between language and the world – that is, between words or other expressions and the things or situations that they refer to. **Representational** approaches try to model how meaning is represented in the human mind – in other words, they are mentalistic in nature. Both types of approach are to be found in both philosophy and linguistics, but it is fair to say that much of the modern linguistic tradition is more representational than denotational, and that most denotational approaches have their hearts in philosophy and mathematical logic. (It is interesting to note how many of the key thinkers discussed in this book were trained as mathematicians.)

The traditions that we cover here include those that are most often taught in English-speaking universities – particularly, formal, generative, structural and cognitivist approaches. **Formal approaches** are those that use a formal language, that is, a type of mathematical logic, in order to represent meanings in an unambiguous way. Such approaches tend to be denotational, and they are strong in the philosophical tradition, but have been imported into linguistic semantics, particularly in the guise of Montague grammar. **Cognitivist approaches** are at the other end of the scale – they aim not only to represent linguistic meaning, but to get to the nature of human conceptualization, and in doing so they often rely on representations that are far more flexible than formal. Approaches linked with the **generativist** (Chomskyan) tradition in linguistic study seek to account for the acquisition and generation of an infinite potential for linguistic meaning, but the approaches under this heading vary quite a bit, and many have not had the blessing of mainstream Chomskyan linguistics. Finally, **structural semantics** focuses on the relations among units of a language and how meaning arises through these relations, and can be considered to be in the Saussurean tradition. Having defined these categories, some approaches defy categorization into these traditions. For instance, the Conceptual Semantics of Ray Jackendoff has many goals in common with the cognitivist enterprise, but it comes from the generativist tradition.

Another way do categorize semantic approaches is whether they are **componential** or not, that is, whether they hold that complex meanings are built out of smaller meaningful units. On a componential account, we might consider *eat* to include simpler semantic elements like CAUSE, GO and IN (since eating involves causing something to go into someone), and these elements could also be used in representing the meanings of *drink* and *insert*, among other expressions. In a non-componential approach, we might look at the relation between the word *eat* and instances of 'eating' or between *eat* and other words (like *food* and *meal* and *drink*), without reference to an internal componential structure for *eat*.

The remainder of this book is divided into key terms, key thinkers and key texts, which include the texts suggested in the key terms and key thinker entries. In such a new field, it is unavoidable that many of the key thinkers are still at work and the 'key'ness of some of that work may not be evident for some years yet. We have included a selection of important philosophers of language in addition to linguistic semanticists, although this selection is, inevitably, restricted. The key texts are ones that have shaped particular discussions in the field. In addition to those texts, we suggest in the 'further readings' below a number of helpful introductions to aspects of the field. Additional topic-specific further readings are suggested in the key terms and key thinkers entries.

In our years of teaching semantics to undergraduate students, we have found that some naturally take to the kind of precise, abstract thinking and communicating required by the field, while others work at it for a while before having a 'Eureka!' moment when it comes together for them. We wish you the best in your studies and dedicate this book to our students, from whom we have learnt so much.

References

Allott, Nicholas (2009) *Key terms in pragmatics*. London: Continuum.

Luraghi, Silvia and Claudia Parodi (eds) (2008) *Key terms in syntax and syntactic theory*. London: Continuum.

Martin, Bronwen and Felizitas Ringham (2006) *Key terms in semiotics*. London: Continuum.

Further reading on semantics

Allan, Keith (2001) *Natural language semantics*. Oxford: Blackwell.

Allwood, Jens, Lars-Gunnar Andersson and Östen Dahl (1977) *Logic in linguistics*. Cambridge: Cambridge University Press.

Bennett, Paul (2002) *Semantics: an introduction to non-lexical aspects of meaning*. Munich: Lincom Europa.

Chapman, Siobhan (2000) *Philosophy for linguists*. London: Routledge.

Croft, William and D. A. Cruse (2004) *Cognitive linguistics*. Cambridge: Cambridge University Press.

Cruse, Alan (2000) *Meaning in language*. Oxford: Oxford University Press.

Evans, Vyvyan and Melanie Green (2006) *Cognitive linguistics*. Edinburgh: Edinburgh University Press.

Frawley, William (1992) *Linguistic semantics*. Hillsdale, NJ: Erlbaum.

Lappin, Shalom (ed.) (1997) *Handbook of contemporary semantic theory*. Oxford: Blackwell.

Löbner, Sebastian (2002) *Understanding semantics*. London: Arnold.

Portner, Paul H. (2005) *What is meaning? Fundamentals of formal semantics*. Oxford: Blackwell.

Saeed, John I. (2008) *Semantics, 3rd edn*. Oxford: Blackwell.

Key Terms in Semantics

Absolute

A PROPERTY (or an expression – particularly an ADJECTIVE – that denotes a property) is **absolute** if the having of that property is an all-or-none affair. For example, in mathematics an integer is either *odd* or *even*, and one cannot say that *Three is just a little odd*. This is opposed to **relative** (also called SCALAR or GRADABLE) properties, like *poor* or the 'peculiar' sense of *odd*, which can be had to different degrees, as in *That statue looks very odd*.

Abstract

The term *abstract* is used in semantics in two different ways. In one sense, **abstract** refers to concepts that are not CONCRETE, that is, entities or experiences that cannot be perceived through the senses, such as TRUTH, MONTH, SIMPLICITY, SUPERSEDE or MARRIED.

Sometimes **abstract** is also used in a sense that does not contrast with *concrete*, but rather refers to representations of concepts that are very general or schematic, that is, not specified in rich detail. In this sense, the concept PHYSICAL OBJECT is more abstract than CUP, and MOVEMENT is more abstract than RUNNING.

Accident

See DEFINITION.

Accomplishment

See **VENDLER CLASSES**.

Achievement

See **Vendler classes**.

Active voice

See **voice**.

Activity

See **Vendler classes**.

Adjective

Adjective can be briefly defined as referring to the grammatical class of words that modify nouns in either **attributive** (*the **red** ball*) or **predicative** (*the ball is **red***) position. In many languages, like English, adjectives comprise a large, **open class**, while in others, like Swahili, the range of adjectives is small and fixed. Still other languages, like Mandarin Chinese, arguably have no adjectives.

Like other grammatical word classes, semantic generalizations or tendencies can be observed within the adjective class. Prototypically, adjectives describe **properties** that an entity might have – for example, being *big*, *obstinate* or *late*. Less typically – most often when the adjective is derived from a noun – adjectives can indicate membership in a subordinate category – for example, *financial* in *financial crisis* describes the type of crisis, rather than a property of the crisis.

The property-denoting adjectives can be classified according to whether they denote **gradable** or **absolute** properties.

See also **antonym, comparison, scale**.

Adjunct

See **argument**.

Affect

Affect (or **affective meaning**), following the psychological use of the term, refers to the emotional attitudes expressed through language, as opposed to DENOTATIVE meaning. This can be expressed through lexical or grammatical choices, or through paralinguistic means, such as intonation, pauses or body language. For example, consider the following two ways of describing the same situation.

Those toilets haven't been cleaned in some time.

and

Those toilets are FILTHY!

These sentences convey different levels of disgust toward the toilets or those responsible for them.

Affect is often considered to be an aspect of CONNOTATION, although it can also be classified as a type of SOCIAL MEANING, in that it expresses something about the speaker – their emotional state.

Affirmative

See POLARITY.

Agent

See SEMANTIC ROLE.

Aggregate

An **aggregate** noun is a noun that refers to a collection of the same type of thing when those things do not function as a group (cf. COLLECTIVE NOUN). Most plural forms represent aggregates – for example, the word *keys* denotes a number of individual keys. Some aggregates are not plural forms of singular nouns – for example *cattle*. Nevertheless, these are treated semantically and grammatically as plural: *The cattle are lowing,* not **The cattle is lowing.*

See also COUNTABILITY, AGREEMENT.

Agreement

Linguistic **agreement** (also called **concord**) is the matching of features between elements of a phrase or clause – for example, between a subject and its verb or an adjective and the noun it modifies. While this is generally treated as a grammatical phenomenon, the morphological categories that force agreement often carry some semantic value. For example, English verbs agree with their subjects in NUMBER and PERSON and PRONOUNS agree with their ANTE-CEDENTS in NUMBER and GENDER. In some cases, agreement can be observed between the semantic, rather than morphological, values of the expressions involved. In some dialects of English (particularly in British English), for example, semantic agreement between collective noun subjects and their verbs is preferred over morphological agreement. For example, in the sentence

The committee have agreed to meet monthly.

the verb *have* is in the plural form, while the subject, *the committee*, is morphologically singular. The trigger for the plural form of *have* is therefore not the form of the subject, but the knowledge that committees are collective entities, made up of a number of individuals. Similarly, under certain conditions, natural gender trumps grammatical gender in French, as in the following sentence where grammatical considerations should make *distrait(e)* 'distracted' agree with the masculine *phenomène*, but instead it agrees with the feminine person that the adjective describes.

Ton	phenomène	de fille	est bien	distraite/*distrait.
your.M	phenomenon[M]	of girl[F]	is quite	distracted.F/*.M

'That character of a daughter of yours is quite absent-minded'

(Hulk and Tellier 1999)

Aktionsart

Verb senses fall into different categories based on how the situation described by the verb unfolds in time. This dimension of a verb's meaning is called its **lexical** ASPECT and lexical aspect categories are often called by the German term **Aktionsarten** (singular: **Aktionsart**), meaning 'types of action'. Diagnostic tests involving grammatical and other means of expressing aspect are used to categorize verbs according to *Aktionsarten*. (See discussions at particular aspectual categories: STATIVE, TELIC, PUNCTUAL.)

The notion that particular verbs have particular aspectual properties is most associated with works by the philosopher Zeno Vendler, who described several categories of EVENT. Since then it has been regularly noted that the verb's ARGUMENTS also play a role in the temporal qualities of the action. For instance, in English an *in* time phrase can be used to describe an action that can be completed in full, and a *for* time phrase can be used to describe an action that can continue without completion. Whether *drive* can take a *for* or an *in* time phrase depends on whether there is an argument indicating the goal of the driving action:

> Eve drove for/*in an hour.
> Eve drove to Rochester in/*for an hour.

Nevertheless, some aspectual properties are determined by the meaning of the verb. For example, *watch* describes a potentially lengthy activity, but *notice* describes an abrupt change of state – from non-perception to perception.

> Joe watched the gulls (for a while/*in an instant).
> Joe noticed the gulls (in an instant/*for a while).

See also **VENDLER CLASSES**.

Ambiguity, ambiguous

If an expression has more than one SENSE, then it is **ambiguous**. There are several sources for ambiguity in language.

Lexical ambiguities involve a word form having more than one possible meaning, due to POLYSEMY or HOMONYMY. For instance, *fire* could mean 'discharge a bullet from', 'bake in a kiln' or 'terminate the employment of'. Thus sentences that contain the verb *fire* are usually ambiguous. For example,

She could not fire the gun.

While the 'discharge a bullet' meaning may seem like the most likely one in this sentence, the others are perfectly possible, particularly in certain contexts:

She could not fire the gun because the trigger was stuck.
She could not fire the gun because her kiln was broken.
She could fire the employee who had shot her, but **she could not fire the gun**.

Structural ambiguities arise because there is more than one possible constituent structure for a complex expression. One type of structural ambiguity is an attachment ambiguity, in which there are (at least) two possible ways of linking a constituent to the rest of the sentence. For example, the headline *COMPLAINTS ABOUT NBA REFEREES GROWING UGLY* can be interpreted as a noun phrase that refers to people complaining that the referees are getting uglier, or an abbreviated sentence about a situation in which the complaints about referees are growing ugly, as shown in Figure 1.

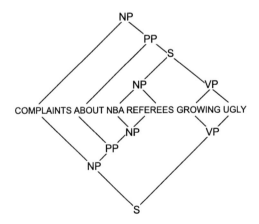

Figure 1 Structural ambiguity

In this example (Figure 1), regardless of the interpretation of the phrase, the words have the same meanings and belong to the same word classes.

Lexical-categorial ambiguities involve both structural and lexical differences. In this case, a word or words in the phrase could belong to more than one grammatical class. Because of this, the phrase can be parsed in more than one way. A headline from the 1980s, *BRITISH LEFT WAFFLES ON FALKLAND ISLANDS*, illustrates this point. *British*, *left* and *waffles* each have possible meanings in more than one word class. If *British* is interpreted as an adjective here, then it combines with the noun *left* (as in the left wing in politics) to make a subject for the verb *waffles*. But if *British* is a noun meaning 'British forces' or 'British people', then *left*, the past tense of *leave*, is the verb and *waffles* is a noun denoting a kind of griddled cake. The differences in the words' meanings, then, make for differences in the structure of the sentence, as shown in Figure 2.

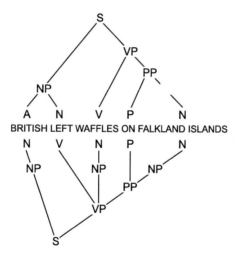

Figure 2 Lexical-categorial ambiguity

See SCOPE and NEGATION for discussion of **scopal ambiguities**.

See also VAGUENESS.

Amelioration

See SEMANTIC CHANGE.

Analytic

Analytic PROPOSITIONS are those that require no external verification, which is to say that their truth or falsity can be established by examining only their linguistic matter and internal logic, rather than appealing to our senses in order to verify the claims they describe. Consider, for example, the following:

No dead person is alive.
Every dog is a canine.
Everything is either a dog or not a dog.

All of the above examples are **analytic truths**, that is, they can never be false as long as the words in them are used in the CONVENTIONAL ways.

See also SYNTHETIC.

Anaphor, anaphora, anaphoric

In **anaphora**, a linguistic expression (called an **anaphor** or **anaphoric pronoun**) is understood to have the same REFERENCE as another linguistic expression (its **antecedent**), which typically precedes it in the same sentence or in the earlier discourse. Thus in the sentence below, we would most likely understand *he* and *Neil* to be CO-REFERENTIAL because the anaphoric pronoun *he* refers back to *Neil*, its antecedent.

Neil couldn't remember the name of the girl **he** met last night.

It is also possible to get an anaphoric interpretation without an overt anaphor. For instance, in *Abby closed the door and locked* it, we understand Abby to be the subject of *lock*, even though no overt anaphoric pronoun occurs in the subject position. Such cases involve **zero anaphora**.

In some uses, *anaphora* is taken to include **cataphora**, but when a distinction is made, *anaphora* is specifically defined as involving 'backward' reference to an antecedent that precedes the anaphor, while in cataphora the reference is 'forward', to a co-referent that occurs later in the discourse. In the following example of cataphora, *they* refers forward to *the children*:

> As **they** walked through the garden, **the children** were careful not to tread on any flowers.

Anaphoric uses of pronouns are distinct from **exophoric** uses, where the pronoun refers to something in the extralinguistic CONTEXT, rather than the surrounding linguistic context. Thus in the first sentence below, *she* is anaphoric, but in the second sentence it is exophoric:

> Natalie promised **she** would do the washing up.
> **She** (speaker points to Natalie) promised to do the washing up.

See also DEIXIS.

Animacy, animate

Animacy is a semantic category that can have semantic and grammatical effects. A noun or noun phrase can be classified as **animate** if it denotes something that can act of its own accord – most typically a human or animal. Some languages, such as the North American Athabaskan languages or the Bantu languages of Africa, have an **animacy hierarchy** by which humans are the 'most animate' beings and animals are 'less animate' than humans. Animals may differ among themselves in animacy, but they are still more animate than objects like trees and rocks. The effects of such hierarchies can be seen in the ordering of ARGUMENTS of the verb, such that noun phrases that denote 'more animate' beings must precede those that denote 'less animate' beings – this means that, for example, a sentence expressing 'The dog bit Mary' would be more likely in some languages to be expressed in the passive VOICE so that the more animate noun phrase would occur first: *Mary was bitten by the dog*.

Anomalous, anomaly

A semantically **anomalous** linguistic expression is one that has an abnormal meaning or fails to make sense, despite being grammatically well-formed.

This is due to a semantic incompatibility between some of the constituent parts of the linguistic expression, as in the examples below:

> #My brother is pregnant (clash between the property of maleness and the possibility of becoming pregnant).
> #The rain fell upwards (clash between directions of vertical movement in the verb and adverb).

The hash (#) symbol is used to mark semantically anomalous but grammatically well-formed expressions.

Semantic anomalies are sometimes accounted for as violations of SELECTIONAL RESTRICTIONS that words place on other words that they occur with. Thus *The telephone ate my gingerbread* is anomalous because the verb *eat* is restricted to only occur with subjects that refer to animate beings – unless the expression is to be interpreted FIGURATIVELY.

Antecedent

An **antecedent** is something that comes before something else. In reference to ANAPHORA, it refers to an earlier expression to which a pronoun CO-REFERS. It is also a term for the first clause in a CONDITIONAL sentence – that is, the *it rains* portion of *If it rains, it pours*.

Antonym, antonymous, antonymy

Antonymy is the PARADIGMATIC LEXICAL RELATION between two LEXEMES that are opposite in meaning, such as *big/little*, *female/male* and *down/up*. It is sometimes called a relation of **minimal difference** in each member of the antonym pair shares most of its semantic properties with the other member of the pair, except for one that causes the two words to be semantically INCOMPATIBLE. So, for example, *down* and *up* are similar in that they both describe vertical directions, but they are different in terms of the particular direction they indicate. *Left* also describes a direction, but it is not the opposite of *down* because it is more than minimally different from *down*: not only does *left* describe a different direction from *down*, but it also describes a different orientation (horizontal).

Several types of antonym relation can be distinguished on the basis of their logical and referential properties. **Complementary** (also called **contradictory**) antonyms are those for which the assertion of one ENTAILS the NEGATION of the other and *vice versa*, as for *even* and *odd* in their mathematical senses:

That integer is even. → That integer is not odd.
That integer is not odd. → That integer is even.

In other words, every integer is either odd or even, there is no middle ground.

Contrary antonyms are those, like *long/short* and *new/old*, for which the assertion of one entails the negation of the other, but the negation of one does not entail the assertion of the other, as illustrated for *long* and *short* below:

The Nile is long. → The Nile is not short.
The River Thames is not long. → The River Thames is short.

In other words, there is a middle ground between *long* and *short*, so that some rivers can be described as *neither long nor short*. Some authors restrict the use of the term *antonym* to only contrary antonyms. In this case, they may use the term OPPOSITE to refer to other antonym types.

Some antonym pairs have properties of both complementarity and contrariety. For example, *honest* and *dishonest* seem to contradict each other (*X is not honest* entails *X is dishonest*, and *vice versa*), but a middle ground seems to exist, since we can assert that some person is *neither honest nor dishonest*. Such cases are sometimes called **gradable complementaries**. Even classic examples of complementarity, like *dead/alive*, sometimes take on GRADABLE qualities (e.g. *he's more dead than alive*).

Converse antonyms describe the same relation or activity from different perspectives, and follow patterns like: if X is *p* to Y, then Y is *q* to X. These include examples like *buy/sell*, *child/parent* and *above/below*. **Reversive** opposites involve the undoing of some action, such as *mask/unmask*, *embark/disembark*. Converse and reversives antonyms are sometimes grouped, along with other miscellaneous examples (e.g. *come/go*), in a general category of **directional** antonyms.

See also ADJECTIVE, SCALE.

Key texts: Cruse 1986; Murphy 2003.

Apodosis

See CONDITIONAL.

Arbitrariness, arbitrary

The connection between a linguistic form and its meaning is **arbitrary** if there is no necessary causal reason for that meaning to be signified by that particular form. For instance, the connection between the English word *road* and the meaning 'a route used by travellers to get from one place to another' is arbitrary as English might have used any other form to signify that meaning instead. Indeed, the same meaning is designated by different forms in different languages: *väg* in Swedish and *tie* in Finnish, for instance. Therefore, the connection between the forms and their meanings is a matter of CONVENTION; something that has to be learned by speakers of each of the languages.

FERDINAND DE SAUSSURE defines language as a system of arbitrary SIGNS. While most linguistic signs are indeed arbitrary, there are some exceptions. **Onomatopoeic** words are ICONICALLY motivated, in that there is a resemblance between the sound that the word designates and the word's phonological form, as in the case of *hiss*, *bang* or *miaow*. However, even onomatopoeic words involve an element of arbitrariness: the sound of a chicken is *cluck cluck* in English, but *kot kot* in Finnish.

While arbitrariness is an important **design feature of language** (Hockett 1960), it is important to recognize the limits of arbitrariness and how arbitrariness and **motivation** interact in language. For instance, Saussure acknowledges that while individual signs are arbitrary, compound expressions (e.g. *whiteboard*) are partially motivated by their connection with the individual signs (*white* and *board*) or with other, associated signs (e.g. *blackboard*). Arbitrariness in language therefore relates specifically to the semiotic link between a form and a meaning, while many aspects of the relations between linguistic signs and their forms and meanings are motivated. A case in point is meaning extension and POLYSEMY: while it is arbitrary that the form *head*, and not some other form, is used to designate the uppermost part of the body, there is a motivated reason (based on METAPHOR) for why *head* is also used to designate 'a person in charge of an organization'.

See also SEMIOTICS.

Key text: Saussure 1916.

Argument

In a PROPOSITION or SENTENCE, (semantic) **arguments** are the participants in the EVENT or STATE expressed by the PREDICATE. For example, an event of stroking involves two participants, the entity that strokes and the entity that is stroked, and therefore in *Samantha stroked her kitten*, *Samantha* and *kitten* are the two arguments of *stroke*. Predicates vary in the number of arguments they require in order to form a complete proposition – for instance, while *stroke* requires two arguments, *purr* requires only one, the entity doing the purring (see VALENCY).

Within a sentence/proposition, arguments play particular roles, called SEMANTIC ROLES. For instance, we might say that in *Samantha stroked her kitten*, *Samantha* is an AGENT, the intentional initiator of the action, while *her kitten* is a PATIENT, the entity that undergoes the action. The number and type of arguments that a predicate requires and their syntactic realization is known as **argument structure**.

In determining the number of arguments in a sentence/proposition, an important distinction is made between arguments and **adjuncts**. Adjuncts are expressions of time, place or manner that may modify a proposition. In the examples below, the arguments are enclosed in square brackets while adjuncts are indicated in bold:

[Samantha] stroked [the kitten] **on her lap**.
[The kitten] purred **with pleasure**.
On Wednesday [Samantha] gave [the kitten] [a ball of yarn].

Adjuncts are always optional and not required by the predicate to form a complete proposition. Leaving out an argument, on the other hand, often results in an ungrammatical sentence: *Samantha stroked*, *Purred*. However, in some cases an argument may be left unexpressed syntactically, if the semantic argument can be understood implicitly. For instance, in *The kitten ate*, the kitten is understood to have eaten **something**, even if the argument is not realized syntactically.

Key texts: Grimshaw 1990; Levin 1993.

Aspect, aspectual

The SITUATIONS described by PROPOSITIONS can take place in time in different ways. The internal organization of a situation with relation to time – that is, *how* the situation unfolds in time or the temporal perspective taken on the situation – is its **aspect** as opposed to its TENSE, which is the *when* of the situation. For example, an action could happen in a prolonged way or a repetitive way; we could describe the onset of the action or its continuation; and the action could happen in a flash or very slowly. English has many ways of marking aspect in sentences, including the following:

Through auxiliary verbs and verbal inflection:
Jane **is** bak**ing** a cake. (on-going)
Jane **has** bak**ed** a cake. (completion)

Through repetition of the verb:
The clock **beeped and beeped**. (repetition)
The cake **rose and rose**. (elongation of the event)

Through verb particles:
They ate **up** the cake. (completion)

Through certain 'helping' verbs:
Arthur **kept** eating. (continuation)
Enid **used to** bake. (habit)

Through adverbial words and phrases, such as *continuously, intermittently, in the blink of an eye*, and so forth.

And through the verb's own inherent aspectual properties, or **lexical aspect**, which is also called **AKTIONSART**.

See also IMPERFECTIVE/PERFECTIVE, PERFECT, INCHOATIVE, ITERATIVE, HABITUAL, VENDLER CLASSES.

Key texts: Comrie 1976; Verkuyl 1993.

Atelic

See TELIC.

Atomic

An **atomic** semantic entity is one that is not analysed in terms of smaller COMPONENTS that it is made of.

See also ATOMISM, PRIMITIVE.

Atomism

Atomism, as opposed to HOLISM, is a philosophical term for the position that complex meanings can be built up out of simpler parts.

See also COMPOSITIONALITY, COMPONENT.

Attributive (adjective)

See ADJECTIVE.

Base

See Cognitive Grammar, figure/ground.

Basic level

The term **basic level** relates to the hierarchical organization of concepts or categories from the more general, or inclusive, to the more specific, as in the hierarchy living being > animal > cat > siamese cat. Within a taxonomic hierarchy, the basic level is a level of categorization that is maximally informative and economical and in some respects cognitively basic. The basic level is situated between the most inclusive and most specific concepts: in the hierarchy above, cat is a basic-level concept. Similarly, car is a basic-level concept in the hierarchy object > vehicle > car > sports car. Concepts below the basic level are called subordinate and the ones above are superordinate-level concepts.

The basicness of the basic level is indicated by a number of cognitive and linguistic effects. For instance, in most contexts, speakers are more likely to name objects using basic-level terms, such as *cat*, rather than superordinate- (*animal*) or subordinate-level terms (*Siamese*). Linguistic labels for basic-level concepts also tend to be short and consist of a single lexeme: compare *car* and *sports car*. Furthermore, concepts at the basic level are typically the first to be acquired by children and arguably the first to be lexicalized in a language. Members of basic-level categories also share a large number of common properties, compared to their superordinates. For instance, different kinds of cars share a similar shape, parts and function, whereas vehicles in general have far fewer properties in common. Concepts at the subordinate level, on the other hand, only add a small number of additional properties to the basic-level concept. Compared to subordinate-level concepts, basic-level concepts also contrast more strongly with their neighbouring concepts at the same level of categorization. Thus the members of subordinate-level categories siamese cat, persian cat and manx cat are more similar to each other than are the members of the basic-level categories cat, dog, horse and cow.

The notion of basic level is associated with the Prototype Theory and particularly the work of Eleanor Rosch and her colleagues. Prototypes and the basic level interact, in that basic-level concepts are the most likely to have clear prototypes. Within anthropological work on folk categorization of plants and animals, the basic level is often referred to as the **generic level**.

See also Prototype Theory.

Key texts: Berlin et al. 1973; Rosch et al. 1976; Lakoff 1987.

Beneficiary

See semantic role.

Biconditional

The **biconditional** is a logical operator that joins two propositions by mutual entailment, that is, P is true **if and only if** Q is true. In logic, this is symbolized as $\leftrightarrow$ or $\equiv$. In semantic literature, *if and only if* is often abbreviated as **iff**. The biconditional operation can be paraphrased in terms of the material conditional and conjunction:

P is true iff Q is true (P$\leftrightarrow$Q) =
If P is true, then Q is true AND if Q is true then P is true. ((P$\rightarrow$Q) $\wedge$ (Q$\rightarrow$P))

In order for a biconditional proposition like P$\leftrightarrow$Q to be true, either both P and Q must be true, or both must be false.

See logic, truth condition.

Binary feature

See component.

Bind, bound

In syntactic theory, **binding** generally refers to the dependency relations between antecedents and anaphora. The term is also used this way in some semantic approaches that distinguish a semantic level of binding.

Binding can also refer to the relation between a quantifier or similar logical operator and a variable. The variable is a semantically empty expression in this case, which must be **bound** to a quantifier in order to be interpretable. (Note: **bound** is not the same as BOUNDED – see that entry for further information.)

Bleaching, semantic

See SEMANTIC CHANGE, GRAMMATICALIZATION.

Blending Theory

See CONCEPTUAL BLENDING THEORY.

Bounded, boundedness

Bounded, and its opposite, **unbounded**, are frequently used as semantic components or descriptions of semantic properties, applying to a wide range of different meaning types. In general terms, something is bounded (or **+bounded**) if the boundary between being that thing (or property or action) and not being that thing (etc.) is clearly identifiable, and if compromising that boundary results in changing the nature of the thing. It is unbounded (or **non-bounded**, or **-bounded**) if its boundaries are not fixed in this way.

For nouns, especially those that describe concrete things, the property of boundedness can describe the difference between count nouns, like *cat* and *cup*, and non-count nouns, like *water* and *flour* (see COUNTABILITY). Here, we can tell that *cup* refers to a bounded entity because if we break the cup in half, we no longer have *a cup*, nor even *two cups* – the loss of the original boundaries of the cup makes it no longer a cup. But if we divide some *flour* into two piles, or even add more flour to it, we still have *flour* – not *half a flour* or *two flours*.

In the case of EVENT descriptions, boundedness refers to whether or not the event is completed – so *I am eating lunch* is not bounded, but *I ate lunch* is.

These concepts have been applied as well to PROPERTY and intensifier meanings. The intensifier *very* is unbounded and thus modifies unbounded adjectives; so one can say *very tall* because there's no inherent limit on how tall a *tall* thing is. *Absolutely*, on the other hand, marks boundedness; so one cannot say *absolutely tall* because of the mismatch in boundedness of the intensifier and the adjective, but one can say *absolutely clean*, because there is an upper bound on how clean something can be.

See also COUNTABILITY, TELICITY.

Key texts: Jackendoff 1991; Paradis 2001.

Broadening

See SEMANTIC CHANGE.

Case

Case can be used to refer to the morphological marking of the role of the noun phrase in a sentence, or, in some theories, to an underlying abstract relational category that may or may not be morphologically marked. In the abstract sense, it is usually spelt with a capital 'C' and sometimes called **deep case**.

'Deep' Case is a theoretical notion that provides a bridge between semantics and syntax in approaches such as CHARLES FILLMORE's Case Grammar and in the Chomskyan generative tradition. It is the means by which SEMANTIC ROLES are assigned by PREDICATES to their ARGUMENTS. Such approaches hold that Case is assigned to any argument (regardless of whether the language morphologically marks such roles) and that the assignment of Case is constrained in certain ways – for example, any phrase can have only one Case.

Traditional terminology for morphologically marked cases include **nominative**, typically for the subject position in a sentence, **accusative** for the object position, **genitive** for relations such as possession and origin, and **ablative** for locative or instrumental roles.

In English, semantic roles are generally made clear through word order rather than case marking, but the remains of a morphological case system are seen in the pronominal system – for example, the distinction between *I* and *me* or *she* and *her*. Finnish is an example of a modern language with a morphological case system that makes very fine distinctions – for instance, between the nominative *käsi* 'hand', the **inessive** *kädessä* 'in a hand', the **illative** *käteen* 'into a hand', the **elative** *kädestä* 'from inside a hand' and the **ablative** *kädeltä* 'from a hand'.

Key texts: Fillmore 1968; Blake 2001.

Cataphor, cataphora

See ANAPHOR.

Category

Category refers to a set of entities, properties or experiences that are grouped together and distinguished from other entities or experiences on some coherent basis. For example, the category CAT consists of all things in the world that are cats and not dogs, lizards, microphones, job applications, and so on. Categories are determined by **CONCEPTS**: we can categorize an entity as a member of the category CAT by virtue of being in possession of the concept CAT.

See also CLASSICAL THEORY OF CONCEPTUALIZATION, PROTOTYPE THEORY, 'THEORY' THEORY, FUZZINESS, TAXONOMY.

Causal chain

In one approach to **PROPER NAME** meaning, the ability of a name to designate a real or imaginary thing is not the product of a **SENSE** represented in the speaker's mind, but the product of the name's history of use in the speech community, called a **causal chain**. In this case, names are **RIGID DESIGNATORS**, which is to say that they always point out the same real or imaginary individual.

A causal chain starts when an individual receives a name through some act of **dubbing**. For example, when individual X was born, someone, let's say her mother, said or thought 'I'll call her *Arden*', and started using the name to refer to her. When X's father needs to talk about X, because he's heard the mother call X *Arden* he'll use *Arden* to designate her too, and then others experience the name as designating that person and use it too. Another causal chain is started when X is assigned the nickname *Ardie*. Once a causal chain is established, the name always points to the original 'dubbee', no matter how they are described. So, for example, imagine that someone says *Arden is in the kitchen* when in fact X is in the bedroom. *Arden* still points to X in spite of the fact that there is no Arden who is in the kitchen. In order for us to succeed in referring to Arden all that matters is that this act of calling her *Arden* is a link in the historical chain that started with her mother dubbing her *Arden*.

The reliance of causal chains on the initial dubbing act creates some problems. For example, *Madagascar* originally referred to part of the African mainland. Somewhere along the line, there was a miscommunication, in which someone understood *Madagascar* to refer to a large island off the African coast. The error was then spread far and wide, and now we only refer to the island as *Madagascar*, in spite of the fact that there has been a continuous history of the use of the name that started with an act of dubbing that pointed out a different place.

Key texts: Kripke 1980; Evans 1973.

Causative

A verb like *kill* is said to be **causative** in that it CONFLATES two EVENT descriptions:

(1) an EVENT in which something dies, and
(2) an EVENT in which something caused EVENT (1).

In other words, *kill* can be paraphrased as 'cause (something) to die', and it requires one more ARGUMENT than the verb *die*, because it requires something to take the SEMANTIC ROLE of 'causer'. Lexical causative verbs like *kill* or *raise* ('cause to rise') incorporate the causative meaning without special morphological marking. In some languages, productive causative morphemes can be used to turn non-causative verbs into causatives. For example, the causative morpheme *-is-* is found in many Bantu languages, so that in Sesotho, for example, *hlwekisa* 'to clean' is derived from *hlweka* 'to become clean'. English and other languages also make use of causative constructions with support verbs like *make*, as in *The film made him cry*. The 'causer' semantic role is usually represented as the highest role in role hierarchies.

Classical theory of conceptualization

The foundations of the **classical theory of conceptualization** and categorization can be traced back at least as far as the philosopher ARISTOTLE. According to the classical theory, CONCEPTS are defined in terms of **necessary and sufficient conditions** or features. For instance, the concept TEENAGER might be defined by the features 'human', 'aged thirteen or older', 'aged nineteen or younger'. These features are individually necessary, which means that for any entity to be categorized as a teenager, that entity must necessarily possess each of these features. Necessary features will therefore not include any properties that are true only of some of the members of the category (e.g. a feature such as 'is grumpy' is not true of all teenagers).

The set of features must also be jointly sufficient, which means that taken together, they should adequately distinguish the concept they define from other neighbouring concepts. For instance, the features 'human' and 'aged thirteen or older' would not be sufficient to distinguish teenagers from adults, who are also older than thirteen.

The classical theory has been very influential in philosophy, psychology and linguistics, particularly with respect to its assumption that concepts are built up from smaller features or COMPONENTS. However, it is subject to a number of significant criticisms. In particular, many authors, including LUDWIG WITTGENSTEIN, have pointed out that many concepts cannot be defined by necessary and sufficient conditions (see FAMILY RESEMBLANCE). For example, we might attempt to define CHAIR with the features 'is an item of furniture', 'has legs', 'has a back', 'has a seat', 'is a seat for one person'. However, there are such things as backless chairs (e.g. some office chairs that you kneel on), which would mean that the feature 'has a back' is not a necessary feature for something to be a chair. However, without this feature the definition does not sufficiently distinguish CHAIR and STOOL. Furthermore, the classical approach entails that the categories that concepts define should have clear-cut boundaries: an entity either is or is not a member of a category, depending on whether it possesses all the relevant definitional features. As all members of a category also possess the same features, they should be equal and it should make no sense to distinguish between 'better' and 'worse' members of a category. As a consequence, the classical theory is unable to account for PROTOTYPE EFFECTS, which suggest that category boundaries are often FUZZY and categories may indeed have central and marginal members.

Further reading: Margolis and Laurence 1999.

Closed and open classes

Linguistic items can be divided into **closed and open classes** on the basis of the kinds of roles they play in language, the kinds of meaning they express and the ease with which a language adds new words to that class. Closed-class items generally include prepositions, conjunctions, determiners, auxiliary and modal verbs, and inflectional and derivational affixes, while open-class items include nouns, verbs, adjectives and adverbs. In the sentence below, closed-class items are indicated in bold, while all the other items are open class:

> **The** small rabbit **was** nibbl**ing on a** carrot **and some** blade**s of** grass.

Open-class items, such as *small, rabbit* and *nibble*, express rich, more definite meanings, while the meanings of closed-class items, such as *the, and*, *of* or the plural *-s* are more schematic. That is, closed-class items often have meanings that are very general or not easily definable. This distinction is, however, to some extent a matter of degree in that some members of some closed classes have relatively specific meanings – consider, for instance, the prepositions *inside* or *below*.

Closed-class words are also called **function words** or **grammatical words**, which reflects the fact that they have a grammatical function in a sentence (e.g. indicating definiteness or conjoining phrases or sentences together). Open-class words, on the other hand, are called **content words** or **lexical words**, in reflection of their more contentful meanings. The terms *closed* and *open class* themselves refer to the fact that a language can easily develop new open-class items (consider some of the recent nouns and verbs that have entered the English language, such as *metrosexual* or *blog*), while closed classes are relatively stable and not easily added to. Subclasses of the NOUN, VERB, ADJECTIVE and ADVERB classes may differ in how open they are, and languages may vary somewhat in the openness of particular classes. For example, the ADJECTIVE class is closed in many languages (see Dixon 1982).

Clusivity

See PERSON.

Cognitive Grammar

Cognitive Grammar is a COGNITIVE LINGUISTIC theory of language developed by Ronald Langacker. It assumes that grammar is meaningful and an integral part of cognition. Thus the theory posits that no fundamental distinction can be drawn between lexical and grammatical knowledge (and, as a result, it has much to say about issues that are beyond what is traditionally considered to be 'grammar').

Central to Cognitive Grammar is the idea that the fundamental unit of language is a symbolic unit, a pairing of a linguistic form with a meaning. Both lexical and grammatical knowledge is assumed to be represented in terms of such form-meaning pairings, an assumption Cognitive Grammar shares with CONSTRUCTION GRAMMARS. Linguistic knowledge is then modelled as a structured inventory of symbolic units of varying degrees of schematicity and complexity. The Cognitive Grammar conception of language is **usage-based** – linguistic knowledge is viewed as being extracted from and as reflecting language use (see ENTRENCHMENT). Given its assumption that grammar is meaningful and reflects conceptualization, Cognitive Grammar also argues that grammatical categories and relations such as noun, verb, subject and object can be characterized in terms of their conceptual content, rather than just their syntactic properties. (A similar view is taken in LEONARD TALMY's approach to COGNITIVE SEMANTICS.)

Cognitive Grammar equates meaning and conceptualization and stresses that linguistic expressions reflect our CONSTRUAL of situations and experiences. Meaning is also argued to be encyclopaedic in nature. Thus no distinction is made between **linguistic** (or DEFINITIONAL) **meaning** and ENCYCLOPAEDIC MEANING: any aspect of encyclopaedic knowledge may form part of the semantic value of a linguistic form, although some knowledge specifications are more central than others. The conceptual content evoked by linguistic expressions is seen as being structured in terms of conceptual DOMAINS. Furthermore, the meaning of a linguistic expression is viewed as consisting of a **profile** and a **base**, the base being the conceptual material necessarily presupposed by the profile. For example, the meaning of *elbow* presupposes and is profiled against the concept of the arm. The base of a concept profile may include specifications in one or more domains (e.g. BODY, SPACE, SHAPE, etc. for 'elbow'). The notion of profiling constitutes one kind of FIGURE/GROUND asymmetry.

Key texts: Langacker 1987–1991, 2008; Taylor 2002.

Cognitive linguistics

Cognitive linguistics refers to a cluster of related theoretical approaches that assume that linguistic structure reflects human conceptualization and experience. While most modern approaches to linguistics are 'cognitive' in the more general sense that they aim to model the mental representations and processes that underlie language, cognitive linguistics is 'cognitive' in a more specific sense, by virtue of the assumptions it makes about the relationship between language and cognition.

Cognitive linguistics arose in the 1980s as a reaction to formal linguistic approaches such as GENERATIVE GRAMMAR and FORMAL SEMANTICS. Consequently, cognitive linguistic approaches can in some respects be characterized by their rejection of many of the assumptions of generative linguistics (see NOAM CHOMSKY), including the notion of language as an autonomous faculty of the mind. Instead, cognitive linguists see language as an integral part of cognition and seek to explain linguistic structures and patterns through general cognitive principles that relate to conceptualization, perception and categorization. Other key commitments of cognitive linguistics include the view that human concepts are EMBODIED, which is to say they are grounded in human bodily experience and partly determined by the nature of our bodies and the way we experience the world.

Central to cognitive linguistic approaches is the focus on meaning and the conceptual structures and processes that are involved in meaning construal. The focus on meaning is also evident in the treatment of linguistic units of all sizes, including bound morphemes, lexical items and grammatical constructions, as pairings of forms and meanings. Cognitive approaches therefore see grammar as inherently meaningful, and maintain that the lexicon and grammar differ only in terms of how richly specified or schematic the forms and the meanings are.

See also COGNITIVE SEMANTICS, CONCEPTUAL METAPHOR THEORY, FRAME SEMANTICS, MENTAL SPACE THEORY, CONCEPTUAL BLENDING THEORY, COGNITIVE GRAMMAR, CONSTRUCTION GRAMMAR.

Key thinkers: GEORGE LAKOFF, CHARLES FILLMORE, LEONARD TALMY.

Further reading: Croft and Cruse 2004; Evans and Green 2006.

Cognitive meaning

See DENOTATION.

Cognitive semantics

Cognitive semantics refers to COGNITIVE LINGUISTIC approaches to the study of meaning in language. Rather than one unified theory of semantics, cognitive semantics, like cognitive linguistics in general, is a group of related theoretical approaches that make similar theoretical assumptions. Central to cognitive semantics is the view that meaning is conceptual in nature, and as a consequence, work in cognitive semantics aims to model the conceptual structures and processes that underlie linguistic meaning. In this respect, cognitive semantics contrasts with TRUTH-CONDITIONAL semantic approaches that consider only the relation between word and world and do not include the role of human perception and conceptualization. Furthermore, unlike many other approaches to semantics, cognitive semantics also holds that no meaningful, non-arbitrary distinction can be made between **linguistic** (OR DEFINITIONAL) **meaning** and ENCYCLOPAEDIC MEANING. As meaning is instead seen as being constructed in the context of language use by activating parts of conceptual structure, cognitive semantics also blurs the distinction between semantics and PRAGMATICS, or context-independent and context-dependent meaning.

See also CONCEPTUAL METAPHOR THEORY, MENTAL SPACE THEORY, CONCEPTUAL BLENDING THEORY, FRAME SEMANTICS, COGNITIVE GRAMMAR.

Key thinkers: GEORGE LAKOFF, LEONARD TALMY, CHARLES FILLMORE.

Further reading: Croft and Cruse 2004; Evans and Green 2006.

Co-hyponym, co-hyponymy

See HYPONYM, CONTRAST.

Co-index

See CO-REFERENCE.

Collective noun

A **collective** noun is a singular noun that refers to a group of things (and for this reason, they are called **group** nouns by some semanticists). A collective noun is sometimes treated as plural in AGREEMENT relations. For example, *committee* and *crowd* are singular but refer to groups of individuals. In some dialects of English, such nouns are variable in their agreement with verbs – either agreeing semantically with plural verbs and pronouns (*The committee are meeting today*) or grammatically with singular verbs and pronouns (*The committee is meeting today*). In dialects that allow both forms, the singular verb usually indicates that the collective is being referred to as a single entity, without reference to individuals in it (*The committee is responsible for the budget*) and the plural verb indicates that the individuals are relevant to the situation (*The committee are discussing the problem* – where *discussing* indicates a number of individuals saying different things).

See also COUNTABILITY, NUMBER.

Comment

See TOPIC.

Common noun

A NOUN is a **common noun** if it typically designates a category or kind, rather than an individual. That is, common nouns can be used to refer to any or all members of the class of things picked out by the noun's SENSE, or they can be used without referring at all. If a noun is not a common noun, it is a PROPER NAME, which denotes a unique individual. So, *aviatrix* is a common noun that can be applied to any female aeroplane pilot, but *Amelia Earhart* is a proper name that can be understood to refer uniquely to one particular person. In English, common nouns typically occur in noun phrases with determiners (QUANTIFIERS) and/or with plural marking (e.g. *an aviatrix, the pilot, five planes, airports*) in order to indicate their referential status.

See also COUNTABILITY, DEFINITENESS, REFERENCE.

Comparative, comparison

Any category that can exist in different quantities or to different degrees can be compared. Comparative forms are often associated with ADJECTIVES, since gradable adjectives indicate properties that can be possessed at different levels:

positive	I am **happy**.	He is **depressed**.
comparative	I am **happier than** he is.	He is **more depressed than** me.
superlative	I am the **happiest** of all.	He is the **most depressed** of all.

The positive form, such as *happy*, can be said to be inherently comparative, in that this happiness is measured in relation to some neutral emotional state (see SCALE). The comparative compares two explicit ARGUMENTS, in these examples, 'him' and 'me'. The superlative is comparison of one thing to all others. Negative versions of the comparative and superlative are also available: *less happy* and *least happy*.

Comparison can also be effected for noun quantities (*I have more cakes than he does; I have the most cakes*) and the STATES and EVENTS described by verbs. The latter can be compared in terms of extent or intensity through the use of adverbial *more/less*: *I sang less than he did* (i.e. my singing took less time than his did); *I loved her more than he did* (i.e. my love was more intense than his).

See also GRADABILITY.

Complementary (antonym)

See ANTONYM.

Component, componential, componential analysis

In approaches to semantics that incorporate **componential analysis**, it is assumed that word SENSES are composed out of smaller units of meaning called **semantic components** or **semantic features**. For example, the meaning of *woman* might consist of the components [FEMALE, HUMAN, ADULT]. Some meaning components may themselves be broken down into smaller components, but central to many componential approaches is the assumption that there is a restricted and finite inventory of PRIMITIVE components. An unlimited number of meanings can then be generated by combining these basic building blocks of meaning and the larger semantic components in different configurations. In some approaches, components take the form of **binary features** that have a possible value of + or –. This reduces the number of components required: for instance, instead of needing separate features [MALE] and [FEMALE] to define *man* and *woman*, they can be defined as having the same feature, with a different value:

man [+human, +adult, –female]   *woman* [+human, +adult, +female]

One of the benefits of compositional semantics is that it allows for the relations between meanings to be represented by certain configurations of shared features. Thus the relationship of ANTONYMY between *man* and *woman* is shown by the fact that they share all the same features and feature values except for one. The HYPONYMY relation between *man* and *husband*, on the other hand, would be represented by *husband* having all the features of *man* plus one additional one, [+married].

Componential analysis provides one kind of METALANGUAGE for describing the semantics of natural language. The basic notion that word senses can be decomposed and defined owes much to the CLASSICAL THEORY OF CONCEPTUALIZATION. But with the assumption that word senses can be precisely defined, some approaches (such as the early and influential componential analysis of JERROLD KATZ and JERRY FODOR) also inherit from the classical theory the problems associated with necessary and sufficient conditions. Current componential approaches to semantics include NATURAL SEMANTIC METALANGUAGE, CONCEPTUAL SEMANTICS and the GENERATIVE LEXICON approach.

Key texts: Katz and Fodor 1963; Katz 1972.

Compositional, compositionality

The principle of **compositionality** states that the meaning of a complex linguistic expression is built up from the meanings of its composite parts in a rule-governed fashion. This entails that one should be able to work out the meaning of a sentence such as *The cook steamed the fresh carrots* if one knows the meanings of each of the words and their inflections and the syntactic rules that combine them, such as the rule for the subject-verb-object word order or for modifier-noun combinations. Well-known exceptions to the compositionality of complex expressions are IDIOMS such as *spill the beans* or *pull someone's leg*, whose meanings are not composed out of the meanings of their parts.

The principle of compositionality is a foundational assumption in many FORMAL and COMPONENTIAL approaches to semantics. Some COGNITIVE LINGUISTIC approaches, however, reject strict compositionality as they question its underlying assumption that words can have fixed, context-independent meanings that they contribute to any syntactic context.

Key thinker: GOTTLOB FREGE.

Concept

Concepts are mental representations of knowledge about CATEGORIES of entities and experiences. For instance, the concept ELEPHANT incorporates information about the size, body shape, colour and typical habitats of elephants. The concept allows us to identify and categorize things in the world as elephants, label them by the linguistic form *elephant* and make INFERENCES about them. Although the application of linguistic forms to entities and experiences depends on concepts of those entities and experiences, not every concept has a single LEXEME associated with it: consider, for instance, THE PLEASANT COOLNESS OF THE OTHER SIDE OF THE PILLOW, which is a concept in many people's minds, but not one conventionally labelled by a single word.

The preceding definition reflects a perhaps typical understanding of what concepts are, but there is no consensus about the definition of *concept* among philosophers, linguists and psychologists. For instance, for some philosophers (e.g. GOTTLOB FREGE), concepts are abstract, non-mental entities. On the other hand, some cognitive psychologists question the assumption that concepts are static representations in long-term memory, and instead see them as being created dynamically in on-line processing (see, for example, Barsalou 1993).

See also CATEGORY, CLASSICAL THEORY OF CONCEPTUALIZATION, PROTOTYPE THEORY, 'THEORY' THEORY.

Further reading: Margolis and Laurence 1999; Murphy 2002.

Conceptual Blending Theory, Conceptual Integration Theory

Conceptual Blending Theory (also known as **Blending Theory** or **Conceptual Integration Theory**) is a COGNITIVE LINGUISTIC theory developed by Gilles Fauconnier and Mark Turner in the 1990s. It aims to account for the creative conceptual processes that underlie the construction of meaning. Conceptual Blending Theory assumes that meaning construction involves the selective integration or blending of conceptual elements and employs the theoretical construct of **conceptual integration networks** to account for this process. For example, the process of understanding the sentence *In the end, VHS delivered a knock-out punch to Betamax* would involve a basic network consisting of four MENTAL SPACES, as shown in Figure 3. This includes two **input spaces** (one relating to boxing and another to the competition between rival video formats in the 1970s and 1980s). A **generic space** represents what is common to the two input spaces. Elements from the input spaces are mapped to each other and projected selectively into the **blended space**, to derive an integrated conceptualization where the video formats are seen as being engaged in a boxing match, which VHS eventually wins.

Blending Theory can be seen as a development of MENTAL SPACE THEORY, and it is also influenced by CONCEPTUAL METAPHOR THEORY. However, unlike the latter, Blending Theory focuses specifically on the dynamic construction of meaning. Blending Theory has also been applied to many other kinds of linguistic phenomena besides metaphor, such as COUNTERFACTUALS and jokes and also to non-linguistic phenomena such as the design of computer interfaces.

Key texts: Fauconnier and Turner 1998, 2002; Grady et al. 1999.

Conceptual meaning

See DENOTATION.

Conceptual metaphor, Conceptual Metaphor Theory

Conceptual Metaphor Theory is a COGNITIVE LINGUISTIC theory of METAPHOR and METONYMY. It was first developed by GEORGE LAKOFF and Mark Johnson in their 1980 book *Metaphors we live by*. Conceptual Metaphor Theory holds that instead of being just a feature of literary language, metaphor is an

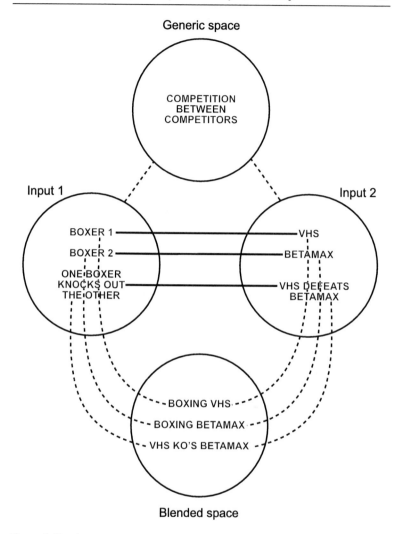

Figure 3 Blend

important cognitive tool, used to provide structure for the conceptualization of more abstract notions via more concrete ones. Consequently, metaphorical expressions in language are seen as reflections of underlying conceptual metaphors, as in the following sentence:

The company plans to **prune** its workforce by 1,800 employees.

The choice of words and images in this sentence is motivated by the conceptual metaphor AN ORGANIZATION IS A PLANT. Conceptual metaphors take the form of **mappings** between **source** and **target** DOMAINS, so that in AN ORGANIZATION IS A PLANT elements from the source domain of PLANT are mapped onto the target domain of ORGANIZATION:

Source	Target
PLANT	ORGANIZATION
PARTS OF PLANT	PARTS OF THE ORGANIZATION
GROWTH OF PLANT	DEVELOPMENT OF THE ORGANIZATION
PRUNING, CUTTING	REDUCING THE ORGANIZATION

According to Conceptual Metaphor Theory, source concepts are typically more **CONCRETE** or physical, while the targets are more **ABSTRACT** and lack sensory content. The mappings from the source concepts are therefore argued to provide structure for conceptualizing and talking about the target concepts. The mappings are assumed to be unidirectional: for instance, WARMTH is mapped metaphorically onto AFFECTION (*We got a very warm welcome*), but not the other way around. (*My tea has gone unsympathetic* does not mean the tea has gone cold.) Importantly, the mappings between the source and the target are not arbitrary, but rather motivated by and grounded in physical and cultural experiences. For instance, the metaphor MORE IS UP, LESS IS DOWN (*That's a really **high** price to pay for a cup of tea*, *The company's profits are set to **fall***) is motivated by the fact that an increase in quantity is often accompanied by an increase in height: consider, for instance, how the level of water in a glass rises when you add water to it.

See also **IMAGE SCHEMA, EMBODIMENT**.

Key texts: Lakoff and Johnson 1980; Lakoff 1993; Kövecses 2002.

Conceptual Semantics

Conceptual Semantics (CS) is a linguistic semantic theory that has been developed by **RAY JACKENDOFF** since the 1970s. Its goal is to represent 'how linguistic utterances are related to human cognition, where cognition is a human capacity that is to a considerable degree independent of language, interacting with the perceptual and action systems as well as language' (Jackendoff 2006: 355).

The architecture underlying CS is formed of three interlinking systems: a phonological system, a syntactic system and a conceptual system. The conceptual system is not a specifically *linguistic* system – and so in representing the conceptual system, Jackendoff aims to provide a 'grammar of thought'. **Lexical concepts**, that is, concepts that are represented by words, comprise a subset of concepts – those that are linked to phonological and(/or) syntactic information. Because there is no linguistic representation of meaning that is separate from the conceptual representation, this approach does not make the traditional distinction between DEFINITION and ENCYCLOPAEDIC MEANING. Because it is a mentalistic approach, it aims to represent meaning as it is in the mind of an individual (idealized) language user, rather than as an object in the culture or in terms of notions of truth and falsity.

The semantic descriptions in Conceptual Semantics utilize a small number of major ONTOLOGICAL CATEGORIES, such as EVENT, STATE, PLACE, AMOUNT, THING, and PRO-PERTY, which serve as universal semantic PRIMITIVES. Any CS analysis of a concept begins with these primitive ontological categories, which interact through a COMPONENTIAL metalanguage that employs a PREDICATE-ARGUMENT structure. To take a simple sentential example (ignoring the TENSE/ASPECT properties), the meaning of *Ray entered the room* can be represented as (1):

(1) $[_{EVENT} \text{ GO } ([_{THING} \text{ Ray}], [_{PATH} \text{ TO } ([_{PLACE} \text{ IN } ([_{THING} \text{ the room}])])])]$

And from this, the meaning of *enter* can be abstracted as follows:

(2) $[_{EVENT} \text{ GO } ([THING], [_{PATH} \text{ TO } ([_{PLACE} \text{ IN } ([THING])])])]$

Here GO, TO and IN are primitive semantic predicates that require certain numbers and types of arguments.

Work in CS has included treatments of major grammatical-semantic phenomena including predicate-argument structure, BOUNDEDNESS in COUNTABILITY and verbal ASPECT, and ANAPHORA.

Key texts: Jackendoff 1983, 1990, 2002.

Concord

See AGREEMENT.

Concrete

Concrete CONCEPTS (as opposed to ABSTRACT) are ones that relate to entities or experiences that can be seen, heard, touched, tasted or smelled, such as APPLE, KNEE, BABOON, AIR, DAUGHTER, EAT or SOFT. Words that refer to concrete entities can also develop abstract senses, for instance, through METAPHOR: *field* has a concrete sense that designates a piece of farmland, and an abstract sense that refers to an area of study, as in *the field of linguistics*.

See also CONCEPT.

Conditional

A **conditional** clause describes a condition or a hypothetical situation, as in the first clause of the following sentence:

> **If you eat too much chocolate**, you will get sick.

Conditional (sentence) is also used to refer to the whole complex proposition in these cases, that is, 'If X, then Y'. The X clause is called the **antecedent** or **protasis**, and the Y clause is the **consequent** or **apodosis**. The example above is a case of a **causal conditional**, which can be paraphrased as 'if you eat too much chocolate, it will cause you to become sick.' The MATERIAL CONDITIONAL does not indicate causality, but simply the truth relations between two propositions (e.g. *If it's Thursday, Jim is in Tokyo*). **Counterfactual conditionals** include a false antecedent – for example, *If I had twelve fingers, I'd type faster*.

Conditional is also the traditional grammatical term for special verb forms that express hypothetical situations, as would be used in the antecedent of a conditional sentence.

See also COUNTERFACTUAL.

Conflate, conflation

Conflation refers to the incorporation of more than one element of a complex conceptualization within a single linguistic unit. The term is particularly associated with the work of **LEONARD TALMY** on the semantics of motion **EVENTS**. According to him, languages such as English have motion verbs that conflate the fact of motion with the manner of motion (consider, for example, *run*, *swim*, *skip*, *roll*). Verbs in other languages may conflate motion and the path of motion (e.g. Spanish *entrar* 'go in' and *salir* 'go out'), or motion and the entity that moves (e.g. Atsugewi has distinct verbs for the motion of small shiny spherical objects or of runny icky material).

Conjunction

Conjunction is the 'and' relation between **PROPOSITIONS** or **SENTENCES** or components thereof: *P and Q*. It is also the name of the grammatical class of **CONNECTIVE** lexemes that can join two constituents – in which case it is used to include other relations besides semantic conjunction (e.g. **DISJUNCTION**). In formal **LOGIC**, conjunction is indicated by the symbol $\wedge$ (or sometimes &).

In natural language, conjunction may be communicated by *and* or other lexemes, like *but* or *yet*, which indicate that both of the connected propositions are to be understood as true. But any of these conjoining lexemes differs from the 'pure' conjunction of logic in terms of the conventionalized implicatures (see **IMPLICATURE**) that they carry. For instance, *and* often carries with it an implication of temporal ordering, so that it is interpreted as meaning 'and then' (*Quentin combed his hair and looked in the mirror*) and sometimes a further implication of causation (*Orla laughed and Peter got embarrassed*).

See also **LOGICAL OPERATOR**.

Connective

A **connective** is a **LOGICAL OPERATOR,** or its natural language equivalent, that joins two propositions. See **LOGICAL OPERATOR** for a list of connectives.

Connotation

The term **connotation** generally refers to aspects of meaning that do not contribute to the DENOTATION of an expression. In other words, connotations are semantic associations of an expression that do not change the EXTENSION or range of possible referents of that expression. For instance, *child* and *kid* (in their human offspring senses) refer to the same range of people, but using one rather than the other may lead to a different mental picture for the following contexts:

> Gus is a good child.
> Gus is a good kid.

On reading *a good child*, one might imagine a more quiet boy in a more formal setting than one might for *a good kid*, which might call to mind a more outgoing, playful child – though the particular associations may vary considerably among and within English-speaking communities. In this example, the associations can be traced to the more formal/informal status of the words *child* and *kid* in English.

Connotation can be used as a cover term for any type of non-denotational meeting, but some linguists use it specifically to refer to associations that have to do with the nature of the referent, rather than the attitude (AFFECT) or social properties (SOCIAL MEANING) of the person who has chosen the word.

Consequent

See CONDITIONAL.

Constant

See LOGICAL CONSTANT.

Construal, construe

In COGNITIVE LINGUISTICS, **construal** refers to the particular way in which a person attends to and conceptualizes an experience for the purposes of representing that experience in a linguistic utterance. Thus the pairs of sentences below portray different construals of the same situation:

The car is behind the tree – The tree is in front of the car
Sarah has bought a new laptop – Sarah has bought a new electronic device

Here, the first pair of sentences involves different perspectives on the relative location of the car and the tree. The second pair, on the other hand, involves different degrees of abstraction whereby Sarah's purchase is attended to and construed at different levels of detail. The cognitive linguists LEONARD TALMY and Ronald Langacker have proposed various different types of construal operations that can effect alternative construals.

See also FIGURE/GROUND.

Key texts: Langacker 1987–1991; Talmy 2000.

Construction grammar

Construction grammar refers to a group of related approaches to grammar that treat the **construction** as the basic unit of grammar. A construction consists of a linguistic form and the meaning associated with that form. For example, the **ditransitive** construction (as in *Paula gave Louisa a pencil*) has the grammatical form [Subject + Verb + Indirect Object + Direct Object], which is associated with the **constructional meaning** 'X causes Y to receive Z' (where X is the subject argument, Y the indirect object and Z the direct object argument).

Construction grammars therefore see grammatical structures (including morphological, phrasal and clause-level structures) as being directly associated with meanings, in the same way as lexical forms are associated with their meanings. Lexical and grammatical knowledge are consequently seen to differ only in that grammatical knowledge generally involves more schematic forms and meanings. This blurring of the distinction between syntax and the LEXICON distinguishes construction grammars from many

GENERATIVE approaches. Many construction grammars are associated with and share the key assumptions of COGNITIVE LINGUISTICS.

Key thinker: CHARLES FILLMORE.

Key texts: Fillmore et al. 1988; Goldberg 1995; Kay and Fillmore 1999; Croft 2001.

Content word

See CLOSED AND OPEN CLASSES.

Context

Context refers to the background against which the meaning of an UTTERANCE is interpreted. This includes the physical setting of the speech event (where and when it takes place), the identity and social relationship of the participants in the speech situation, the surrounding utterances in the same discourse situation (the **linguistic context**, also sometimes called **co-text**), and the background knowledge shared by the participants (their **common ground**). Interpreting an utterance such as that below relies on the context in various ways:

> I called the landlord about the bathroom and he said he'd come round tomorrow to fix the tap.

Here the hearer must, for instance, attend to the preceding linguistic context in order to figure out that *he* most likely refers to the landlord (see ANAPHORA). The interpretation of *tomorrow*, on the other hand, relies on knowing when the utterance is spoken (see DEIXIS). Shared background knowledge may be required to assign REFERENCE, including for inferring that the tap is probably the one in the bathroom. The field of PRAGMATICS is concerned specifically with the interpretation of linguistic utterances in context. Some semantic theories, however, hold that no definite distinction can be made between context-independent linguistic meaning and the contextual interpretation of that meaning (see COGNITIVE SEMANTICS).

Contradiction

One meaning of **contradiction** is a type of PROPOSITIONAL RELATION. A PROPOSITION P **contradicts** another proposition Q if and only if the truth of P ENTAILS the falsity of Q. For example, any sentence is contradicted by its negation:

Jean ate snails   contradicts   Jean did not eat snails.

Some propositions involving ANTONYMS are contradictions:

Elvis is alive   contradicts   Elvis is dead.
Elvis died in 1977   contradicts   Elvis was alive in 1980.

Contradiction can also refer to a property of a single proposition. In this case, a **contradictory proposition** is one that can never be true. For instance, *Hughie was dead when he was alive* is a contradiction if we take 'dead' and 'alive' in their literal senses. This sense of *contradiction* is the opposite of TAUTOLOGY.

Contradictory (antonym)

See ANTONYM.

Contrary (antonym)

See ANTONYM.

Contrast

Two expressions are in a relation of semantic **contrast** if they are not in a relation of semantic INCLUSION, and particularly if they have opposite POLARITY or are otherwise INCOMPATIBLE. For instance, one might say that the CONJUNCTION relation in natural language is inherently **contrastive** in that the two conjuncts are assumed to be semantically incompatible. Thus it is odd to say *dogs and canine animals* because the EXTENSION of *dog* is included in the extension of *canine animals*. But note how this expression is improved if it is changed to *dogs and other canine animals*, since *other canine animals* in this context does not refer to dogs. Some authors use the term *contrast* specifically to refer to the LEXICAL RELATION of non-binary CO-HYPONYMY as opposed to the binary relation of OPPOSITION or ANTONYMY. In this case, incompatible terms at the same level of a TAXONOMY are in a **contrast set** – for example, *red/yellow/blue* is the contrast set of primary colours.

Pragmatically, *contrast* can refer to relations in which differences in assumptions underlying inferences are highlighted. For example, in *He is wealthy, but kind* the *but* signals a contrast between the usual assumptions about wealthy people and the proposition that a wealthy person is kind. (See also IMPLICATURE.)

Contrastive focus

See FOCUS.

Convention, conventional

Convention generally refers to a pattern of behaviour that is established as a shared, common practice within a community (and it is part of common knowledge that this is so). Applied to language, we can say that a linguistic expression and/or its meaning is conventional if it is part of the shared knowledge of the language community that that particular form should be used, to designate that particular meaning. Conventions are generally ARBITRARY: in English, we conventionally use the form *dog* to designate 'a canine animal', but any other form could have been chosen to designate that meaning instead (or, the form *dog* could equally designate some other meaning). Conventions therefore have to be specifically learned by the members of the community.

Key thinker: **DAVID LEWIS**.

Key text: Lewis 1969.

Converse (antonym)

See ANTONYM.

Copula

A **copula** is a word that is used to link a subject and a PREDICATE – an expression that describes the identity or some property of the subject. In English, the verb *to be* is a copula – in the examples below, it serves the function of linking the subject *Cassie* with the predicates that follow it.

> Cassie **is** a bowling champion.
> Cassie **was** exhilarated.

Note that not all uses of the verb *to be* are copular: exceptions are its use as an auxiliary verb to mark passive VOICE (e.g. *This jigsaw **is intended** for ages 3 to 6*) or progressive ASPECT (*Christopher **was dusting** behind the bookcase*). Apart from the copula *to be*, other verbs can also be used as **copular verbs** – for example, *seem*, *become* and *remain*.

Co-refer, co-reference, co-referent

Two expressions **co-refer** (which is to say, they are each other's **co-referents**) if they refer to the same (set of) thing(s). This term is used especially with reference to ANAPHORS and their ANTECEDENTS, and is symbolized in linguistics texts by identical lower-case subscripted letters, usually starting with the letter *i*, as in:

> Joe$_i$ tried to wash himself$_i$ with his$_i$ last sliver of soap.

This notation indicates that *Joe*, *himself* and *his* all refer to the same person. Note that this notation has DISAMBIGUATED the sentence, which could also be interpreted as:

> Joe$_i$ tried to wash himself$_i$ with his$_j$ last sliver of soap.

The *j* subscript (in contrast to the *i* on *Joe*) indicates that *his* refers to someone other than Joe.

See also ANAPHOR, REFERENCE.

Co-text

See CONTEXT.

Count noun

See COUNTABILITY.

Countability

In English and many other languages, there is a grammatical and semantic distinction between words that denote individual things that can be counted and words that denote stuff that is not individuated and counted. *Cup* falls into the first category, called **count nouns**, and *rice* into the second, traditionally called **mass nouns**. Count nouns can be pluralized and preceded by numerals or other 'counting' QUANTIFIERS, like *several*, *many* or *a few*:

There are fifty/many cups in the cupboard.

Mass nouns are not pluralized (at least not in their 'mass' senses) and occur with no determiner or with non-counting quantifiers, such as *much*, or with **partitive** constructions, such as *cup(s) of* or *pound(s) of*.

I ate rice.
I ate too much rice. (#I ate too many rices.)
I ate three cups of rice.

However, English also allows for nouns that usually refer to countable entities to be reinterpreted as 'mass' substances and *vice versa*. For instance, if we use *china cup* with the morphological markings of a mass noun, we interpret it as something non-countable:

There was china cup all over the floor.

In this case, the reader is likely to construe *china cup* as referring to broken pieces of cup – not a whole cup that one could look at and count as 'one cup', since the inherent boundary (see BOUNDEDNESS) of the cup has been lost. The process by which descriptors of individuals are used to refer to substances is sometimes called the **Universal Grinder**. On the other hand, by a process sometimes called the **Universal Packager**, mass nouns can be interpreted as countable when they occur with count morphology. For example, *I drank three teas* can be interpreted as 'I drank three cups of tea.' Although the count noun *cup* has not occurred in this sentence, a countable meaning is inferred from the numeral and plural marking on *tea*. Another possible interpretation of this sentence is 'I drank three types of tea' – which similarly involves understanding a countable unit 'types' based on the plural marking on the usually non-countable *tea*.

The traditional count/mass dichotomy ignores a range of other types of (non-)countability. These include categories for non-pluralizable singular words for classes of unlike things (*furniture*, *cutlery*), always-plural words for single things with a symmetrical, double design (*trousers*, *scissors*) and words for groups made up of individuals (*committee*, *team*) – all of which have their own grammatical-countability and AGREEMENT properties. The extent to which some or all of these morphological categories are semantically motivated or ARBITRARY is subject to some debate.

See also BOUNDEDNESS.

Key texts: Wierzbicka 1985; Jackendoff 1991.

Counterfactual

A **counterfactual** statement is one that is meant to be understood as being inconsistent with reality, such as the first clause in *If pigs could fly, I'd be happy*.

See also CONDITIONAL.

Decompositional

A semantic theory is **decompositional** if it attempts to identify a semantic METALANGUAGE through the identification of meaning COMPONENTS in natural language meanings.

Definite, definiteness

A noun phrase is **definite** or **indefinite** if it is formally marked in order to indicate that the referent of the noun phrase is or is not unique for the purposes of that context. The use of a **definite** noun phrase PRESUPPOSES that the referent of the noun phrase is unique and identifiable in that context. PROPER NAMES are definite – unless explicitly marked otherwise. COMMON NOUNS are morphologically marked for definiteness or indefiniteness in many languages, including English, although in some languages definiteness is marked in more oblique ways, such as word order, CASE and TOPIC/FOCUS marking in Finnish. Such morphological marking may include a definite determiner (e.g. *the* in English: *the apple*), possessive determiners (*my baton*, *his cat*), DEMONSTRATIVE determiners (*this dictionary*, *those eggs*) and universal QUANTIFIERS (*all farmers*, *every girl*). Personal (*she*, *it*, *you*, *we*) and demonstrative (*this*, *those*) PRONOUNS are also definite. So, in uttering the following sentence, the speaker presupposes the existence of a unique referent for each of the bold noun phrases:

(1) **Jill** said that **the king of Spain** ate **her sandwich** before **she** could eat **it**.

Indefinite noun phrases indicate that the addressee cannot be expected to be able to uniquely identify the referent. In English indefinite noun phrases may be the combination of a common noun and the indefinite determiner *a(n)* (*a house*, *an inkspot*), other indefinite quantifiers (*some junk*, *many keys*, *five llamas*) or a plural without a determiner (*men*). Indefinite PRONOUNS typically share the same form as indefinite quantifiers (*one*, *some*). The bold noun phrases below are all indefinite:

(2) **A friend of mine** said that **a European king** ate **three of her sandwiches** before she could eat **one**.

Within a discourse, indefinite noun phrases are characteristically only used in the first instance of referring to a certain thing. After reference has been established through that initial indefinite noun phrase, the referent is unique and identifiable within the context. So, note that in example (2), *she* refers to the same person as *a friend of mine*. If we substitute an indefinite noun phrase for *she*, we have no choice but to interpret it as referring to a different person from *a friend of mine*.

(3) **A friend of mine**ᵢ said that **a European king** ate **three of her sandwiches** before **a friend**ⱼ could eat **one**.

Not all uses of the definite and indefinite articles indicate definite/indefinite reference – see REFERENCE.

Key texts: Russell 1905; Lyons 1999.

Definition

A **definition** is a statement of the meaning of a linguistic expression that explains what the expression refers to and what it does not refer to. The term to be defined is called **definiendum** and the explanation of its meaning **definiens**.

In semantics and LEXICOGRAPHY, a definition is typically expected to include only as much information as is necessary to explain the meaning of the word or phrase and exclude irrelevant information. This reflects ARISTOTLE's proposal that a definition should explicate the **essence** of the thing that is being defined – that is, those properties make the thing the kind of thing it is (stated as necessary and sufficient conditions – see CLASSICAL THEORY OF CONCEPTUALIZATION). This is distinct from **accidents**, properties that some instances of a kind may have but that are not necessary and do not determine whether the entity is an instance of its kind. For instance, the colour of a horse is an accidental property in that a horse is still a horse regardless of whether it is white, bay, chestnut – or blue. The general distinction between essential, defining properties and additional properties also correlates with a distinction many approaches to semantics make between the **linguistic meaning** or **dictionary meaning** of a word or a phrase and its ENCYCLOPAEDIC MEANING.

In lexicographic practice, definitions traditionally consist of two parts: **genus** and **differentiae**. The genus term states what kind of thing the defined entity is in general while the differentiae part distinguishes it from other members of that broader category. For example, in the definition of *pilot* as 'A person who flies an aircraft', the genus is *a person* and the differentiae part is *who files an aircraft* – this distinguishes pilots from other persons, such as chefs or teachers. Other principles or guidelines for defining include the avoidance of circularity (e.g. not defining *frying pan* as 'a pan used for frying') and formulating definitions in such a way that they reflect the grammatical function of the definiendum and can, in principle, be substituted for the definiendum in context. For example, the definition of the noun *pilot* above is itself a noun phrase and can be substituted for the word *pilot* in context: *At the party yesterday I met a pilot/person who files an aircraft.*

See also DENOTATION, SENSE, INTENSION.

Deictic, deixis

Deixis refers to the phenomenon where the meaning of some linguistic item relies inherently on the extralinguistic CONTEXT. Thus understanding **deictic expressions** like *that book*, *here*, *yesterday* or *I* depends on knowing where the utterance is spoken, when it is spoken and who is speaking. This kind of reference to the extralinguistic context is called **exophoric** (as opposed to ANAPHORIC) reference.

A distinction can be made between different **deictic categories**. **Spatial deixis** involves reference to the physical location and is commonly expressed by demonstratives (e.g. *this*, *that*) or deictic adverbs (*here* and *there*). Many languages make a distinction between **proximal** and **distal** spatial deixis. Hence *this book* refers to a book that is closer to the speaker than *that book*. **Temporal deixis** relates to the time of the utterance. Temporal deictic expressions include adverbs of time (e.g. *today*, *now*, *then*). Since TENSE expresses the relation of a situation to time (now, before now or after now), it can also be viewed as GRAMMATICALIZED expression of temporal deixis. PERSON **deixis** relies on the identity of the speaker and the addressee and is typically expressed by personal pronouns such as *I*, *we*, *you* or *they*. However, not all uses of personal pronouns are deictic – exceptions are anaphoric uses and impersonal uses, such as *you* in *You have to be under 16 years of age to qualify for a child discount*. **Social deixis** points to the social relationship between the speaker and the addressee. In many languages this is marked by formal and informal terms of address (e.g. the French second-person pronouns *vous* and *tu*), while languages such as Japanese and Korean employ extensive morphological markings on verbs and nouns to indicate degrees of deference and politeness.

The default interpretation of deictic expressions is **egocentric** in that it is assumed that the **deictic centre** – the reference point for interpreting the expression – is the speaker, her location and time of speaking. However, the deictic centre can be shifted: for instance, *come* and *bring* usually denote motion towards the speaker, but in *I'll bring some wine when I come over to your place* the deictic centre is shifted to the addressee.

Deixis straddles the boundary between semantics and PRAGMATICS in that the meanings of deictic expressions are conventionalized (e.g. *I* refers to 'the speaker'), but they at the same time rely inherently on the context for their interpretation.

See also REFERENCE, INDEXICAL.

Key texts: Lyons 1977; Levinson 1983; Fillmore 1997.

Demonstrative

Demonstratives are expressions such as *this, that, those* and *these*. A distinction can be made between **demonstrative determiners** and **demonstrative pronouns** – the former occur with a noun in a noun phrase (*this book, those boxes*), while the latter substitute for a whole noun phrase and therefore stand alone (*This is nice.*). Demonstratives are typically used for spatial DEICTIC reference, where the speaker refers to something in the physical CONTEXT, often while pointing (e.g. *Could you put this into that box?*). Demonstratives can also be used ANAPHORICALLY – that is, with reference back to something else mentioned in the preceding discourse (e.g. *I lost my favourite pen yesterday. I really loved that pen.*). A third use of demonstratives is for **discourse deixis**, where the reference is to parts of the preceding or following discourse, as in the example below, where *this joke* and *that* both refer to the joke:

> A: Listen to this joke: Two birds were sitting on a perch; one says to the other, 'Can you smell fish?'
> B: That was a stupid joke.

See also INDEXICAL.

Denotation

Denotation can be used to mean **denotative** (also called **conceptual** or **cognitive**) **meaning**, that is, the relation between an expression and the things (or properties or actions or concepts) that it refers to. Broadly speaking, a word's denotative meaning is its 'literal' meaning, the kind of meaning that is most directly represented in dictionary DEFINITIONS of a word. The process of **denotation** is thus the use of an expression to single out some thing or concept and refer to it. Denotative meaning contrasts with CONNOTATION.

The **Law of Denotation** states that if more information is added to a definition (or **sense**), its **extension** will shrink in size – that is, the more specific a definition, the fewer things it will denote. For example, the noun *dog* can be defined as 'a canine animal belonging to a domesticated breed' and *puppy* can be defined as 'a young canine animal belonging to a domesticated breed'. Since *puppy* has a more specific definition than *dog*, it cannot refer to as many animals as *dog* can, but instead refers to a subset of dogs.

See also REFERENCE.

Denotational versus representational

Semantic approaches can be divided into two main types. **Denotational** approaches attempt descriptions of the relation between language and the world – that is, between words or other expressions and the things or situations that they refer to (see DENOTATION). **Representational** approaches try to model how meaning is represented in the human mind – in other words, they are **mentalistic** in nature. Denotational approaches tend to derive from philosophy and mathematical logic (and thus FORMAL SEMANTIC approaches are often denotational), but much of the modern linguistic tradition in semantics is more representational than denotational – for example, COGNITIVE LINGUISTICS, CONCEPTUAL SEMANTICS and NATURAL SEMANTIC METALANGUAGE approaches are all representational.

Deontic

See MODALITY.

Dictionary meaning

See DEFINITION.

Disambiguate, disambiguation

An AMBIGUOUS expression, that is, an expression with more than one possible interpretation, can be **disambiguated** through the provision of contextual cues that indicate which of the possible meanings is preferable in the context. For example, in *I went to the bank to deposit some money*, the phrase *to deposit some money* makes it less likely that *bank* in the sentence means 'river bank'. Note, however, that, strictly speaking, the sentence is still ambiguous because it is logically possible that I went to a river bank to deposit money, even if it is unlikely.

A PARAPHRASE or formal representation of a sentence may **disambiguate** it, which is to say it provides a non-ambiguous alternative.

Discourse

In general terms, a **discourse** is a series of written or spoken UTTERANCES. Usually, this refers to a series of utterances on a specific occasion, but it can also refer to a series of utterances on a certain topic (either within or across an occasion). The term in this sense is most relevant to investigations of meaning that involve consideration of PRAGMATICS or of interactions of meaning between sentences (as in DISCOURSE REPRESENTATION THEORY).

In formal terms, **discourse** can be used as a synonym for UNIVERSE OF DISCOURSE.

Discourse Representation Theory

Discourse Representation Theory (**DRT**) is a MODEL-THEORETIC approach that was developed by Hans Kamp and colleagues in the 1980s. DRT has the particular aim of accounting for problematic cases of ANAPHORA, including DONKEY SENTENCES and anaphoric reference across sentences. Discourse meaning is represented as a series of **Discourse Representation Structures** (DRS) that are composed of discourse referents (i.e. the things being referred to) and PREDICATES that apply to those referents. With each successive sentence in a discourse, a new DRS is created based on the previous ones. A DRS is a partial model, which is true if it fits with the larger model created by the sequence of DRSs. DRT can be considered to be an early example of DYNAMIC SEMANTICS.

Key texts: Kamp 1981.

Disjunction

Disjunction is the 'or' relation between PROPOSITIONS or SENTENCES or components thereof: P or Q. Or can be interpreted as **exclusive**, in which case it is interpreted as 'P or Q but not both' or **inclusive**, in which case it is interpreted as 'P or Q or possibly both'. In formal LOGIC, the symbol $\vee$ stands for inclusive 'or'; exclusive 'or' can be stated in terms of inclusive disjunction, CONJUNCTION and NEGATION, although some logicians use special symbols as a shortcut. In natural language, it is often the case that we understand or as exclusive. For instance, if someone says to you *Please choose cake or pie*, you may assume that you may only have one. Nevertheless, *or* (and similar CONNECTIVES in other languages) is often AMBIGUOUS in natural language. In order to make clear that we mean inclusive or exclusive *or* in English, we can use phrases like *P and/or Q* and *either P or Q*, respectively.

See also LOGICAL OPERATOR.

Distal (spatial deixis)

See DEIXIS.

Domain

In FORMAL and computational approaches to semantics, a **domain** is a part of a MODEL against which an expression can be interpreted. This may be interpreted as a partially ordered set of PROPOSITIONS.

In COGNITIVE LINGUISTICS, a **domain** is a coherent knowledge structure that relates associated conceptual content. In CONCEPTUAL METAPHOR THEORY, *domain* is used to refer to conceptualizations of areas of experience that may function as the **source** and **target** of a conceptual metaphor. For instance, in the metaphor ORGANIZATION IS A PLANT (e.g. *After last year's phenomenal growth, the company is seeking to branch out to new areas*), PLANT is the source domain and ORGANIZATION is the target domain. In COGNITIVE GRAMMAR, *domain* is used in a more specific sense to refer to a coherent area of conceptualization that provides the background for understanding other concepts. This notion of domain is similar to the notion of FRAME and IDEALIZED COGNITIVE MODEL, but in Cognitive Grammar, it is specifically argued that domains are themselves understood relative to other domains. For instance, the concept PLANT may be understood relative to the domain of LIVING BEING, which for its part would presuppose an understanding of the domains of LIFE and PHYSICAL OBJECT.

Donkey sentence

The term **donkey sentence** refers to a class of sentences that share a particular problem for FORMAL analysis. The term is a reference to a classic example of such sentences: *Every farmer who owns a donkey beats it*. Such a sentence is impossible to translate into a first-order LOGIC (see PREDICATE CALCULUS) without representing the indefinite determiner in *a donkey* as a universal QUANTIFIER, while in most circumstances it would be treated as existential quantification. In other words, it must be translated to be equivalent to: *For every farmer and every donkey, if a farmer owns a donkey, then he beats it*. The pronouns in such examples are sometimes called **donkey pronouns** or **donkey ANAPHORA**.

See also DISCOURSE REPRESENTATION THEORY.

Dual

See NUMBER.

Durative, durativity

A **durative** EVENT is one that takes place over a course of some time, rather than in an instant (see PUNCTUAL). For instance, *eat an apple* and *dance* are both durative. Durativity is a property that contributes to **AKTIONSART** and **VENDLER CLASSES**.

See also ASPECT.

Dynamic

In discussions of ASPECT, an EVENT (as opposed to a STATE) is **dynamic** in that it describes a situation that involves something *happening* – that is, there is change over time, such as an action like *running* or a change of state like *blackening*. Its opposite is STATIVE.

The term **dynamic** is also used with reference to MODALITY and the theory of DYNAMIC SEMANTICS – see the related entries for further discussion.

See also **VENDLER CLASSES**.

Dynamic semantics

Dynamic semantics refers to formal approaches to meaning that rest on the assumption that the uttering of a sentence brings about a change, and that meaning should be understood in reference to the changes that a sentence makes – or a sentence's potential to make change. Smaller units than sentence are meaningful to the extent that they contribute to the change created by the sentence. How 'change' is interpreted here depends more particularly on the approach, but it might be understood in terms of what information is now present in the discourse that was not there earlier. Such views contrast to the TRUTH-CONDITIONAL approaches, which hold that meaning is a static relation between expressions and reality, or some model(s) of reality.

See also DISCOURSE REPRESENTATION THEORY.

Key texts: Groenendijk and Stokhof 1991; Muskens 1996.

Dysphemism

A **dysphemism** is a LEXEME that is selected for its derogatory CONNOTATIONS as compared to a more neutral description. For example, *vomit* is a neutral term, but *puke* is a dysphemistic way of referring to the same thing.

See also EUPHEMISM.

Embodiment

Embodiment refers to the idea that the human conceptual system is shaped by and reflects our bodily experience of the world. We experience the world in a particular way by virtue of having the kinds of bodies we do – bodies with fronts and backs, an upright orientation and particular kinds of limbs, sensory organs, and so on. Our CONCEPTS are then argued to reflect this embodied experience, as opposed to being purely objective representations of entities, categories and relations in the world. Thus what makes concepts like FRONT and BACK meaningful for us is the fact that we understand frontness and backness relative to our bodies.

The notion of embodiment is employed by many philosophers and cognitive scientists, and it forms a key assumption in COGNITIVE LINGUISTIC approaches. Cognitive linguists have proposed, for example, that the meaning of MODAL VERBS such as *must* or *may* is grounded in basic physical experiences of force and removal of restraint. Such basic sensory-motor experiences give rise to IMAGE SCHEMAS, very basic conceptual structures.

See also COGNITIVE LINGUISTICS, IMAGE SCHEMA, CONCEPTUAL METAPHOR THEORY.

Key thinker: GEORGE LAKOFF.

Key texts: Johnson 1987; Varela et al. 1991; Lakoff and Johnson 1999.

Emphatic, emphasizer

See INTENSIFIER.

Encyclopaedic meaning

In many approaches to semantics, a distinction is made between a word's DEFINITION or **linguistic meaning** and its **encyclopaedic meaning**. According to this distinction, linguistic meaning (sometimes also called **dictionary meaning** or **core meaning**) is something that we know by virtue of knowing a language, while encyclopaedic meaning is general world knowledge, known by virtue of our experience of the world. Linguistic meaning is often held to consist of defining properties that distinguish the word's DENOTATION from the denotations of other words. Thus the linguistic meaning of *triangle*, for example, might be 'a shape with three angles and sides', whereas the encyclopaedic meaning would include properties such as that the angles of the triangle add up to 180 degrees or that traffic warning signs are often triangle-shaped.

While the distinction between linguistic and encyclopaedic meaning is assumed in many approaches, not all semanticists draw the distinction in the same place. For instance, according to the NATURAL SEMANTIC METALANGUAGE approach, the linguistic meaning of *mouse* includes the fact that cats want to catch them (Wierzbicka 1996). Some approaches also argue against the distinction between encyclopaedic and linguistic meaning and see all meaning as encyclopaedic (e.g. COGNITIVE SEMANTICS, FRAME SEMANTICS, CONCEPTUAL SEMANTICS).

Key texts: Fodor et al. 1980; Haiman 1980; Peeters 2000.

Entailment

Entailment is the PROPOSITIONAL RELATION in which if one PROPOSITION is true, then it is always the case that the related proposition is true. This can be stated as the MATERIAL CONDITIONAL.

If P is true then Q is true (P → Q)

For example, *Fifi is a dog* entails *Fifi is an animal*, since part of the meaning of *dog* is that it is an animal, and thus it can never be the case that it is true that something is a dog without it also being true that that something is an animal. The entailment relation goes in one direction only (so, it is not the case that Q entails P too). **Mutual entailment**, in which P and Q entail each other, is also called (logical) PARAPHRASE.

Entrenchment

The term **entrenchment** is used in COGNITIVE LINGUISTIC approaches to refer to the way in which mental representations of linguistic units become established and how salient those representations are in the mind. Every cognitive event, including hearing some lexical form and understanding its meaning, leaves behind a memory trace of the pattern of conceptual activation involved. If the same cognitive event recurs repeatedly, that memory trace becomes strengthened and the cognitive activation becomes more routinized. This strengthening and routinization is called *entrenchment*. The term was coined by Ronald Langacker as part of the **usage-based** conception of language that is assumed in COGNITIVE GRAMMAR. This theory stresses that linguistic representations in the mind are abstracted from contexts of language use and that the degree of entrenchment of a particular linguistic unit or pattern is a function of its frequency. One of the implications of this view is that the mental LEXICON may be assumed to include representations of frequent compositional expressions, such as regular plurals (e.g. *cats*).

Key texts: Langacker 1987–1991; Barlow and Kemmer 2000.

Epistemic

See MODALITY.

Essence

See DEFINITION.

Etymology

Etymology refers either to the origin and history of a word or to the study of the origins of words as a branch of historical linguistics. Describing the etymology of a word involves explaining how it entered a language and the changes it has undergone in its meaning and form.

See also SEMANTIC CHANGE.

Euphemism

A euphemism is an alternative way of describing something so that the thing sounds more pleasant than it really is. For example, in different dialects of English, *powder room*, *restroom* and *cloakroom* are all euphemisms for *toilet* that avoid any mention of the bodily functions that take place there.

See also DYSPHEMISM.

Event

An **event** is a type of SITUATION that is DYNAMIC – that is, in which something happens. In this sense it can be contrasted to a STATE. Descriptions of events include some predicating element and its arguments – thus full sentence meanings are usually described as representing events, although a noun phrase like *the collapse of the building* could also be said to describe an event ('the building collapsed'). Types of events, in terms of their ASPECT qualities, can be described by the **VENDLER CLASSES**. Other types of events include CAUSATIVE and INCHOATIVE.

Evidential, evidentiality

Evidentiality is a type of MODALITY that indicates the speaker's source of the knowledge that is expressed in a PROPOSITION or SENTENCE – for instance, through personal observation, by hearsay or by inferring it from other knowledge. Languages like Turkish have morphological markers of evidentiality, but in English it can only be marked by lexical means (e.g. *apparently*) or through constructions such as *be supposed to*: *Daisy's stew is* **supposed to be** *delicious* (i.e. 'I have heard that it is, but I do not have experience of it myself').

Exclusive 'or'

See DISJUNCTION.

Exclusive pronoun

See PERSON.

Existential quantifier

See QUANTIFICATION.

Exophoric reference

See ANAPHORA, DEIXIS.

Experiencer

See SEMANTIC ROLE.

Explicature

See IMPLICATURE.

Extension

The extension of an expression is the set of all potential REFERENTS of the expression with respect to some world or MODEL. For example, the extension of *French cities* contains exactly those things that both qualify as cities and are in France. The extension of *water that does not contain hydrogen*, on the other hand, is the empty set, and therefore it has the same extension as any other expression that refers to nothing, such as *headless living people*. An **extensional semantics** is an approach to meaning that only deals with the relation between language and models of reality and possible realities, and not with the issue of how the expression describes and limits the expression (i.e. INTENSION).

Family resemblance

Family resemblances are similarities or shared properties among the members of a CATEGORY. The notion comes from the philosopher LUDWIG WITTGENSTEIN's discussion of the concept GAME. He argued that GAME cannot be defined by properties that are shared by all games (in other words, **necessary and sufficient conditions** – see CLASSICAL THEORY OF CONCEPTUALIZATION), since not all games involve an element of skill, nor luck, and not all involve competition or winning and losing. Instead, different members of the category share properties with various other members: for example, chess and poker (but not roulette) share the property 'involves skill' while poker and roulette (but not chess) both have the property 'involves luck'. Family resemblances have also been shown to correlate with PROTOTYPE EFFECTS: the more properties a member of a category shares with the other members, the more prototypical it is.

Key texts: Wittgenstein 1953; Rosch and Mervis 1975.

Feature

See COMPONENT, PRIMITIVE.

Figurative, figure of speech

Figurative language is commonly understood to refer to language that is embellished and poetic and uses imagery to achieve a special effect. **Figurative meaning** is meaning that is not **literal**. While the literal meaning of an utterance is variously understood to mean its CONVENTIONAL meaning or meaning that is truthful or directly meaningful, figurative meaning is non-conventional, not truthful and may need to be inferred in the context of the utterance (and is therefore often considered part of PRAGMATIC meaning). That is, if someone describes someone named Ed by saying *Ed is a skyscraper*, the sentence is untruthful with respect to its literal meaning (because Ed is a human being, not a very tall building) and should instead be understood figuratively, as describing Ed as being very tall.

Figurative meanings are often assumed to arise through the use of **figures of speech** such as METAPHOR (as in the example above), METONYMY (*I love to read Dickens*), **irony** (*I really hate these chocolate muffins you've made, but if* *you insist, I'll eat another one*), **hyperbole** (exaggeration: for example, *This book weighs a ton!*) and **understatement** (*Michael was a bit cross after the builders accidentally bulldozed his house*).

The distinction between literal and figurative meaning is debated and disputed in many theoretical approaches. Cognitive linguists in particular disagree with the notion that figurative language is derivative or supplementary to literal language and instead argue that figurative language, particularly metaphor and metonymy, reflect the way we conceptualize abstract notions in terms of more concrete ones (see Conceptual Metaphor Theory).

Key texts: Searle 1978; Gibbs 1994.

Figure/ground

Within a perceived scene or situation, there is typically some entity, known as the **figure**, that is more salient or stands out against the rest of the scene, the **ground**. Imagine, for instance, a spider running across the carpet – the spider is the figure and the carpet is the ground. The figure is perceived to contrast with the ground: it is typically smaller than the ground, has a more clearly defined shape, and may be moving while the ground remains stationary. Importantly, figure/ground organization is not an objective property of a scene but is rather imposed by the conceptualizer. This is demonstrated by the fact that it is possible to assign figure status to different elements in a scene, as in Rubin's face/vase illusion (Figure 4) where either the faces or the vase can be construed as the figure.

The notion of figure/ground organization is applied to the description of linguistic structure by some cognitive linguistic theories, particularly in Leonard Talmy's approach to cognitive semantics and in Cognitive Grammar. In Talmy's work on the lexicalization of motion events, the figure refers to an object that is conceptualized as moving or as potentially moving, while the ground is the reference point against which the figure's movement or location is described. Talmy points out that language imposes certain expectations of figure/ground asymmetry on locational expressions, which explains the oddity of the second sentence below:

The football is by the tree.
?The tree is by the football.

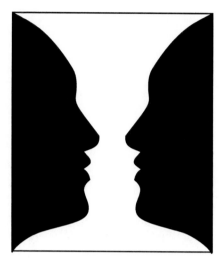

Figure 4 Face/vase illusion

Cognitive Grammar, on the other hand, applies the notion of figure/ground organization to multiple levels of linguistic structure. For instance, at the clausal level, the subject can be identified as the figure (or **trajector**, in Ronald Langacker's terminology) while the object is the ground (or **landmark**). Langacker also maintains that the meanings of all linguistic items are **profiled** against a **base** of background knowledge. This relationship between profiled aspects of meaning and the background constitutes one kind of figure/ground asymmetry.

See also **construal**.

First-order logic

See **predicate calculus**.

Focus

Focus is the marking of important new information in a sentence. In some languages, for instance, the West African language Hausa, focus can be marked with particular focus morphemes. In English, it is common to use stress in pronunciation to indicate focus, as in (1) or to use cleft constructions as in (2) and (3) in order to put the focused item in a special position.

(1) I ate **the cake**, not the pie.
(2) It was **the cake** that I ate.
(3) What I want is **a cake**.

Focus can be **contrastive** or **presentational**. In contrastive focus, the focused element is implicitly or explicitly contrasted to something else that has been referred to or implied in the discourse. Example (1) shows an explicit case, where *cake* is focused in order to contrast it with discourse expectations that the speaker instead ate pie. Presentational focus introduces new information without the contextual contrast. Example (3) might be used in this way.

See also TOPIC.

Formal semantics

A **formal semantic** theory is one that uses a formal METALANGUAGE – that is, a LOGIC or similar mathematical language – in order to represent natural language meanings. Such approaches are valued for their precision. Since the metalanguage has very clear rules and its elements have very specific meanings, formal representations avoid the problem of AMBIGUITY and are very testable. Formal approaches typically rely on the notions of truth and falsity in defining PROPOSITIONAL meaning and pay a good deal of attention to the types of phenomena that can be translated using LOGICAL OPERATORS.

See also TRUTH CONDITION, MODEL-THEORETIC SEMANTICS, MONTAGUE GRAMMAR, SITUATION SEMANTICS, DYNAMIC SEMANTICS, DISCOURSE REPRESENTATION THEORY.

Frame, Frame Semantics

Frame Semantics is a theory of linguistic meaning developed by CHARLES FILLMORE. Its key claim is that the meanings of LEXEMES are understood relative to background **frames**. Frames are coherent systems of related concepts that represent schematizations of experience. For example, the cultural notion of the SEVEN-DAY WEEK is a frame that provides the background for understanding the meanings of the names of days of the week, as well as the terms *weekend*, *fortnight* and even *Monday morning blues*.

To the extent that it describes a structured complex of knowledge, Fillmore's notion of FRAME is related to the use of this term in psychology, as well as to notions such as SCRIPT, DOMAIN and IDEALIZED COGNITIVE MODEL. Fillmore specifically sets up Frame Semantics in opposition to COMPONENTIAL and TRUTH-CONDITIONAL SEMANTICS by arguing that a complete understanding of the meanings of linguistic items requires reference to the ENCYCLOPAEDIC MEANING provided by frames. Frame Semantics also contrasts with STRUCTURAL SEMANTICS in that the meanings of words are seen to derive from their associations with the background frame, not from associations with other words.

Applications of the notion of FRAME include its use in describing the meanings of related verbs. For example, the meanings of *buy*, *sell*, *cost* and *pay* are all understood against the COMMERCIAL TRANSACTION frame, which specifies that a commercial transaction involves the participants BUYER, SELLER, GOODS and MONEY. Each of the verbs highlights different participant roles: *buy*, for instance, focuses on the BUYER and the GOODS (*Michelle bought a bouquet of flowers*) while *cost* focuses on GOODS and MONEY (*The flowers cost £10*).

The description of the frames evoked by different lexemes is the focus of the recent work in Frame Semantics under the FrameNet project at University of California, Berkeley.

See also SEMANTIC FIELD.

Key texts: Fillmore 1982, 1985; Fillmore and Atkins 1992.

Function word

See CLOSED AND OPEN CLASSES.

Future tense

See TENSE.

Fuzziness, fuzzy

The term **fuzziness** is used to describe the boundaries of CATEGORIES: **fuzzy** boundaries are ill-defined, rather than sharp. For instance, is rhubarb a fruit? Different speakers may give different answers, may be uncertain of their answer or give different answers depending on the context (e.g. in a cooking versus gardening context). This suggests that the boundaries of the category FRUIT are fuzzy. A well-known illustration of the fuzziness of category boundaries is a study by William Labov that considered the boundaries of the categories CUP and BOWL. Labov asked his informants to categorize pictures of vessels of varying widths, and discovered that there was no consensus over the width at which a vessel should be called a *bowl* rather than a *cup*. The notion of the fuzziness of category boundaries is a key argument used against the CLASSICAL THEORY OF CONCEPTUALIZATION and for the PROTOTYPE THEORY.

See also FAMILY RESEMBLANCE, VAGUENESS.

Key texts: Labov 1973; Rosch 1975.

Gender

Gender is a means of classifying nouns and pronouns that is important to AGREEMENT relations. Frequently, but not always, these include **feminine**, **masculine** and **neuter** categories. There are two varieties of gender. **Natural gender** is the use of gendered forms to match the sex of the thing that is described. For example, in English third-PERSON pronouns generally (with the exception of some more poetic uses) reflect natural gender – we use *she* for females, *he* for males and *it* for sexless things.

Grammatical gender is the assignment of a gender category to a word form, which may or may not reflect the natural gender of the item in question. For instance, in Spanish every noun is designated as feminine or masculine – most female and male things are referred to using feminine and masculine nouns, respectively, but names for inanimate objects are also marked as *feminine* or *masculine*. For instance, *el sofá* 'the sofa' is masculine, while *la silla* 'the chair' and *la mesa* 'the table' are feminine. Some grammatical gender systems do not relate to the sex of the referents at all. For example, in Swedish, the grammatical genders are 'common gender', which includes most ANIMATES as well as many other nouns like *en bok* 'a book', and 'neutral gender', which includes many ABSTRACT nouns, but also others, like *ett bord* 'a table'. Bantu languages, like Swahili, are noted for their large numbers of grammatical gender categories, which are usually called **noun classes**. Languages with grammatical gender systems tend to require nouns to agree with their modifiers and sometimes to agree within subject–verb relations.

Traditionally, the relation between the grammatical gender of a noun and the natural gender of the object it refers to is considered to be ARBITRARY and may have more to do with the form of the noun than its meaning. However, many gender or noun class categories tend to include certain types of words – for instance, most of the body part words in a language might be in a particular gender category. This is thought to reflect less arbitrary categorizations at some earlier point in the language's development, but the arbitrarily assigned gender of a noun may also influence its CONNOTATIONS.

Key text: Corbett 1991.

Generalization

See SEMANTIC CHANGE.

Generative, generative grammar

A linguistic theory is **generative** if it consists of a finite set of rules and principles that generate all of the possible expressions in a language while ruling out those that are not possible. The term is particularly associated with **generative grammar**, a cover term for approaches to syntactic theory that rely on generative rules – in particular those associated with **NOAM CHOMSKY**. Most generative approaches to syntax involve what is known as an **interpretive semantics** – that is, the assumption that semantic interpretation happens to already-generated syntactic structures (particularly at a level of analysis called **Logical Form** or **LF**). This is opposed to the role of semantics in **GENERATIVE SEMANTICS** (and related theories that followed it), where it is assumed that semantic structures generate the syntactic structures.

Key texts: Chomsky 1965, 1995; Hornstein 1995; Newmeyer 1995.

Generative Lexicon (theory)

The **Generative Lexicon** approach is a theory of semantics developed by computational linguist James Pustejovsky. One of its particular concerns is accounting for POLYSEMY and the fact that words have different SENSES in different contexts. In the Generative Lexicon approach, senses are generated in context through the composition of semantic COMPONENTS that are encoded in the lexical entries of each of the words within a phrase or clause. The model is GENERATIVE in the sense that it aims to account for the flexibility of word meaning through finite means – the components and the lexical rules for combining these at the phrasal level.

In this approach, lexical entries consist of multiple levels of representation. For instance, the level of **argument structure** gives the number and type of logical arguments a word has. The level of QUALIA structure includes a number of roles that characterize the properties of the referent of the lexical item, such as the general category the entity belongs to, its function and any factors involved in its origin or creation. For example, the lexical structure for *book* would be represented as shown in Figure 5.

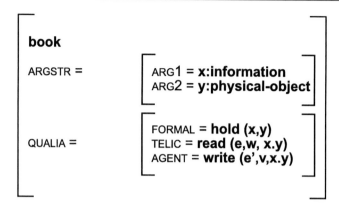

Figure 5 A Generative Lexicon representation of *book*

The argument structure representation specifies that *book* is associated with two readings of different types; a book as a unit of information and as a physical object. The telic role indicates that the purpose of a book is to be read by an individual, while the agentive role specifies that a book was created by being written. The different qualia roles then account for the different readings of *Eleanor began a book*, where she may have begun to either read it or write it. The representation of *begin* specifies that one of its arguments must be an EVENT and therefore *begin* combines with either the event given under the telic role or the agentive role in the lexical representation of *book*. This also means that the nominal *book* is given an event reading, effecting what is called **type coercion**.

See also COMPOSITIONALITY.

Key texts: Pustejovsky 1991, 1995.

Generative Semantics

Generative Semantics was an important approach to the relation between meaning and syntax that was active in the 1970s as a reaction to the interpretive semantics of GENERATIVE GRAMMAR. In Generative Semantics, as in early generative grammars, the first level of syntactic generation is a **deep structure** to which various changes (transformations) happen in order to make a grammatical **surface structure** representation – that is, the grammatical form that one experiences when a sentence is used. Generative Semanticists held that deep structure is a semantically motivated level, and that the means of semantic representation are universal – that is to say, that the deep structure for a sentence meaning 'I love that hat' would be the same no matter what language it was composed in, regardless of any syntactic differences across the languages. This meant that syntactic transformations would be wholly responsible for moving the parts of the sentence into a form that is grammatical for a particular language and that the number of syntactic categories available at the deep level was minimal.

NOAM CHOMSKY (or, more directly, several of his influential students) opposed the Generative Semantic enterprise from its start, and it ran into a number of explanatory problems, such as accounting for QUANTIFIER SCOPE changes that come with certain transformations and lack of evidence that sentences that require more transformations are any more difficult to psychologically process than those that do not. However, many of the assumptions of Generative Semantics were to re-emerge in the COGNITIVE LINGUISTICS movement, which abandons many of the assumptions of generative grammar.

Key thinker: GEORGE LAKOFF.

Key texts: Lakoff 1971; McCawley 1973; Harris 1993.

Generic

The term *generic* is applied to several semantic phenomena. **Generic reference** is a type of reference (see REFERENCE) that involves reference to a class, rather than an individual member of a class. **Generic aspect** is a type of HABITUAL ASPECT that involves broad, general statements about a class, as in *Elephants live in Africa and Asia*. **Generic level** is another term for the BASIC LEVEL.

Given/new information

See TOPIC.

Goal

See SEMANTIC ROLE.

Gradability, gradable

ADJECTIVES like *early*, *easy* and *eager* are **gradable**, as they denote PROPERTIES that can be had to greater or lesser degrees. This can be tested by using the adjectives with INTENSIFIERS like *very* and *somewhat* or by using them in a comparison: *This class is earlier than that one*. Adjectives like *dead*, *perfect* and *non-gradable* are **non-gradable** in that they denote properties that a thing either has or does not have. These categories of adjective are linked to contrary and contradictory ANTONYMS, respectively.

See also SCALE.

Grammaticalization, grammaticalize, grammaticalized

A notion that is **grammaticalized** in a language is expressed as part of the language's CLOSED-CLASS system. For example, the notion that something happened before now is grammaticalized in English in the morphological past TENSE, usually marked with the past tense suffix *-ed*.

The term **grammaticalization** (or **grammaticization**) refers to the process in which lexical, open-class items come to be used as closed-class, grammatical items. For example, the English verb *will*, which is today used to refer to the future, derives from the Old English lexical verb meaning 'want'. This process of grammaticalization was accompanied by semantic bleaching (see SEMANTIC CHANGE) in that the modal auxiliary verb *will* no longer designates wanting or desiring anything.

Key text: Hopper and Traugott 2003.

Grammatical word

See CLOSED AND OPEN CLASSES.

Ground

In METAPHOR, the **ground** is the similarity between the TENOR and the VEHICLE. For example, in *Rob is a beanpole*, the similarity between Rob (a person) and a beanpole is that both are remarkably tall and thin.

For the use of **ground** in contrast with *figure*, see FIGURE/GROUND.

Habitual

Habitual ASPECT indicates that a type of EVENT happens regularly over time, in a repeated or on-going way. In other words, it marks a type of event that typically happens. Habitual is marked by special verb morphology in some languages. The past tense *used to* is the closest thing that standard English has to a straightforward habitual marker on the verb:

> I used to go to that restaurant. (i.e. 'I went there regularly')

English also often marks habituality through the use of the simple present or past marking on a DYNAMIC VERB, as in the following sentences:

> The bus comes at six (every day).
> Ivan rides his bike to work.
> Jen whistled when she worked.

When such examples are interpreted as habitual, they are understood to mean that the activity described is typical, but not necessary. For example, the *whistled* example is not interpreted as meaning that Jen whistled from the moment she started work and did not stop until the end of her shift, and it would not be falsified by evidence that Jen whistled only 50 per cent of the working day.

See also GENERIC, ITERATIVE.

Historical present

See TENSE.

Holism

Semantic **holism** (as opposed to ATOMISM) is the position that meanings are not composed of semantic COMPONENTS – that is, that any subparts that may be discerned in a meaning cannot exist without reference to the whole meaning or to the arrangements of meanings in a semantic network. This position has been promoted by a number of philosophers of language, where it is usually discussed in relation to PROPOSITIONS. In linguistic semantics, holism is rarely applied to sentential meanings, where the principle of COMPOSITIONALITY is usually a precept, but a form of holism can be argued to exist in some treatments of lexical meaning, such as in some forms of SEMANTIC FIELD theory within STRUCTURAL SEMANTICS. Holism has been challenged on psychological grounds – that it does not provide an explanation for how people learn new meanings.

Key texts: Quine 1951; Putnam 1975; Fodor and Lepore 1992.

Holonym, holonymy

See MERONYM.

Homonym, homonymous, homonymy

A **homonym** is a LEXEME that shares the same form as another, separate lexeme. An example of this is *tattoo*$_1$ 'an ink drawing in the skin' and *tattoo*$_2$ 'a military drum signal'. **Homonymy** and POLYSEMY both involve one lexical form that is associated with multiple senses and as such both are possible sources of lexical AMBIGUITY. But while homonyms are distinct lexemes that happen to share the same form, in polysemy a single lexeme is associated with multiple senses. The distinction between homonymy and polysemy is usually made on the basis of the relatedness of the senses: polysemy involves related senses, whereas the senses associated with homonymous lexemes are not related. Whether the senses associated with some lexical form are related or not can be determined either diachronically (by establishing if the senses have a common historical origin) or synchronically (by considering whether there is a plausible semantic relation between the senses today). For example, the senses of *adult*, 'grown up' and 'sexually explicit' (as in *an adult movie*) are polysemous because they are related both historically and semantically. In contrast, neither a historical nor semantic relation exists between the two senses of *tattoo* above: the two *tattoo* words entered English at separate times and from separate sources (Polynesian and Dutch, respectively), and it is difficult to think of a plausible semantic connection between ink drawings and military drum signals. Therefore these two senses belong to distinct homonymous lexemes.

Homonyms may share either the same phonological or the same written form – or both, as in the case of *tattoo*. **Homophones** are pronounced the same, but not necessarily written the same, as in *cash* and *cache*. **Homographs** have the same written form, but not necessarily the same phonological form, as in *wind* /wɪnd/ and *wind* /waɪnd/. The identity of the forms of homonyms often arises accidentally through phonological change so that words that were originally pronounced differently come to be pronounced the same. Another source of homonymy is lexical borrowing when a borrowed word has the same form as another existing word in the language. Homonymy may also arise when the senses of a polysemous lexeme diverge so they are no longer perceived as belonging to the same word. For instance, although the 'metal spike' and 'hard flat plate at the end of a finger or toe' senses of *nail* are related historically, the semantic relation may not be obvious to all speakers, and so the different senses may be associated with different homonymous lexemes in their mental LEXICONS. Such cases, however, mean that the distinction between homonymy and polysemy is not always clear-cut because what looks like a polyseme from a historical perspective is synchronically a homonym, at least for some speakers. Furthermore, because in some cases the semantic relation between the senses is more obvious than others, it has been argued that the distinction between polysemy and homonymy should be viewed as being a matter of degree.

Further reading: Lyons 1977.

Hyperonym, hyponym, hyponymy

Hyponymy is the LEXICAL RELATION that expresses a relationship of INCLUSION between two LEXEMES, such as *bird* and *swan* or *cup* and *teacup*. The lexeme with the more general or inclusive meaning is called a **hyperonym** (or, in some texts, **hypernym**), while the lexeme with the more specific or less inclusive meaning is a **hyponym**. Thus *swan* is a hyponym of *bird*, and conversely, *bird* is the hyperonym of *swan*. Lexemes that are hyponyms of the same hyperonym, at the same level of categorization (and that are therefore 'semantic sisters' and in a relationship of CONTRAST) are called **co-hyponyms** – thus, for example, *swan*, *robin* and *pigeon* are all co-hyponyms.

Although hyponymy is defined in terms of inclusion, what-includes-what is dependent on whether hyponymy is viewed in terms of EXTENSIONS (the categories that the words refer to), or in terms of INTENSIONS or SENSES (the semantic content associated with the words). From the extensional perspective, we can say that the category BIRD includes all the members of the category SWAN. Viewed intensionally, however, the inclusion relation is reversed: the hyponymous sense includes the sense of the hyperonym. If we define *bird* as 'a winged animal that lays eggs', the meaning of *swan* would include this semantic content plus some other more specific properties, such as that swans are usually white, have long necks and webbed feet.

Hyponymy typically gives rise to unilateral ENTAILMENT whereby the hyperonym entails the hyponym, but not vice versa. So *Paul was attacked by a swan* entails *Paul was attacked by a bird*, but if we know that Paul was attacked by a bird, we do not know that the attacker was necessarily a swan – it could have been a pigeon or a blue tit. Cases of **functional hyponymy**, however, are exceptions to the idea that truth of the hyponym entails the truth of the hyperonym. This is because in functional hyponymy the hyperonym defines what the hyponym can be 'used' as, rather than what it is. Thus although *doll* can be seen as a hyponym of *toy*, knowing that something is a doll does not entail that it is a toy because not all dolls are toys – consider, for example, the life-sized dolls used to train people in resuscitation.

Key texts: Wierzbicka 1984; Cruse 2002; Murphy 2003.

See also TAXONOMY, TAXONYMY.

Iconic, iconicity

Iconicity refers to the phenomenon in which the form of a linguistic expression (or of any other kind of SIGN) has some kind of resemblance to the meaning associated with it. Iconicity therefore contrasts with ARBITRARINESS in that in iconicity there is a motivated reason for why the meaning is designated by that particular form.

Onomatopoeic words such as *bang*, *smash* or *hush* are examples of **iconic signs** in that their phonological forms resemble the sounds that they produce. **Sound symbolism** refers to the idea that iconic motivations may exist at the level of individual sounds; it has, for example, been proposed that high front vowels like [i] are often associated with meanings that relate to smallness (e.g. *little*, *tiny*).

Iconicity can also be involved at the level of grammatical structure. For example, the order of events is typically reflected in the order in which they are mentioned: compare *Tina opened the door and put on her sunglasses* and *Tina put on her sunglasses and opened the door*. The morphological process of **reduplication** can also be seen as being iconically motivated insofar as it involves a correlation between more form and more meaning. This is seen most clearly in cases where reduplication is used to mark plurality or ITERATIVITY (examples from Moravcsik 1978):

> Sundanese: *paturunan*, 'descendant'; *paturunanpaturunan*, 'descendants'
> Tzeltal: *-pik* 'touch it lightly'; *-pikpik* 'touch it lightly repeatedly'

See also ARBITRARINESS, SEMIOTICS.

Key texts: Jakobson 1965; Haiman 1983.

Idealized cognitive model

The notion of **idealized cognitive model** or **ICM** comes from the work of COGNITIVE LINGUIST GEORGE LAKOFF. An ICM is a complex conceptual structure that represents an abstraction or idealization of experiential knowledge. Lakoff's ICMs are in many respects similar to CHARLES FILLMORE'S FRAMES. However, one of Lakoff's particular concerns is using the notion of ICMs to explain PROTOTYPE EFFECTS and in this he extends Fillmore's account considerably.

Lakoff's general proposal is that prototypes are not explicitly represented in the mind, as is assumed in the Pʀᴏᴛᴏᴛʏᴘᴇ Tʜᴇᴏʀʏ. Instead, prototype effects may arise because a category member does not fit the content of the ICM (or cluster of ICMs) that the category is defined against. For example, Catholic priests and men in long-term co-habiting relationships are not typical members of the category ʙᴀᴄʜᴇʟᴏʀ, even though they are unmarried male adults. Lakoff maintains that this is because ʙᴀᴄʜᴇʟᴏʀ is defined relative to an ICM that represents idealized background conditions against which we judge a person to be a bachelor. This background ICM does not take into account vows of celibacy or the possibility of moving together with your partner before you are married. In other cases, prototype effects arise due to ᴍᴇᴛᴏɴʏᴍɪᴄ ICMs in which a typical, stereotypical, ideal or salient subcategory stands for the category as a whole (e.g. ʀᴏʙɪɴ stands for the category ʙɪʀᴅ).

Key text: Lakoff 1987.

Idiom, idiomatic

An **idiom** is a complex, multiword expression whose meaning is **non-ᴄᴏᴍᴘᴏsɪᴛɪᴏɴᴀʟ**, that is, not predictable from the meanings of the constituent parts. For example, one cannot work out that *spill the beans* means 'reveal the information' or *cut the mustard* means 'meet an expected standard' just on the basis of knowing the meanings of each of the individual words in the expressions and the rules of English grammar. Instead, one has to learn the expressions as whole units and store them in the lexicon as ʟᴇxᴇᴍᴇs. Because idioms are fixed expressions, the idiomatic meaning is typically not preserved if any of the component words are replaced with a (near) sʏɴᴏɴʏᴍ, as in *spill the **pulses***. The grammatical form of an idiom is also usually restricted. For example, *Peter kicked the bucket* cannot be put into passive ᴠᴏɪᴄᴇ while still retaining the idiomatic meaning: *The bucket was kicked by Peter* does not mean 'Peter died'. Some idioms are ᴍᴇᴛᴀᴘʜᴏʀɪᴄᴀʟʟʏ motivated – for example, *let off steam* 'release pent-up emotions' can be seen as involving a metaphorical conceptualization of a person as a pressurized steam cooker.

Key text: Nunberg et al. 1994.

Image schema

The term **image schema** is used in COGNITIVE LINGUISTICS to refer to very basic conceptual structures that represent recurring patterns in our experience of the physical world. Image schemas are multimodal representations; they are not based on a single sensory modality such as vision, but on a holistic awareness of the motion and location of our own bodies and the experience of other things moving and acting on each other. Examples of image schemas include CONTAINER, SOURCE-PATH-GOAL and FORCE schemas. The CONTAINER schema, for instance, represents the basic notion of containment. It is derived from the subjective experience of our bodies as containers (for air, food, etc.) and things contained (in rooms, inside our clothes, etc.). The basic structure of the CONTAINER image schema consists of an interior, a boundary and the exterior. This structural configuration gives rise to basic logical notions such as the transitivity of containment (if I am in a room, and the room is in a house, then I am in a house). Image schematic structure is derived from concrete physical experience but can be projected onto abstract concepts and serve as the **source** DOMAIN of CONCEPTUAL METAPHOR. We may, for example, conceptualize emotional states as containers: *I am **in** love*.

See also EMBODIMENT.

Key texts: Johnson 1987; Lakoff 1987; Hampe 2005.

Imperfective

Imperfective is a category of ASPECT in which the internal structure of an EVENT is relevant. In English, the progressive can be considered to be an imperfective aspect:

> Karen was singing a song.

In using this sentence, we refer to a time during the singing of the song. Even though it is in the past tense, it makes no reference to the completion of the event (and it remains possible that the song was never completed).

See also PERFECTIVE, PERFECT.

Implicature

Implicature is a PRAGMATIC type of INFERENCE – that is, a means of communicating more than is literally said. In implicating something and interpreting an implication, speaker and addressee (respectively) depend on aspects of the non-linguistic CONTEXT. For example, say a friend invited you to lunch and made soup for you both. After you both have had your first taste, he says as follows:

I don't know about this soup. Do you want some salt?

You would probably understand your friend to additionally mean 'I'm worried that you'll find this soup too bland.' This interpretation of what has been communicated does not arise from any of the particular words or structures in the sentences alone, but from one's knowledge of (among other things) the responsibilities of a host, the usual preferred properties of a soup and the role of salt in making food more flavourful.

Implicature is usually used to mean **conversational implicature**, in which the inference is calculated from knowledge of conversational principles and the context, as in the soup example. Unlike ENTAILMENTS, conversational implicatures can be cancelled. To illustrate this, consider the example of a **scalar implicature**. In a scalar implicature, we interpret expressions that denote a degree or quantity of something as expressing the highest degree/quantity that is true in the context. We do this because of assumptions we make about the nature of communication – that is, that people try to be as informative as is possible and relevant in that context. So, for example, if someone says *Lex has two children*, we understand them to mean that he has only two children, because if he had three, it would be more informative to say *Lex has three children*. But this 'two and only two' interpretation is cancellable if contextual properties make it appropriate to do so, as in the following dialogue:

A: You need to have two children to qualify for a tax break.
B: Lex has two children – in fact, he has three.

Conversational implicatures can be divided into generalized and particularized implicatures. A **generalized implicature** is not limited to the particular context at hand. So, a scalar implicature is generalized in that no matter the context, when we say *two*, we can usually be understood to intend to mean 'exactly two'. The soup example, on the other hand, is a case of a **particularized implicature**, since the same implicature would not arise if the speaker were in a supermarket, reading the label on a can of soup.

The term **conventional implicature** is opposed to *conversational implicature*, and refers to inferences that are attached by CONVENTION to particular linguistic forms. For example, in *She was poor, but honest*, the connective *but* is logically equivalent to *and*, but it also communicates the conventional implicature that being poor and being honest are not an expected combination. Conventional implicatures are not cancellable.

Some theoreticians distinguish between implicatures and **explicatures**. When the term is used in contrast with *explicature*, *implicature* refers to cases like the soup example above, which communicate other PROPOSITIONS that are additional to the one(s) directly communicated through the form of the utterance. Explicatures, in contrast, involve the 'filling in' of information that is left unsaid in the utterance, so that a complete proposition is understood. For instance, if your friend said *I ate already* in the afternoon, you would fill in the information that what he ate was *lunch*. Scalar implicatures, on this view, are really explicatures, as they can be expressed by adding *exactly* (or something like it) to the utterance: *Lex has exactly two children*.

The philosopher H. P. Grice famously proposed a communicative principle – the **Co-operative Principle** – and a number of maxims of communication in order to account for the ways in which speakers and hearers produce and understand implicatures, and his work is the basis for much pragmatics research today – either as developments of his principle and maxims or alternatives to it.

Key texts: Grice 1975; Sperber and Wilson 1995; Levinson 2000.

Inceptive

See INCHOATIVE.

Inchoative

Verbs (or PREDICATES) whose meanings involve 'beginning' or 'becoming' are referred to as **inchoative** (also **inceptive**) from the Latin verb for 'begin'. Inchoative verbs describe a change of state or a beginning of having a state. For example *redden* means 'become red' and *open* denotes the change from being closed to not being closed. CAUSATIVE verbs can also be considered to be inchoative.

Inclusion, inclusive

The terms **inclusion** and **inclusive** can apply to a number of semantic phenomena. In SEMANTIC (particularly LEXICAL) RELATIONS, a relation of inclusion is when the EXTENSION of one term is a proper subset of the extension of another. For example, the things denoted by *kitten* are also among the things denoted by *cat* (see HYPONYM). **Proper inclusion** is when a SUBORDINATE CATEGORY is wholly contained within another, SUPERORDINATE category. The set of *blue pens* is properly included within the set of *pens* because there is nothing that is in the set of blue pens that is not also in the set of pens.

See also DISJUNCTION for discussion of **inclusive disjunction** and PERSON for discussion of **inclusive pronouns**.

Incompatibility

Incompatibility is a SEMANTIC RELATION between two expressions in which both expressions can never refer to the same thing. For example, *book* and *hiccup* are incompatible because if something is a book, then it is not a hiccup, and vice versa. Incompatibility is an important concept in the definition of ANTONYM or OPPOSITE.

See also CONTRADICTION.

Indefinite

See DEFINITE.

Indeterminacy

See VAGUENESS.

Indexical

Indexicals are expressions whose reference depends on the context of use. Therefore, DEICTIC expressions are indexical: in *I want you to stand there*, what *I*, *you* and *there* refer to is dependent on who is talking to whom and the physical location. A distinction is sometimes made between **pure indexicals** and **demonstratives** – the referent of pure indexicals such as *I*, *today* and *now* can be determined just on the basis of the general context, whereas demonstratives such as *this* and *that* require the speaker to direct the hearer's attention in order to fix reference.

In SEMIOTICS, **indexical SIGNS** are ones that involve a direct connection between the sign's form and its meaning. For example, smoke is an **index** of fire.

See also DEIXIS.

Indicative

See MOOD.

Inference

Information that follows from a PROPOSITION or UTTERANCE without being directly communicated through its form is **inferred**, and the content or process of inferring is **inference**. Inferences can arise through semantic relations or pragmatic processes.

See PROPOSITIONAL RELATION (ENTAILMENT, CONTRADICTION, PARAPHRASE), IMPLICATURE, PRESUPPOSITION.

Instrument

See SEMANTIC ROLE.

Intensifier

An **intensifier** is an expression that modifies another expression for degree. For instance, *very* and *really* are intensifiers that can modify adjectives: *very hot, really tall*. This term can be used generally to include all degree modifiers or specifically to refer to those like *too* and *very* that indicate intensity of degree but not completeness – those, like *totally* and *completely* are also called **emphasizers**. Generally, *intensifier* is used to indicate any level of intensity – including not-very-intense levels like *barely* and *somewhat*.

Some authors also use **intensifier** to refer to emphatic uses of reflexive pronouns, as in *He wanted to do it himself* or *She herself could not see the point of it.* In these cases *himself* and *herself* are not grammatically required and are not assigned SEMANTIC ROLES by the verb.

Intension

The term **intension** (not to be confused with INTENTION) or **intensional meaning** is sometimes used in linguistic semantics as equivalent to SENSE – that is, to refer to whatever representation of a word meaning allows for its reference to be determined. The term comes from philosophy of language, in which it is used to refer to the DEFINITION of a term, that is, the properties that allow the EXTENSION of the term to be determined.

Key text: Carnap 1947.

Intensional logic

An **intensional logic** is a system of LOGIC that distinguishes the INTENSION and EXTENSION aspects of meaning. First-order logics like PREDICATE CALCULUS are not intensional; they map between quantified (see QUANTIFICATION) expressions and their extensions – that is, individuals that the expression refers to.

See also **MONTAGUE GRAMMAR**, MODAL LOGIC.

Intention

Any UTTERANCE is uttered with a particular **intention** on the part of the speaker in terms of how they wish their audience to interpret the utterance.

The relation between speaker's intention and the addressee's INTERPRETATION of a sentence is a major concern of PRAGMATICS. This term should not be confused with the semantic term INTENSION.

Interpretation

Interpretation often refers to the contextual (PRAGMATIC) process of determining the intended meaning of an utterance in context. This includes determining the particular SENSE of an AMBIGUOUS expression, the intended REFERENTS of the expressions and the IMPLICATURES that the speaker intends.

Interpretation can also refer to the mapping of grammatical structures to semantic representations in the interpretive semantics of GENERATIVE GRAMMAR.

Interpretive semantics

See GENERATIVE GRAMMAR.

Iota operator

The **iota operator** is a LOGICAL CONSTANT, symbolized by the Greek letter ι. It is used in some FORMAL SEMANTIC systems in order to express DEFINITE reference by BINDING to a VARIABLE. For example,

$\iota x(Px)$

can be translated into English as 'the x that has the property P'. So, if *P* here stands for 'is Prince of Wales', then this formula can be interpreted as 'the unique individual that is Prince of Wales'. The formula can then be used to represent an individual (in the same way that symbols like *a*, *b* and *c* do in PREDICATE CALCULUS) as an argument of a predicate. For example, if Q stands for 'is quiet', then

$Q(\iota x(Px))$

can be read as 'the Prince of Wales is quiet.'

Iterative

Iterative means 'repeating', so in the study of ASPECT it refers to the repeated occurrence of an EVENT. This may be marked in English by an adverbial phrase like *again and again* in *She watched the film again and again*, but iterative readings can also emerge from the combination of a verb describing a PUNCTUAL event with a grammatical or lexical form that indicates duration or continuation, such as the progressive in *The light was blinking*.

Lambda, lambda calculus

Lambda calculus or **λ-calculus** is a mathematical system that was developed by Alonzo Church in mid-twentieth century. It is widely used in computer programming, but also in some branches of FORMAL SEMANTICS, such as MONTAGUE GRAMMAR. It allows for the definition of sets. For example, say that P stands for 'is purple'. Then the **lambda expression**

$$(\lambda x \, (P(x)))$$

can be read as 'the set of all x such that x is purple' – in other words, the set of all purple things. This can be interpreted as the representation of a PROPERTY, and in order to represent a PROPOSITION in which something has that property, the variable x can be specified (here as an individual named *Barney*), using the following notation:

$$(\lambda x \, (P(x)))(Barney)$$

This is equivalent to the predicate calculus expression *P(Barney)* 'Barney is purple.' The process of getting from the **lambda-abstracted** expression to the predicate calculus version in which all of the lambda-bound variables are specified is called **lambda conversion**. Since other properties as well as referring expressions can be **abstracted** using the **lambda-operator** λ, more complex interactions than those demonstrated here can be represented, which solves certain ambiguity problems in MODAL LOGIC and in the representation of the ellipsis of natural language predicates (*The steak is ready to eat and my dinner guests are too*), for example.

Further reading: Chierchia and McConnell-Ginet 1990.

Landmark

See FIGURE/GROUND.

Lexeme

A **lexeme** (cf. LEXICAL ITEM) is a unit of language that is represented in the LEXICON. If we see the (mental) lexicon as analogous to a dictionary, lexemes are the headwords in that dictionary. Traditionally, lexemes differ from other units of language in that they are non-COMPOSITIONAL, that is, a lexeme's meaning cannot be derived from the meanings of its parts. On this view, lexemes may be simple MORPHEMES or WORDS (e.g. *cat*), complex words whose meanings are not clear from their constituent morphemes (e.g. *greenhouse*) and IDIO-MATIC phrases (e.g. *on the fly* to mean 'without preparation'). A phrase like *the steep hill*, however, would be seen as composed of three lexemes, since the overall meaning can be derived from the meanings of those words and the grammatical structure in which they sit.

Like other linguistic *-eme* terms, *lexeme* refers to an abstraction from the actual spoken or written language – that is, it refers to the word as it is represented in the mind, rather than in the mouth or on the page.

Lexical field

See SEMANTIC FIELD.

Lexical gap

A **lexical gap** is a concept for which a language has no word, especially in cases where there is a gap in a pattern of lexicalization of other similar concepts. For example, English has general terms for *limb* and *digit* as well as specific terms for the upper- and lower-body versions of these – but no such general term that encompasses *hand* and *foot*. Thus, there is said to be a lexical gap in the SEMANTIC FIELD – as in Figure 6.

Figure 6 Lexical gap

Lexical item

Lexical item refers to a unit of language that is represented in a language's LEXICON. It is often used as a synonym for LEXEME, although it may also be used without the mentalistic overtones of *lexeme*, to mean an item of **lexis** (see LEXICON).

Lexical relation

A **lexical relation** is a SEMANTIC RELATION in which two or more words have some aspect of meaning in common. The term is most often used to refer to PARADIGMATIC RELATIONS such as ANTONYMY, HYPONYMY or SYNONYMY, but is sometimes used to refer to SYNTAGMATIC RELATIONS, for example, between a VERB and its ARGUMENTS.

Lexical semantics

Loosely speaking, **lexical semantics** is the study of WORD meaning, but more technically it is the study of the semantics of LEXEMES, including words and multiword lexical expressions.

See also LEXICON.

Lexical word

See CLOSED AND OPEN CLASSES.

Lexicalization, lexicalize

A language **lexicalizes** a concept if it has a LEXEME (or WORD) for that item. The process by which a language comes to have a word for a particular concept is called **lexicalization**.

Lexicography

Lexicography refers to the theory and practice of dictionary writing. Lexicography can be seen as **applied** LEXICOLOGY insofar as lexicographers draw on the research of lexical semanticists or other scholars studying the nature and structure of vocabulary. Dictionaries have, however, existed in some form for centuries, although the earliest ones were focused on either giving translational equivalents in another language or just providing definitions of 'difficult' words. Early dictionaries also often took a **prescriptive** approach and aimed to stipulate how language 'should' be used, whereas modern general-purpose dictionaries are usually **descriptive** and aim to record the way a language is used by its speakers.

A standard dictionary entry for a word may include information about its spelling and pronunciation, grammatical information, DEFINITIONS of the word's meaning(s), different derivational forms (e.g. *adjective*, *adjectival*) usage (including the dialect the word belongs to or whether the word is formal or informal or perhaps offensive) and its ETYMOLOGY. How much of this information is given varies depending on the dictionary – for example, dictionaries aimed at non-native speakers typically omit etymologies, but often give more detailed grammatical information. The most important part of a dictionary entry is the definition, and much of lexicographic theory and practice is concerned with establishing how definitions may be stated in as clear, comprehensive, accurate and concise way as possible (see the discussion under DEFINITION).

Key texts: Zgusta 1971; Bejoint 2000; Landau 2001.

Lexicology

Lexicology is the study of the LEXICON – usually interpreted as the study of the mental lexicon. This includes investigation of the following questions: What kind of information is part of lexical knowledge, as opposed to grammatical or (in some theories) conceptual/ENCYCLOPAEDIC knowledge? How is information organized within the lexicon? What is the nature of LEXICAL RELATIONS? Loosely speaking, it can also include LEXICAL SEMANTICS.

See also LEXEME.

Lexicon

Traditionally, the **lexicon** is a collection of information about a language's LEXEMES, that is, the expressions that are learnt by the language's users, rather than derived anew each time they are used. The term *lexicon* can refer to the following:

- a) a dictionary, especially a dictionary of a classical language; or
- b) the vocabulary of a language (also known as **lexis**); or
- c) a particular language user's knowledge of her/his own vocabulary, as stored in her/his mind – the **mental lexicon**.

The last two definitions are both relevant to the study of LEXICAL SEMANTICS, as different scholars and theories assume one or the other or the interrelation of both in their use of the term. In most contemporary linguistic theories, it is the mental lexicon that is most relevant, though the most formal semantic approaches concentrate on the relation between language and world – without much attention to the mediation by the mind – and usage-based approaches may be more concerned than others with the speech-community-based lexis.

Traditionally, the (mental) lexicon had been seen as a 'dictionary in the mind', which contains much of the same information for each expression as a dictionary would: its pronunciation, (in a literate language user) its orthography, grammatical information such as its word class, social information such as its register (e.g. formal versus informal), and, importantly, its DEFINITION. On this view, like a dictionary, the lexicon would include only those linguistic expressions that are not derivable via the language's grammar – that is, those that are non-COMPOSITIONAL (see LEXEME) and ARBITRARY. This traditional lexicon-as-dictionary approach has been challenged in many recent linguistic theories.

Increasingly, mentalistic semantic theories eschew a semantically rich mental lexicon that is separate from conceptual knowledge. (See the discussion at ENCYCLOPAEDIC MEANING.)

The traditional notion of lexicon-as-dictionary has also been challenged recently by theories that hold that abstract grammatical constructions, like words and idioms, are meaningful. In such approaches – called CONSTRUCTION GRAMMARS – the lexicon/grammar distinction is not made. Instead, we might think of our knowledge of linguistic constructions – from words to abstract grammatical constructions – as part of a '**constructicon**' of form-meaning associations.

From a language-processing point of view, it is questionable whether the mental lexicon should only include expressions that are non-compositional. It would be expedient for frequently used but compositional expressions – for example, regular past tense forms of common verbs or oft-used phrases like *I love you* – to be stored in a ready-to-use form.

Lexis

See LEXICON.

Linguistic meaning

See DEFINITION.

Literal

See FIGURATIVE.

Location

See SEMANTIC ROLE.

Logic

FORMAL, TRUTH-CONDITIONAL approaches to semantics often use a logical language as a METALANGUAGE for the description of natural language meanings. Such languages include PROPOSITIONAL LOGIC, the first-order logic PREDICATE CALCULUS and higher-order logics like MODAL LOGIC.

One advantage of using such metalanguages is the avoidance of the AMBIGUITY that is endemic in natural languages. For example, the ambiguity in the SCOPE of QUANTIFICATION in *Everybody loves somebody* is not available in a logical language like predicate calculus, in which one can represent only one of the meanings at a time. So if Px = 'x is a person' and Lxy = 'x loves y', then:

$$\exists x \, (Px \wedge \forall y \, (Py \wedge Lyx))$$

= 'there exists a person x such that any person y loves x'

$$\forall y \, (Py \rightarrow \exists x \, (Px \wedge Lyx))$$

= 'for any person y, there is a person x such that y loves x'

See also LOGICAL OPERATOR.

Key text: Tarski 1944.

Further reading: Allwood et al. 1977; McCawley 1981.

Logical constant

A LOGICAL CONSTANT is an expression that (within a particular theory) has the same value in all semantic MODELS or POSSIBLE WORLDS – for instance, LOGICAL OPERATORS are generally held to be logical constants.

Logical form

See GENERATIVE GRAMMAR.

Logical operator

A logical operator is an element of a LOGIC that is used to create new PROPOSITIONS by performing a semantic function on one or more propositions. The following basic operators are common to different forms of logic, although there is some variation in how they are written in different texts.

Negation applies to a single proposition and reverses its TRUTH VALUE.

$\neg$**P** (variant: **~P**)   NEGATION: 'it is not the case that P'

Logical **connectives** combine two propositions to give rise to a new one.

P$\wedge$**Q** (variant: **P&Q**)   CONJUNCTION: 'P and Q'
P$\vee$**Q**   DISJUNCTION: 'P or Q'
P$\rightarrow$**Q** (variant: **P**$\supset$**Q**)   MATERIAL IMPLICATION: 'if P then Q'
P$\leftrightarrow$**Q** (variant: **P**$\equiv$**Q**)   BICONDITIONAL: 'P if and only if Q'

QUANTIFIERS are another type of operator.

See also IOTA OPERATOR, LAMBDA.

Logical relation

See PROPOSITIONAL RELATION.

Markedness

The concept of **markedness** originated in the early twentieth-century Prague School of linguistics, and was originally applied to phonological systems. It has come to be used across linguistic subdisciplines in order to try to account for asymmetries in the distribution, complexity or frequency of linguistic forms that contrast as pairs. The **unmarked** member of a contrasting pair is the one that is more 'basic' or 'natural' in a context, while the **marked** member deviates from that 'basicness' in some way. The more marked member of a pair may be more morphologically complex, have a more restricted grammatical distribution, be less frequent, or some combination of these properties. Semantically, the unmarked member of the pair may be 'neutralizable', and thus more polysemous. For example, *man* can mean 'a male human' or 'a human', but the gender of *woman* is not neutralizable – thus *man* is the unmarked term in that pair. Unmarkedness can also be linked to PROTOTYPICALITY.

Many scholars have assumed or claimed that the markedness of a linguistic form reflects the cognitive markedness of the meaning that the form represents – in other words, that formal markedness is ICONIC for cognitive complexity or unusualness. For example, it has been noted that words for evaluatively positive properties like TRUTH, HAPPINESS and MERIT tend to be less marked and more frequent in language than their evaluatively negative opposites. In this case, one might hypothesize that human cognition classifies negative experiences as deviations from a positive norm, and that human languages reflect this.

Key texts: Lehrer 1985; Haspelmath 2006.

Mass noun

See COUNTABILITY.

Material conditional, material implication

In LOGIC, **material implication** (also called **material conditional**) is the relation of two predicates by means of a LOGICAL OPERATOR that is written → or ⊃. **P → Q** is read as 'if P, then Q'. The P in this case is called the **antecedent** and the Q is the **consequent**. In logical METALANGUAGES, a material implication is false only if the antecedent proposition is true and the consequent is false.

See also CONDITIONAL.

Meaning

Linguistic **meaning** is, of course, the object of study in semantics. However, *meaning* is rarely used as a technical term in semantic study because of its POLYSEMY and generality. For example, it may be used to refer to an expression's DEFINITION or SENSE, but it may instead be used to include non-denotational aspects of meaning, such as CONNOTATION, or to the particular INTERPRETATION of the expression's REFERENCE in a particular CONTEXT. Where it is used, it is usually because a distinction between sense and reference is not needed in the particular discussion or it is used as a synonym for *sense* or *interpretation*.

Meaning postulate

Some FORMAL SEMANTIC approaches employ **meaning postulates** – logical statements that serve as constraints on what can belong to the EXTENSION of an expression. SYNONYMY, ANTONYMY and HYPONYMY and other relations can be described with such statements. So, for example, a condition on the extension of *telephone* would be that that extension is the same set as the extension for *phone*. This would then account for why *A telephone is a phone* is an ANALYTIC PROPOSITION and a TAUTOLOGY.

Key text: Carnap 1947.

Meaning-Text Theory

Meaning-Text Theory (MTT) is a linguistic theory that has its roots in Russian lexicography and machine translation research. Its main developer and proponent is Igor Mel'čuk. In MTT a language's grammar and semantics are driven and constrained by the lexicon, called the **Explanatory Combinatorial Dictionary** (ECD). Lexical entries in the ECD have three **zones**: semantic, syntactic and the lexical co-occurrence zone. The **syntactic zone** contains the word's subcategorization patterns – for instance, whether a verb is transitive. The **semantic zone** includes a definition, which operates on the

Decomposition Principle, that the definition of a word must include only words that are semantically simpler. It is thought that consistent application of this principle will result in the discovery of semantic PRIMITIVES. The **lexical co-occurrence zone** includes a full set of the word's PARADIGMATIC and SYNTAGMATIC relatives, expressed through **lexical functions** (LFs). LFs are tools for representing restrictions on lexical co-occurrence, and so they represent particular arbitrary information. For instance, one LF specifies the intensifiers that a word can take, and thus the entry for *naked* has an LF that specifies *stark* as a possible intensifier, but the entry for *nude* does not include this one, since *stark* and *nude* generally do not co-occur. There were 64 LFs in the mid-1990s, but people working in this theory regularly propose new ones.

Key texts: Mel'čuk 1987; Wanner 1996.

Mental lexicon

See LEXICON.

Mental space, Mental Space Theory

A **mental space** is a temporary, structured conceptualization of some entities and their properties, created in the course of thinking and speaking. The notion was first proposed by Gilles Fauconnier in his work on **Mental Space Theory**, a COGNITIVE LINGUISTIC theory of how meaning is constructed in context. One of the aims of Mental Space Theory is accounting for classic issues in semantics such as REFERENCE, PRESUPPOSITION and COUNTERFACTUALS. The basic assumption is that linguistic expressions trigger the creation of mental spaces, and elements in different spaces can be connected to their counterparts in other spaces. Consider, for example, the sentence *Romeo has broken his leg*, where *Romeo* is used to refer to the actor who plays the character of Romeo in the play *Romeo and Juliet*. This sentence would trigger the building of two mental spaces: one mental space contains a representation of the actor, and his having a broken leg, while the other space has a representation of the character of Romeo in the play. Because the elements 'Actor playing Romeo' and 'Romeo' are connected across the spaces, it is possible to refer to an element in one space by naming its counterpart in the other space – that is, to refer to the unfortunate actor by the name of the character he plays.

Apart from its use in the Mental Space Theory, mental space is also an important construct in Conceptual Blending Theory.

Key texts: Fauconnier 1994, 1997.

Meronym, meronymy

Meronymy is the is-a-part-of or has-a relation. The term refers either to the directional relation from whole to part or collectively to that relation and its converse, **holonymy**. So, for example, *yolk* is a **meronym** of *egg* and *egg* is a **holonym** of *yolk*, and the relation between these two items is meronymy. While meronymy is often included in lists of paradigmatic lexical relations, it is generally regarded as less a relation among words as a relation among things that the words denote. Nevertheless, meronymy is an important relation for definition – for example, it is difficult to define *yolk* without reference to *eggs* or to define *knife* without reference to blades and handles. Different types of meronymy can be distinguished – for instance, the relation between a material and a whole (*cloth–shirt*) or a functional part and a whole (*sleeve–shirt*), and these may differ in the logical relations they give rise to. For instance, *I touched her shirt* entails *I touched her clothing*, but does not entail *I touched her sleeve*.

Key texts: Lyons 1977; Murphy 2003.

Metalanguage

A **metalanguage** is a system used for describing a language without using that language itself. A metalanguage resolves the inevitable circularity that arises if one, for instance, uses English to describe the semantics of English. One could, in principle, use one natural language to describe another (e.g. Finnish to describe Polish). However, this has the problem that the meanings of the **object language** (the language being described) would not necessarily translate in an equivalent way into the other natural language used as a metalanguage. An ideal metalanguage should provide a complete and unambiguous description of the object language. Although no such perfect metalanguage exists, attempts to develop such a language typically take the form of a formalized system of symbols and rules for applying those symbols to the description of natural language. Examples of such metalanguages in semantics are COMPONENTIAL ANALYSIS and the use of LOGIC to describe natural language.

See also METALINGUISTIC.

Metalinguistic

The adjective **metalinguistic** can denote 'being part of or related to a META-LANGUAGE', but it is more frequently used in linguistics to refer to uses of language that are self-referential. For instance, in the example below, *Did Mary ever visit Brighton Beach?* is used to refer to the sentence *Did Mary ever visit Brighton Beach?*:

> The sentence *Did Mary ever visit Brighton Beach?* is used as a mnemonic for remembering the order of ranks in British peerage.

In linguistic writing, metalinguistic uses of expressions are often presented in italics, although in other disciplines and in general English they are often placed within quotation marks (inverted commas).

Metaphor, metaphorical

Metaphor is a form of FIGURATIVE language that involves describing something in terms of another thing, generally on the basis of a perceived resemblance or analogy between those two things. For example, *The internet is a gold-mine* is metaphorical in that the internet is not an actual goldmine – it is instead being described as a resource where you can find countless pieces of valuable information, rather like you can find nuggets of gold in a gold-mine. Traditionally, the thing that is being described (*the internet*) is called the TENOR (or sometimes **topic**) while the thing that is used to describe the something else metaphorically (*goldmine*) is the VEHICLE. The relationship of similarity between the tenor and the vehicle, that is, what they have in common, is the GROUND (here, both the internet and goldmines are locations where one can find valuable things). Insofar as metaphor relies on an implied similarity between the tenor and the vehicle, many approaches view it as implicit SIMILE.

Linguistic work on metaphor is concerned with issues such as how metaphorical language is recognized as such and how it is interpreted. Some approaches hold that metaphorical language, if interpreted literally, results in a semantic ANOMALY, which serves as a trigger for the hearer to look for a figurative way of understanding the sentence. The understanding of metaphors is then viewed as a matter of PRAGMATIC, inferential processing. Exceptions to this are highly conventionalized **dead metaphors**, such as **mouth** of a river or cash **flow**, whose meanings may be assumed to be stored in the LEXICON.

Much of the work on metaphor since the 1980s has taken the perspective of CONCEPTUAL METAPHOR THEORY or other related COGNITIVE LINGUISTIC approaches.

See also SEMANTIC CHANGE.

Key texts: Lakoff and Johnson 1980; Ortony 1993; Glucksberg 2001.

Metonymic, metonymy

In **metonymy**, reference to one entity is used to stand for another entity that is closely associated with the first entity. For example, in I still haven't read the new **Pinker**, the name of the author (Pinker) stands for a piece of written work by the author while in I drank the whole **bottle**, the container stands for its contents (the liquid in the bottle). Metonymy is therefore a type of FIGURATIVE language that relies on a relationship of association or contiguity between the entity that is named (sometimes called the **vehicle**) and the intended referent (sometimes called the **target**). Metonymy is sometimes distinguished from SYNECDOCHE, but many accounts view synecdoche as a type of metonymy.

COGNITIVE LINGUISTS treat metonymy as a conceptual phenomenon where one conceptual entity affords access to another one that is part of the same DOMAIN or IDEALIZED COGNITIVE MODEL (ICM). In this respect conceptual metonymy differs from CONCEPTUAL METAPHOR, which involves mappings across different domains or ICMs.

See also SEMANTIC CHANGE.

Key text: Radden and Kövecses 1999.

Middle voice

See **VOICE**.

Modal logic

Modal logic is a type of **LOGIC** that uses **LOGICAL OPERATORS** to indicate the necessity or possibility of a **PROPOSITION**. There are two modal operators: L or □ for 'it is necessary that' and M or ◊ for 'it is possible that'. These can be defined in relation to each other and negation, as follows:

$$\Box\, P =\neg\; \Diamond\, \neg\, P$$
$$\Diamond\, P =\neg\; \Box\, \neg\, P$$

That is, 'P is necessary' means the same as 'it is not possible that P is not the case' while 'P is possible' means the same as 'it is not necessarily the case that P is not the case.'

See also **MODALITY**.

Modality, modal verbs

In linguistics, **modality** refers to the expression of a speaker's attitude towards a **PROPOSITION**. This involves notions such as obligation, permission, possibility, necessity and ability. In English these notions are typically expressed via the **modal verbs** *may, must, can, will, shall, might, could* and *should*, or semi-**GRAMMATICALIZED** expressions such as *have to, need to* or *had better*. Expressions of **MOOD** may also indicate a type of modality distinction – that between the reality and irreality of a proposition. Modality essentially modifies the meaning of the neutral or declarative proposition: for example, in *You must come home at nine* the notion of obligation is applied to the proposition 'you come home at nine.'

Modality can be divided into different types and, within those types, into different degrees. The most established distinction of modality types is that between **deontic** and **epistemic** modality. Deontic modality involves a duty, obligation, permission or (when negated) prohibition being imposed on someone or something. Different degrees of deontic modality are shown below:

> Tim must take the dog out for a walk. (obligation)
> Tim should take the dog out for a walk. (weaker obligation)
> Tim may/can take the dog out for a walk. (permission)

Epistemic modality, on the other hand, relates to the speaker's judgement of how probable the truth of the proposition is, based on some available evidence. As with deontic modality, there are different degrees of epistemic modality:

> The lights are on in Amber's room; therefore
>> Amber must be home. (necessity)
>> Amber should be home. (probability)
>> Amber may be home. (possibility)
>> Amber might be home. (weaker possibility)

Expressions of epistemic modality can also include EVIDENTIALITY.

Another type of modality that is sometimes distinguished is **dynamic** modality, which refers to the ability or willingness of an individual or whether the surrounding circumstances permit or necessitate the activity, as in *Daisy can cook a wonderful stew* and *The stew must simmer for an hour before it's ready*. Dynamic modality can also be taken to include cases that express the characteristics or habits of the subject: *Whenever they threw a party, Daisy would make guacamole*.

The fact that different types of modality are expressed by the same modal verbs can give rise to ambiguities, as in the examples below:

> Amber should be home by now.
>> **deontic reading:** 'she has an obligation to be home'
>> **epistemic reading:** 'it is probable that she is home'
> Amber can stay in her room for hours.
>> **deontic reading:** 'she is allowed to'
>> **dynamic reading (ability):** 'she has the ability to'
>> **dynamic reading (characteristic):** 'she often does so'

Modality interacts with NEGATION in complex ways. In principle, either the modal or the proposition that the modal modifies can be in the SCOPE of the negation: compare *Amber can't stay in her room* (she is not allowed to stay) and *Amber* can not *stay in her room* (she is allowed to not stay).

See also MODAL LOGIC.

Key texts: Kratzer 1981; Palmer 2001.

Model, model-theoretic semantics

Model-theoretic semantics (also known as POSSIBLE WORLD SEMANTICS) is any TRUTH-CONDITIONAL SEMANTIC approach that considers meaning in terms of interpretations of linguistic expressions with reference to a model, rather than by direct reference to reality. A **model** includes a set of POSSIBLE WORLDS, a set of individuals that can be referred to, a set of times, a set of functions linking individuals to worlds and times in those worlds. Linguistic expressions are interpreted via functions mapping them to EXTENSIONS within a set of possible worlds. In contrast to other formal approaches, model-theoretic semantics can be seen to engage somewhat with the problem of how actual speakers *mean* things via language, given that they do not have complete or accurate knowledge of reality.

See also FORMAL SEMANTICS, MONTAGUE GRAMMAR.

Key texts: Tarski 1944; Montague 1973.

Monosemous, monosemy

See VAGUENESS.

Montague grammar

Montague grammar (also **Montague semantics**) is the common name for the FORMAL (higher-order LOGIC) METALANGUAGE first developed by RICHARD MONTAGUE, a mathematical logician, and further developed and popularized after his death. Montague grammar, and in particular Montague's paper 'The proper treatment of quantification in ordinary English' (or *PTQ*, as it has come to be called), is generally recognized as a breakthrough in integrating formal semantics with a serious attempt to describe natural language. The grammar presents a COMPOSITIONAL means of representing linguistic meaning through the use of a formal system of representation (LAMBDA CALCULUS) combined with set and type theories from mathematics.

This approach is MODEL-THEORETIC and distinguishes between intensional and extensional aspects of meaning. The EXTENSIONS of linguistic expressions are the sets of things (e.g. individuals or, in the case of sentences, TRUTH VALUES) within a model (or POSSIBLE WORLD). INTENSIONS are functions that map between the linguistic expression and the model – that is, which give a means by which to determine which sets or relations among sets in the model are true with respect to the expression.

Key texts: Montague 1973; Partee 1975; Dowty 1979; Dowty et al. 1981.

Mood

The term **mood** is sometimes used synonymously with MODALITY, but when a distinction is made, *mood* refers to the grammatical expression of the degree of reality of a proposition – whether it is real or factual or instead unreal, non-factual. In this regard, mood can be viewed as expressing some aspects of the semantic notion of modality.

One mood distinction that is made in many European languages is between the **indicative** and **subjunctive** forms of verbs. Compare the forms of the verb meaning 'learn' in the Spanish examples below:

Creo	que	**aprende.**
I believe	that	learn.INDICATIVE

'I believe that he is learning.'

Dudo	que	**aprenda.**
I doubt	that	learn.SUBJUNCTIVE

'I doubt that he is learning.'

The subjunctive form is used to indicate that the proposition 'he is learning' is not real or factual. The contrast between subjunctive and indicative forms is largely lost in British English, but is preserved to a greater degree in formal American English:

> The committee insisted that the vote **be** anonymous. (subjunctive; 'they demanded that when the vote happens, it is anonymous')

> The committee insisted that the vote **is** anonymous. (indicative; 'they firmly asserted that the vote [that is currently happening or has happened] is anonymous')

In British English the meaning of the subjunctive above is usually expressed with the modal verb *should*: *The committee insisted that the vote should be anonymous*.

The grammatical forms used to mark questions and commands can also be regarded as expressing kinds of mood, namely, interrogative mood and imperative mood, respectively.

Morpheme

A **morpheme** is a linguistic form that expresses a meaning, but which is not composed of other meaningful linguistic forms. That is, it is the smallest unit of language that is interesting to semanticists. The study of the grammatical and phonological properties of morphemes is **morphology**.

Natural kind

A **natural kind** is a category of things that occur naturally in the world without need for human intervention, like POTATO, PIGEON, GOLD and VIRUS. These can be contrasted to **nominal** (also called **artefactual**) **kinds** – that is, categories of things like MARRIAGE, BEER and LIVESTOCK (which denotes a category based on a particular human relationship to some natural things). Natural kinds have received a lot of attention in the philosophical semantic literature, with Hilary Putnam and others arguing that, like PROPER NAMES, natural kind terms do not have descriptive SENSES. This argument is based on the fact that few people know how to identify all natural things, but we use the terminology for it nonetheless. Putnam gave the example that the facts he knows about elms are the same as the facts he knows about beeches, yet in using the two words he refers to different types of trees. We may also believe false things about natural kinds, but still use the words to denote something. So, for example, if your mental description of *elephant* holds that they are 'the largest mammal species', you do not accidentally refer to the blue whale (which is really the largest mammal) whenever you use the word *elephant*. Another reason why natural kind terms seem special is that people are often happy to concede that they cannot determine what is and is not referred to by natural kind terms, and that only 'experts' know their true meanings – that is, the senses of natural kind terms are external to the speaker who uses the word. So, if you had a glass of clear, drinkable, tasteless, odourless liquid, you might call it *water*. But if a scientist analysed it and told you it is not H_2O in the beaker, but XYZ, you would probably accept that it should not be called *water*.

While this has been an active debate in philosophy, there is little linguistic evidence that people perceive NATURAL KIND as a distinct semantic type. No known language makes any grammatical distinctions strictly on the basis of naturalness/artificiality. It is also not clear that natural kind terms are semantically special, as compared to all nominal kinds. For instance, *marriage* is an artefact, but we still appeal to clerical and legal experts to let us know what is and is not marriage. Furthermore, the fact that it is difficult to pin down the senses of natural kind terms is not reason to conclude that they do not have senses at all – we might just need a more subtle approach to describing those senses. Approaches such as **NATURAL SEMANTIC METALANGUAGE** and **PROTOTYPE**

THEORY represent natural kind and other senses in terms that allow for 'folk' rather than 'expert' use of such expressions.

Key texts: Putnam 1975; Kripke 1980.

Natural Semantic Metalanguage

Natural Semantic Metalanguage (NSM) is a COMPONENTIAL semantic theory that has been developed by **ANNA WIERZBICKA** and colleagues since the 1970s. NSM is concerned with reducing the semantics of all vocabulary down to a very restricted set of universal semantic PRIMITIVES, or **primes**, as they are called in NSM. The primes represent meanings that are hypothesized to exist in every language's vocabulary. Primes are arranged in natural language phrases – called **explications** – in order to represent the SENSE of an expression. The grammar of NSM should reflect universal grammatical relations; however, the grammar of the metalanguage has not as yet received as much attention as the vocabulary (though serious work on it has happened in the last decade). For example, a proposed explication of the past tense verb *broke* is as follows:

> X *broke* Y =
> X did something to thing Y
> because of this, something happened to Y at this time
> because of this, after this Y was not one thing any more

Here we see primes such as THING, TIME, CAUSE, NOT and AFTER. These should be understood as representing universal meanings, rather than the English words – indeed, the NSM claim is that the primes and the explication could be represented using the forms of any other language. The number of primes has grown from 14 in 1972 to more than 60 in current work.

In deriving their metalanguage from natural language, proponents of NSM hold that the relations between semantic universals and natural language are clear and direct, as opposed to the 'obscure' relations between natural and formal languages. Critics argue that natural language expressions are too variable – both from language to language and in themselves (see AMBIGUITY) to support linguistic analysis. NSM has been applied to a wide range of lexical and grammatical phenomena.

See also METALANGUAGE.

Key texts: Wierzbicka 1972, 1996; Goddard 1998.

Narrowing

See SEMANTIC CHANGE.

Necessary and sufficient conditions

See CLASSICAL THEORY OF CONCEPTUALIZATION.

Negation

Negation is the morphological marking of a change in an expression's POLARITY, from **affirmative**, or **positive**, to **negative**. A sentence that is negated is a CONTRADICTION of its affirmative counterpart – for example, *I didn't eat* contradicts *I ate*. Negation is expressed in many ways in English, including the following:

– Adverbials like *not* and *never*, which can negate verbs, adjectives and sentences.

   I did not see that film. (contradicts: I saw that film)
   I never liked that film. (contradicts: I liked that film)

   Note that *not* requires an auxiliary verb, so that when the affirmative version of a sentence would not need an auxiliary, a form of the verb *do* must occur in the negative version in order to support the *not*.
– Several prefixes, which can negate nouns (*a **non**-resident*) and adjectives (***un**happy*, ***dis**satisfied*, ***il**logical*), as well as REVERSIVE prefixes on verbs (*to **un**tie*), which contradict the positive versions of the same verbs, in that *X ties Y* has the OPPOSITE outcome to *X unties Y*.
– The quantifier *no* applied to noun phrases, as in *I ate no bananas*.
– Negative pronouns, such as *nobody*, *nothing* and *none*.

Because negative adverbs are restricted in their position in the verb phrase, they can be the source of AMBIGUITIES of SCOPE, for instance, when modal verbs are used. Thus, in *I can never visit Yolanda*, *never* can have scope over the whole sentence, in which case it means 'It is never the case that I can visit Yolanda' or it can just have scope over the verb phrase *visit Yolanda*, in which case the sentence is interpreted as an offer to not ever visit Yolanda in future. When the negation has scope over the whole sentence, it can (with the support of marked intonation) **focus** on subparts of the sentence. For instance, *I didn't eat pie* can be pronounced (or written, as below) to imply some other **proposition**:

I didn't eat **pie**.	>	I ate something that was not a pie.
I didn't **eat** pie.	>	I did something other than eating to pie.
I didn't eat pie.	>	Someone other than me ate pie.

The scope of negation and its interaction with **quantification** and **modality** can be made unambiguous through the **logical** representations of **formal semantics**. The negative **logical operator** is usually represented by the symbol ¬, but sometimes instead by ~. It has the effect of reversing the **truth value** of the expression that it immediately precedes. For example, a simple proposition P can be negated as ¬P, which means 'It is not the case that P.' One can see differences in scope and interactions of negation and quantification when the negation operator is applied to quantified expressions. For instance, let's say that P stands for 'is in Perugia', so $\exists x(Px)$ means 'there is an x such that x is in Perugia.' Negation of this proposition can occur at two places, with different effects on truth conditions, and these correspond to different English expressions:

$\neg\exists x(Px)$ = 'there is no x such that x is in Perugia', *Nothing is in Perugia.*

$\exists x(\neg Px)$ = 'there is an x such that x is not in Perugia', *There is something that is not in Perugia* (which is equivalent to $\neg\forall x(Px)$ 'for all x, it is not the case that x is in Perugia', *Not everything is in Perugia*).

See also **antonym, polarity item**.

Key text: Horn 2001.

Nominal kind

See **natural kind**.

Non-referential

See REFERENCE.

Non-specific reference

See REFERENCE.

Noun

Noun is an open class (see: CLOSED AND OPEN CLASSES) of words that is often informally defined as including words that refer to persons, places or things. But while words such as *sister, house, apple* and *bookcase* are indeed nouns, so are many words that refer to ABSTRACT concepts, events or states, including *luck, examination, resemblance, commitment* and *nausea*. The category NOUN is therefore usually given a grammatical definition in terms of distributional and inflectional properties. For example, nouns (or noun phrases) may occur as the subjects or objects of verbs (e.g. *An **apple** fell from the tree; He fears **commitment***) and may be inflected for NUMBER, GENDER and CASE in languages that have those inflectional categories. In English, many nouns have singular and plural forms: *a sister, two sister**s***.

However, although most linguists would agree that nouns cannot be adequately defined by general semantic properties that apply to all nouns, the class of nouns is indeed prototypically associated with reference to CONCRETE objects that have clear spatial boundaries and are time-stable (i.e. will stay the same for a period of time). This is to say that there is a high likelihood that the names for tangible objects in any language will be nouns. Nouns that refer to concrete objects are also more likely to exhibit the full grammatical behaviour associated with nouns. Thus in English, many abstract nouns are generally not inflected for number (**lucks, *nauseas*) or they do not occur in the possessive (**the commitment's time*).

Nouns can be subdivided into COMMON NOUNS (such as *bookcase* or *examination*) and PROPER NOUNS (*Susan, Helsinki*), depending on whether they designate a type of entity or an individual entity. Types of nouns are also distinguished on the basis of their COUNTABILITY, thus differentiating **count nouns** (that do inflect for number, such as *sister* and *apple*) and **mass nouns** (e.g. *sugar*, *nausea*).

Key texts: Givón 1984; Schachter 1985; Langacker 1987–1991; Wierzbicka 1988.

Noun class

See GENDER.

Number

Number refers to a grammatical category that reflects quantity. In English, nouns, pronouns and most quantifiers (such as *a* and *some*) have number values, and number AGREEMENT with a subject is marked on present tense verbs. Some other languages mark number more extensively – for example, through greater marking on verbs or agreement with a noun's modifiers, such as adjectives. English distinguishes between **singular** ('one') and **plural** ('more than one') number, but some languages (e.g. classical Arabic and Hmong) mark more number categories – having, for example, separate affixes for singular, **dual** (i.e. 'two') and plural ('more than two').

Number marking in a language is often tied up with GENDER and PERSON marking. The relation between grammatical number and the number or amount of things that are denoted is not one-to-one. For example, the COLLECTIVE NOUN *team* denotes a group made up of several people, but it is morphologically singular. In contrast, *trousers* are one thing, but have plural marking. The interaction between grammatical number and referential number sometimes leads to apparent cases of semantic agreement, as when a British English speaker says *The team are travelling to Rugby for a match*.

See also COUNTABILITY.

Object language

See METALANGUAGE.

Ontological category, ontology

Ontology is the philosophical field that attempts to organize everything that exists into a limited number of general CATEGORIES. An **ontological system** (informally called an **ontology**) is a theory of what general categories there are and how they are structured with relation to each other. A complete onto-logical system would have categories for everything that exists – including abstract 'things' like the property of being green or the state of owning a bicycle. Computer scientists have become major contributors to discussions of ontological categories, as they form the basis of the semantic aspects of many natural language processing efforts.

In semantics, ontological categories may serve as the basis for semantic categories or semantic representations – determining the basic meaning types upon which a semantic system is drawn. While the names of such types may vary from theory to theory, they typically involve categories such as ENTITY, EVENT, STATE, PROPERTY, QUANTITY. Generally, the term *ontological category* is reserved for the highest levels in a TAXONOMY of 'what exists' – in Figure 7 of a small part of an ontology, they are represented by items in small capital letters.

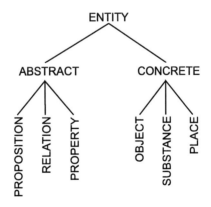

Figure 7 Ontology

Of course, this taxonomy could be carried on down to particular objects like cups, mugs, Tom's mugs, Tom's green mug, and so forth – but such specific items are not likely to be universal in human conceptualization systems, nor do they affect general semantic processes, so they are not treated as general ontological categories.

Opaque context

See REFERENTIAL OPACITY.

Open class

See CLOSED AND OPEN CLASSES.

Operator

See LOGICAL OPERATOR.

Opposite

The term **opposite** can be used either as a synonym of ANTONYM or in contrast with a more restrictive meaning of *antonym*. For example, some authors restrict *antonym* to gradable contrary (see ANTONYM) relations, such as *high/low* and thus use *opposite* for all other cases of binary INCOMPATIBILITY, such as contradictories (*dead/alive*) and directional opposites (*up/down*). Others restrict *antonym* to pairs that are related by lexical form or CONVENTION as well as by semantic opposition (e.g. *dead/alive*, *ascend/descend*), and use **semantic opposite** to refer to pairs like *deceased/alive* or *rise/descend*, in which the meanings are opposed but the word pairings are not the normal ones for the language.

Key texts: Cruse 1986; Murphy 2003.

Paradigmatic, paradigmatic relation

A **paradigmatic relation** is a type of LEXICAL RELATION in which the set of words forms a **paradigm**, particularly a semantic paradigm that contains members of the same grammatical category that share some semantic characteristics in common, but fail to share others. So, for example, the set of basic colour terms forms a paradigm whose members are adjectives (or nouns), each referring to a different section of the colour spectrum. One could also speak of morphological paradigmatic relations, such as the relation that exists between *man* and *men*. Paradigmatically related words are, to some degree, substitutable for each other. For example, *blue*, *black*, and any other member of the colour paradigm can sensibly and grammatically occur in the phrase *a ____ object*. In this way, the term *paradigmatic relation* stands in contrast to SYNTAGMATIC RELATION.

See also ANTONYM, HYPONYM, MERONYM, SYNONYM, TAXONYM.

Paraphrase

In lay terms, a paraphrase is the rephrasing of something in other words.

Logical **paraphrase** (sometimes called SYNONYMY) is the propositional relation of mutual ENTAILMENT; that is, PROPOSITION P entails proposition Q *and* Q entails P. In other words, two propositions paraphrase one another if they are true in exactly the same conditions. For instance, *Mike hugged Ike* paraphrases *Ike was hugged by Mike*. (Not to be confused with PERIPHRASIS.) *Paraphrase* can also be used to refer to the relation between a linguistic expression and a METALANGUAGE representation of it.

Passive voice

See VOICE.

Past tense

See TENSE.

Patient

See SEMANTIC ROLE.

Pejoration

See SEMANTIC CHANGE.

Perfect

Perfect (not to be confused with PERFECTIVE) is a category of ASPECT that expresses a focus on the end or outcome of an event. This is expressed in English through the participial *have VERBed* form. Compare, for example, the perspective on the 'eating' event with and without perfect marking:

(1) I ate lunch.
(2) I have eaten lunch.

Note that both (1) and (2) refer to past events, although *have* in the perfect example (2) is marked for present tense. The simple past tense in (1) could be used to describe an activity that happened at any point in the past, but it would be strange to use the perfect form in (2) to refer to the eating of yesterday's lunch, since we'd expect that the filling effect of yesterday's lunch is not still felt in the present. In other words, the perfect takes a perspective on a past event that is *after* that event happened, but when its effect is still felt. This works as well in other tenses. For example, the future form *I will have eaten lunch* takes the perspective of a time in the future when the future event of eating lunch is already in the past.

Perfective

Perfective (not to be confused with PERFECT) is a category of ASPECT, in which a situation is taken as a whole, without reference to its internal structure. This is expressed in English by the lack of other aspectual marking in the past and present forms: *I ate lunch, I eat lunch*. In using such forms, we consider the event as a whole, as opposed to taking the particular perspective of the beginning, middle or end of the event.

See also IMPERFECTIVE.

Periphrasis, periphrastic

A **periphrastic** expression, from the classical Greek for 'around' and 'tell', is one that communicates something in a wordier way than might be required. For example, *write again* is a periphrastic way of expressing *rewrite*. While periphrasis generally involves a PARAPHRASE relation between the alternative expressions, note that *paraphrase* and *periphrasis* are different words that are used in different contexts.

Person

Person is a grammatical category that reflects DEICTIC reference. It breaks down into three categories, **first, second** and **third person**, whose names reflect a hierarchy among them: first person is reference to the speaker (*I*) or to a group that includes the speaker (*we*); second person refers to the addressee or a group that includes the addressee (*you*); and third person refers to anything that includes neither the speaker nor addressee. The hierarchical relation between these categories means that a group is referred to using a PRONOUN in the 'highest' person category of one of the members of the group. So, if a group contains the speaker and the addressee or others, a first-person (speaker-oriented) pronoun is used to refer to it, rather than a second- or third-person pronoun. Some languages LEXICALIZE the distinction between first-person plurals that include the second person (the **inclusive** first-person plural) and those that include the speaker and others, but not the addressee (the **exclusive** first-person plural). For example, in Chechen, these are *vai* and *txo*, respectively. In pronominal systems, person is often lexicalized in combination with NUMBER (as seen in the *I/we* distinction) and sometimes GENDER categories.

See also AGREEMENT.

Pleonasm, pleonastic

Pleonasm is linguistic redundancy; the inclusion of words or morphemes in an utterance that are not essential and do not add to its meaning. This can give rise to semantic ANOMALY, as in the examples below:

> #a dead corpse
> #a royal king
> ?a bad disaster
> #He kissed me with his lips.

These expressions are pleonastic because the modifying expressions simply repeat a property that is already part of the definition of the noun or the verb: a corpse, for instance, is by definition dead and the meaning of *kiss* includes the fact that it is done with one's lips. Note that the anomaly is avoided if the modifying expression is made more specific: *He kissed me with his **chapped** lips* or *a **terrible** disaster*. Mere repetition is not necessarily pleonastic, as it can often have an intensifying meaning: *She was **very, very** thirsty*.

Plesionym, plesionymy

Plesionyms are near-SYNONYMS that differ enough in their DENOTATION that they cannot be substituted one for the other without affecting the TRUTH CONDITIONS of the PROPOSITION. For example, *mist* and *fog* refer to very similar, perhaps overlapping, categories of things, but some instances of mist could not be described as *fog* – thus they are plesionyms, rather than true synonyms.

Key text: Cruse 1986.

Plural

See NUMBER.

Polarity

Polarity refers to the distinction between the **affirmative** and the **negative**. For example, *I like cookies* is affirmative but *I don't like cookies* is opposite in its polarity – that is, it is negative.

Polarity can also refer to the opposition of the two extremes (**poles**) of a semantic SCALE.

See also NEGATION, POLARITY ITEM.

Polarity item

A **polarity item** is a LEXEME that is sensitive to the POLARITY of the constituent to which it belongs. For instance, the determiner *any* is a **negative polarity item** that can only occur in negated clauses, while the **positive polarity item** *some* must occur in affirmative clauses:

> I have some friends. *But:* #I don't have some friends.
> I don't have any friends. *But:* #I have any friends.

See also NEGATION.

Polyseme, polysemous, polysemy

Polysemy refers to the phenomenon where a single LEXEME (a **polyseme**) is associated with multiple distinct but related SENSES. As a consequence, polysemy is one potential source of lexical AMBIGUITY. For example, the word *window* in *Penelope closed the window* could refer either to 'a glazed opening in the wall of a built structure' or 'a rectangular area of a graphical computer interface'. These senses of *window* are related semantically and therefore they are polysemous senses of a single lexeme. Polysemy is distinguished from HOMONYMY, which involves distinct semantically unrelated lexemes that coincidentally share the same form. Another important definitional distinction is that between polysemy and VAGUENESS. In vagueness, a lexeme can be used with multiple different interpretations, but those interpretations are instantiations of a single general sense, rather than distinct polysemous senses. *Cousin*, for example, can refer to either a male or a female, but most speakers (and linguists) would not view *cousin* as having distinct 'male cousin' and 'female cousin' senses. Instead, we regard it as vague with respect to gender. A number of different methodologies and criteria have been used to draw the line between polysemy and vagueness (see VAGUENESS for some examples), but these are not unproblematic and the demarcation of senses is one of the more controversial issues in lexical semantics.

In **systematic**, or **regular**, **polysemy** the relation between the senses is predictable in that any word of a particular semantic class potentially has the same variety of meanings. For example, words for openable coverings of apertures in built structures (*She rested against the door/gate/window*) are also used to refer to the aperture itself (*Go through the door/gate/window*). In **non-systematic** polysemy, the senses are semantically related, but are not part of a larger pattern: *arm* may refer to a human arm or an arm of a government, but other body-part terms are not used in predictable ways to refer to parts of organizations.

Theories of semantics vary considerably in how they account for polysemy. Some approaches (e.g. GENERATIVE LEXICON THEORY) are particularly concerned with explicating the lexical rules or generative mechanisms that underlie regular polysemy. Other approaches view polysemy as a PRAGMATIC phenomenon and assume that word senses in the lexicon are highly **underspecified** or general and more specific interpretations arise in context through pragmatic inference. In COGNITIVE LINGUISTIC approaches to polysemy, the focus is often on the conceptual processes that motivate the multiple meanings of linguistic forms, such as CONCEPTUAL METAPHOR and METONYMY. Cognitive linguists also argue that categories of senses exhibit the same kind of PROTOTYPE structure as other conceptual categories, and thus the relations of polysemous senses are typically modelled in terms of polysemy networks centred around a prototypical sense. Noting the difficulties in demarcating homonymy, polysemy and vagueness, many cognitive linguists also argue that the distinctions between these phenomena are a matter of degree, rather than clear-cut and stable.

Key texts: Lakoff 1987; Ravin and Leacock 2000; Nerlich et al. 2003.

Possible worlds

Some TRUTH-CONDITIONAL approaches to meaning make use of hypothetical **possible worlds** (or **models**) across which the full range of possible realities can be represented. These imaginary worlds are **possible** in that they are consistent with logical principles. So, for example, there is a possible world in which you are reading *Hamlet* instead of this book, but there is no possible world in which you are reading this book and not reading this book at the same time. The introduction of possible worlds is especially valuable for treating statements that depend on COUNTERFACTUAL statements or expressions of MODALITY. For instance,

If books were made out of lead, they would be heavy

can be judged to be true (in our world) if it is true in any possible world that is exactly like this world except that the books are made of lead.

Possible world semantics is another term for MODEL-THEORETIC SEMANTICS.

Key texts: Lewis 1973, 1986.

Pragmatics

Pragmatics can be defined as the study of language use; how language interacts with CONTEXT. The domain of pragmatics is generally viewed as excluding those aspects of meaning that fall into the realm of semantics. The semantics/pragmatics distinction may be defined in terms of dimensions such as the following:

SEMANTICS	PRAGMATICS
context-independent meaning	context-dependent meaning
CONVENTIONAL meaning	non-conventional meaning
literal meaning (what is said)	speaker meaning (what is implicated)
TRUTH-CONDITIONAL meaning	non-truth-conditional meaning
stored representations in the mind	on-line processing

Central issues for pragmatics include the assignment of REFERENCE, DEIXIS, PRESUPPOSITION and IMPLICATURE. In the dialogue below, pragmatics would, for example, account for aspects such as the fixing of the reference of *the dog* and *I*, the discrepancy between what Anna says literally and what she implicates (i.e. 'I would like you to take the dog out for a walk') and what motivates Anna to make her request implicitly, rather than state it explicitly ('Take the dog out for a walk!').

> Anna: I think the dog wants to go out for a walk.
> Ben: Oh, all right then.

Theorists differ, however, in where they draw the dividing line between semantics and pragmatics (while some, including COGNITIVE LINGUISTS, reject the idea that a definite distinction can be made at all). Many have also pointed out that the various dimensions along which semantics and pragmatics may be demarcated do not exactly overlap. For example, the literal meaning of a sentence is not purely independent of the context, but relies on context-dependent processes such as assigning reference, and resolving any ambiguities.

Key texts: Grice 1975, 1978; Levinson 1983, 2000; Sperber and Wilson 1995.

Further reading: Davis 1991; Huang 2007.

Predicate

In semantics, **predicate** refers to the part of a PROPOSITION that expresses the relation or property that is being ascribed to some entities, ARGUMENTS. For example, in *Emma made a cake*, *make* expresses the predicate; it provides a description of the relation that holds between the two arguments, *Emma* and *a cake*. Predicates are typically expressed by verbs, but may also be adjectives, prepositions and noun phrases. In the examples below, the predicate expressions are in bold:

> Emma **put** the cake in the oven.
> Emma **smiled**.
> The cake is **in** the oven.
> The cake is **delicious**.
> Emma is **satisfied with** the cake.
> Emma is **a baker**.

In English, predicate expressions that are not verbs must occur with the **copular** verb *to be* to make the sentence grammatical. Note that when a noun phrase occurs as a predicate (as in *Emma is **a baker***), it is not a REFERRING EXPRESSION.

Note that in traditional grammar, *predicate* refers to the parts of a sentence other than its subject. Thus, for example, in *Ian ate Emma's cake*, *ate Emma's cake* is the grammatical predicate, whereas 'eat' is the semantic predicate.

See also VALENCY.

Predicate calculus, predicate logic

Predicate logic, or **predicate calculus**, is a logical METALANGUAGE that represents the PREDICATE-ARGUMENT relations within PROPOSITIONS. In this way, it is a development from PROPOSITIONAL LOGIC, whose logical operators and basic syntax it shares. Because it is has a level of complexity above propositional logic, it is known as a **first-order logic**. The predicate-argument structure is written with the predicate first, followed by as many arguments as that predicate requires, usually grouped within parentheses, as in the following representation of the English sentence *Otters love chocolate*:

Love (otters, chocolate)

Usually, such propositions are written using an abbreviated vocabulary:

A, B, C, D, E . . .	represent predicates
a, b, c, d, e . . .	represent individual constants (which have specified referents)
. . . **x, y, z**	represent variables (unspecified reference)

So we could rewrite the *otter* sentence with one of the following formulae:

L(o,c) or Loc

The differences in their punctuation reflect differences in style only – the parentheses add no additional meaning. We have represented the predicate and arguments using the initials of their English translations, but this is just a mnemonic helper; we could use any symbol to represent any predicate, so long as we defined our terms explicitly.

QUANTIFICATION of noun phrases is represented through the use of logical quantifiers ($\forall$ = universal quantification and $\exists$ = existential quantification), and VARIABLES. Every variable must be BOUND to a quantifier – which is to say that if a variable is used as an argument, then there must be a quantifier that indicates the 'amount' of x and that has SCOPE over the predicate for which x is an argument. So $\exists x$ (Lxc) = 'there exists something that loves chocolate.'

Predicative (adjective)

See ADJECTIVE.

Present tense

See TENSE.

Presentational focus

See FOCUS.

Presuppose, presupposition

A **presupposition** is a proposition that must be supposed to be true in order for another proposition to be judged true or false. For example, *The king of France is bald* **presupposes** the proposition that 'there is a king of France.' Unlike ENTAILMENTS, the presupposition remains the same when the sentence is negated. So, *The king of France is not bald* still presupposes that 'there is a king of France.'

Presuppositions have both semantic and PRAGMATIC properties. The fact that presuppositions usually have linguistic **triggers** makes them seem like a semantic phenomenon. In the example above, the determiner *the* triggers the presupposition that the King of France exists. However, the fact that presuppositions are **defeasible** (like IMPLICATURES) makes them seem like a pragmatic phenomenon. For example, usually *before* triggers the presupposition that the event described in the *before* clause actually happened:

> A split second BEFORE **she told Tom she loved him**, Ann crossed her fingers. (presupposes that Ann told Tom she loved him)

But in the following context, the information in the second clause undoes the presupposition:

> A split second before **she told Tom she loved him**, Ann changed her mind. (undoes the presupposition that Ann told Tom she loved him)

See also INFERENCE.

Key texts: Karttunen 1974; Levinson 1983.

Primitive, semantic

A **primitive** or **atomic** unit is one that cannot be broken down or defined further and thus forms the most basic unit of analysis. In semantics, the notion of primitives is particularly important in COMPONENTIAL ANALYSIS, which assumes that the meanings of linguistic items are built out of smaller units of meaning, meaning components. But in order to explain the meaning of those meaning components, they, too, would have to be broken down to their component parts, and so on infinitely. This problem can be avoided by assuming that some meaning components are primitive and undefinable.

Privative

A **privative** meaning expresses the lack of something, especially something that is normally present. For example, *clean* denotes the PROPERTY of lacking filth. **Privative** is sometimes used to describe a type of ANTONYM pair, like *clean/dirty* or *honest/dishonest*, in which one member expresses a lack of something and the other its presence. Morphemes that mark the absence of something can be called *privative* – for example, the *un-* in *unhappy* or the *-less* in *airless*.

Profile, profiling

See COGNITIVE GRAMMAR, FIGURE/GROUND.

Pronoun

Pronouns are linguistic expressions that can stand in place of a NOUN phrase, as illustrated by the bold items in the following examples.

> The fluffy little kitten bit Susan. → **It** bit **her**.
> The students want chocolate. → **They** want **some**.
> These knives are dull, but those knives aren't. → **These** are dull, but **those** aren't.

Pronouns are often used ANAPHORICALLY, which is to say that they refer to something that was mentioned previously in the discourse. But pronouns are also used for DEIXIS, which involves reference to something in the extra-linguistic context. An example of this would be when a speaker says *That was there* while pointing first to an object and then a location.

Personal pronouns like *me*, *she* and *they* have DEFINITE reference, as do the DEMONSTRATIVE **pronouns** *this*, *that*, *these* and *those*. In English, indefinite pronouns are often similar in form to indefinite QUANTIFIERS – for example, *one* or *some* in *I want some*.

See also PERSON.

Proper name, proper noun

A **proper name,** or **proper noun**, is a nominal expression that denotes the same individual (or particular set of individuals) every time it is used. This is opposed to a COMMON NOUN, which indicates a type of thing, and therefore can be used to denote different individuals each time it is used. So, *aviatrix* is a common noun that can refer to any woman who pilots planes, whereas *Amelia Earhart* refers to a particular woman who happened to fly planes. Note that if she had not taken up flying, she could and would still be called *Amelia Earhart*. If something else is also designated *Amelia Earhart*, that is just coincidence (or an homage); it does not mean that the second

Amelia Earhart will have anything in common with the first one. For instance, you could name a houseplant *Amelia Earhart* if you so wished.

There is some debate in the philosophy of language about whether proper names have meaningful SENSES which allow them to refer to individuals who meet the conditions on those senses or whether they are RIGID DESIGNATORS that always refer to the same individual simply by CONVENTION. In linguistic semantics, it is usually assumed either that they are rigid designators or that they have METALINGUISTIC senses – that is, the meaning of *Amelia* is 'something that is called *Amelia*'.

In English, proper names are typically written with initial capital letters and common nouns are not, but this code is not followed in many languages (for instance, German capitalizes all nouns) – nor is it always followed in English. For instance, we spell *Iraqi* with a capital *I*, but it refers to the category of people from Iraq, not any particular individual. Because proper names indicate unique individuals, in English they usually occur without a determiner (*a*, *the*), although there are some proper names that include or allow a definite determiner, such as *The Beatles* or the names of rivers – *the Nile*. In other cases, when proper names occur with determiners (in English) they are usually interpreted as common nouns. For example, *Amelia* can be used to refer to the category 'people named Amelia' when we use it with a determiner, as in *I know three Amelias* or *I know the Amelia that you met yesterday*.

See also INDEXICAL.

Key thinker: SAUL KRIPKE.

Key texts: Kripke 1980; Evans 1973; Abbott 2002.

Property

Property is the name of the ONTOLOGICAL CATEGORY of attributes or characteristics. In English, properties are often LEXICALIZED by ADJECTIVES or some abstract NOUNS. For example, the adjective *Canadian* (as in *Canadian maple syrup*) denotes a single property that a thing or person can have – the property of 'being from Canada' and the noun *Canadianness* can denote that property as well. In contrast, note that the noun *Canadian* (as in *I met a Canadian*) is more complex, in that it denotes a person who has the property of being Canadian. In languages without adjective classes, properties like theses are expressed using nouns or STATIVE verbs. Properties can be SCALAR or ABSOLUTE.

Proposition

A **proposition** may be defined as the meaning of a SENTENCE that makes a statement about some state of affairs. As such, a proposition has a TRUTH VALUE; it can be either true or false. A proposition is independent of the linguistic structure used to express it, which is to say that the same proposition can be expressed by different sentences. Thus all the sentences below express the proposition 'Olivia opened the door':

Olivia opened the door.
The door was opened by Olivia.
It was the door that Olivia opened.
What Olivia did was open the door.

Only declarative sentences express a proposition, because only they make a statement that can be true or false. But interrogative and imperative sentences are sometimes viewed as sharing the propositional content of a corresponding declarative sentence, while either questioning its truth or expressing the proposition as a desirable state of affairs. It is also possible for the same sentence to be used to express different propositions – for example, *I'm opening the door* expresses a different proposition depending on who the speaker is.

A proposition consists of a PREDICATE and one or more ARGUMENTS – for example, in 'Olivia opened the door', the predicate is 'open' and 'Olivia' and 'the door' are the arguments. PREDICATE CALCULUS provides a formal description of the relations between predicates and arguments. PROPOSITIONAL LOGIC studies the relations that can hold between whole propositions irrespective of the internal parts of propositions.

See also UTTERANCE, PROPOSITIONAL RELATION.

Propositional attitude

A linguistic form expresses a **propositional attitude** if it relates an animate being's mental state to a PROPOSITION. For instance, *doubt* in *Norman doubts that Michelle left* indicates Norman's attitude (one of disbelief) toward the proposition 'Michelle left.' Propositional attitudes can also be communicated through markers of MODALITY or MOOD. For example, the use of *must* in *Michelle must have left by now* indicates the speakers level of certainty about the proposition 'Michelle has left by now.'

Propositional logic

Propositional logic is a logical METALANGUAGE that treats PROPOSITIONS as ATOMIC, or unanalysed, entities, which can be combined with LOGICAL OPERATORS. For example, if **P** stands for 'Peter picked peppers' and **Q** stands for 'Quentin quacked' then $\mathbf{P} \rightarrow \neg\mathbf{Q}$ means 'If Peter picked peppers, then it is not the case that Quentin quacked.' The details of the PREDICATES and ARGUMENTS within the propositions are not represented.

See also LOGIC, PREDICATE CALCULUS.

Propositional relation

A **propositional**, or **logical**, relation is a SEMANTIC RELATION of logical necessity between two propositions. These are ENTAILMENT, CONTRADICTION and PARAPHRASE.

Prospective

Prospective ASPECT expresses a perspective on a situation from a time that is earlier than that situation. In other words, it is the converse of PERFECT aspect, which looks back on a past event from a later point. However, the prospective is generally not as GRAMMATICALIZED as the perfect. For the prospective, English uses expressions such as *be about to* [*do something*] or *be going to* [*do something*], as in *He's going to go to Paris*. Since the prospective 'looks at' a situation from the perspective of an earlier time, it is the beginning of that situation that is most salient – and thus the prospective indicates readiness for the future situation. This means that its interpretation may differ slightly from otherwise equivalent simple future TENSE expressions. A simple future form like *Jay will go* turns out to be false if he never goes. But one might say *Jay is going to go* and then feel that one has not been contradicted if Jay was ready to go, but his plans fell through at the last minute. Indeed, in that case, one can contradict a past prospective statement without ANOMALY: *He was going to go, but couldn't.*

Protasis

See CONDITIONAL.

Prototype

See PROTOTYPE THEORY.

Prototype effect, prototypical

The notion of **prototype effects** emerged in the 1970s from the experimental work of cognitive psychologist Eleanor Rosch and her colleagues on CONCEPTS and CATEGORIES. Prototype effects relate to the fact that many categories have a graded, asymmetrical structure; different members of the category may be ranked according to how good they are as members of that category, with the 'best examples' being **prototypical** members.

Prototype effects then relate to the special status of prototypical members in various experimental tasks. For instance, prototypical members tend to be consistently given higher **goodness-of-example ratings** in tasks where subjects are asked to rank or rate members of a category according to how good an example of that category they are. For example, most of Rosch's subjects judged football and tennis to be very good members of SPORT, while fishing and chess were judged to be less good members. Reaction times are also faster for confirming prototypical members as members of the category. Prototypicality has also been shown to be a factor in priming tasks: reaction times for prototypical category members are faster if you see or hear the name of the category shortly before the name of the member. For middle-ranked members, priming with the category name has no effect but for atypical members of the category, priming has an inhibitory effect.

There is also a correlation between prototypicality and FAMILY RESEMBLANCES: the more highly ranked members of categories tend to share more properties with other members of the category. For example, we might say that prototypical fruits, such as apples and oranges, share with many other members of FRUIT properties such as 'seed-bearing part of plant', 'has a peel', 'sweet', 'eaten as a snack', 'about the size of a fist', and so on. More marginal members such as lemons or pumpkins, on the other hand, share fewer of these properties – they are not sweet, would not be eaten as a snack and, in the case of pumpkins, are larger than typical fruit.

The significance of prototype effects lies in how they challenge the CLASSICAL THEORY OF CONCEPTUALIZATION. The empirical findings of prototype effects led to the development of an alternative theory of conceptual representation, the PROTOTYPE THEORY.

Key texts: Rosch 1973; Rosch and Mervis 1975.

Prototype Theory

Prototype Theory is a theory of CATEGORIES and CONCEPTS that arose in the 1970s as a way of accounting for PROTOTYPE EFFECTS. It represents an alternative to the CLASSICAL THEORY OF CONCEPTUALIZATION, which holds that an entity may be categorized as an instance of a concept only if it meets all the necessary and sufficient conditions for that concept. In contrast, the Prototype Theory maintains that category membership is defined in terms of similarity to the **prototype** of the category.

The term *prototype* can be used to simply refer to the category member that shows the highest goodness-of-example rating (see PROTOTYPE EFFECT), without reference to any particular model of conceptual representation. However, in some formulations of the Prototype Theory, prototypes are mental repre-sentations of concepts. According to one view, a prototype is a cluster of properties that represent what members of the category are like on average (e.g. for the category BIRD, the prototype would consist of properties such as 'lays eggs', 'has a beak', 'has wings', 'has feathers', 'can fly', 'chirps', 'builds nests', etc.). Category members may share these properties to varying degrees – hence the properties are not necessary and sufficient as in the classical model, but instead FAMILY RESEMBLANCES. Alternatively, according to some approaches to Prototype Theory, the mental representation of a concept takes the form of a specific, ideal category member (or members), which acts as the prototype (e.g. for BIRD, the prototype might be a representation of a specific robin or sparrow).

Although Prototype Theory provides an explanation for variable goodness-of-example ratings and the FUZZINESS of the boundaries of many categories, it does, however, also have problems. For example, it is not clear how it accounts for COMPOSITIONALITY. Can the prototype of PET FISH (perhaps a goldfish or any other small, colourful aquarium fish) be considered to be compositionally derived from the prototypes of PET (say, a cat or any other furry mammal) and FISH (a trout, perhaps, or any other greyish fish that lives in the wild)? Furthermore, some authors have questioned the conclusion that prototype effects prove that concepts cannot be classically defined. Some concepts that do have classical definitions, such as ODD NUMBER ('a number that cannot be evenly divided by two') also give rise to prototype effects: people typically judge 3 to be a better odd number than 47. The similarity-based view of categorization assumed in the Prototype Theory also has difficulties accounting for category boundaries: although sheep share a number of properties with lions (e.g. 'animate', 'quadruped', 'has hair'), a sheep would never count as even a marginal member of LION. There is therefore a need for some additional measures that allow categories to include all true members and exclude non-members. The so-called **'THEORY' THEORY** of concepts is one approach that tries to account for this.

Key texts: Rosch and Mervis 1975; Rosch 1978; Smith and Medin 1981; Margolis and Laurence 1999.

Prototypical

See PROTOTYPE EFFECT.

Proximal (spatial deixis)

See DEIXIS.

Punctual

EVENTS that happen within a moment are said to be **punctual** (or sometimes **punctive**), as opposed to DURATIVE. For instance, *flash* (as for a light flashing) or *find a parking space* are punctual events (as contrasted to *look for a parking space*, which could take a long time). Punctuality is a property that contributes to **Aktionsart** and **Vendler classes**. Because punctual events are quick, punctual predicates can be **anomalous** in constructions or with lexical items that indicate an on-going event, such as the English progressive:

I am looking for my keys. (durative)
#I am finding my keys. (punctual)

Where punctual predicates do not sound as strange in the progressive, it is usually because the progressive has forced another, durative interpretation. For example, *flash* can be used in the progressive if it is interpreted **iteratively**:

The light is flashing.

See also **aspect**.

Qualia

In philosophy, the term **qualia** generally refers to the subjective qualities of mental experience. In semantics, the term **qualia structure** is used in GENERATIVE LEXICON THEORY to refer to a level of structure in the representation of the meanings of lexical items. Qualia structure consists of four roles that describe aspects of the word's meaning: the basic category the entity belongs to (**formal** role), the parts of the entity (the **constitutive** role), its function (**telic** role) and the factors involved in the origin or creation of the object (**agentive** role). For example, the qualia structure of *sandwich* would be represented as shown in Figure 8.

$$
\begin{bmatrix}
\textbf{sandwich } (x) \\
\text{CONSTITUTIVE} = \textbf{[bread, ...]} \\
\text{FORMAL} = \textbf{physical-object (x)} \\
\text{TELIC} = \textbf{eat (P,w,x)} \\
\text{AGENTIVE} = \textbf{artefact (x)}
\end{bmatrix}
$$

Figure 8 Qualia structure

Quantification, quantifier

A **quantifier** is an expression that modifies a (potentially) REFERRING EXPRESSION in terms of amount. In English, this is achieved through determiners (e.g. *a(n)*, *some*, *every*, *no*) that indicate amount. In LOGIC, QUANTIFIERS are LOGICAL OPERATORS that indicate the quantity of individuals to which a PREDICATE (or other incomplete formula) applies. **Quantification** is achieved by the BINDING of a VARIABLE to such a logical operator. The two basic kinds of quantification in logic are universal and existential quantification. A variable bound to the **universal quantifier** 'picks out' all things in the UNIVERSE OF DISCOURSE. It is symbolized by an upside-down capital A ($\forall$) and read as 'for all'. Consider this example:

$\forall x \, (Px \rightarrow Ex)$

If we take P to mean 'is a physician' and E to mean 'is educated', then this formula can be translated as 'For all x, if x is a physician, then x is educated.' This proposition is true if every physician who exists in the universe of discourse is educated.

The **existential quantifier** is read as 'there is some' – in other words, it asserts the existence of at least one example of something. It is symbolized by a backwards E ($\exists$):

$\exists$x (Px $\land$ Ex)

This can be read as, 'There is some x such that x is a physician and x is educated.' This proposition is true if we can find a single example of an educated physician – and it is not contradicted if we find more than one.

The negative quantifier *no* is expressed as the negation of the existential quantifier. So *No physicians are educated* can be translated as follows:

$\neg\exists$x (Px $\land$ Ex)

'it is not the case that there is some x such that x is a physician and is educated.'

The negated universal quantifier, on the other hand, is the equivalent of 'not all'.

A quantifier that is immediately to the left of a proposition with unbound variables is said to have SCOPE over that proposition. In natural language, quantifier scope can be AMBIGUOUS (see SCOPE for more discussion).

See also PREDICATE CALCULUS.

Key texts: Barwise and Cooper 1981.

Recipient

See SEMANTIC ROLE.

Refer, reference, referent, referential meaning

A linguistic expression **refers** if it 'picks out' a particular something (or set of something) in the world. So, for example, *Trafalgar Square* refers to a particular place in London and *the raisins I just ate* refers to the set of raisins that the author of this sentence consumed just before writing this sentence. The **referent** of an expression is the thing it picks out. The referent of *the only occurrence of the word 'aubergine' on this page in this book* is the thus the seventh word in that example.

GOTTLOB FREGE is attributed with making the firm distinction between **reference** and SENSE as aspects of meaning, demonstrating that it is not sufficient to consider the meaning of an expression to be the thing it refers to. Part of the reason for this is that not all expressions refer, but we still understand them as having different meanings – for example, *the present king of France* and *the goblin who wrote this page* do not refer to anything – their EXTENSIONS are the empty set. If **referential meaning** (i.e. the linking of expressions to extensions) were the only aspect of meaning then those two phrases should mean the same thing – but they do not.

There are a number of ways in which REFERRING EXPRESSIONS can be used to refer. One distinction is that between reference to individuals and reference to whole classes of individuals. The latter type is called **generic reference**, and is illustrated by the sentences below, all of which refer to the class of elephants in general, rather than to a particular individual elephant or elephants:

(1) **An elephant** never forgets. ('any member of the class of elephants')
(2) **The elephant** is the largest land mammal. ('the elephant species')
(3) **Elephants** live in Africa and Asia. ('elephants in general')

Generic reference can take three forms in English: with an indefinite article as in (1), definite article (2) or bare plural (3). These alternatives typically have slightly different interpretations, as indicated above. An important characteristic of generic reference is that it refers to the members of a class 'in general' – that is, it describes typical properties of the class of referents. Therefore, finding one forgetful elephant would not make (1) false.

Generic reference contrasts with **singular reference**, which involves reference to an individual member or individual members of a class, as in (4):

(4) **An elephant** tried to steal my sandwiches.

Singular reference can either be **definite** or **indefinite**. While *an elephant* in the sentence above is indefinite, ***The elephant** tried to steal my sandwiches* would involve definite reference and PRESUPPOSE that the hearer can uniquely identify which particular elephant is being talked about (see DEFINITENESS).

A distinction is typically made between **specific** and **non-specific reference**. A specific referring expression refers to a particular entity which the speaker has in mind while non-specific expressions refer to a hypothetical or virtual entity. Definite reference is usually specific, but indefinite reference may be either specific or non-specific. While (4) above involves specific reference to a particular elephant that took an interest in my sandwiches, in (5) *an elephant* most likely has non-specific reference in that I do not have any particular elephant in mind, any elephant would do:

(5) I'd love to be able to ride **an elephant**.

Non-specific reference can be viewed as being **non-referential** because it does not pick out any particular referent in the world. In some accounts generic reference is also seen as non-referential, but other approaches maintain that generic referring expressions do refer, although to a class.

See also DENOTATION, CO-REFERENCE, REFERENTIAL OPACITY.

Key thinkers: GOTTLOB FREGE, BERTRAND RUSSELL, RUDOLF CARNAP.

Key texts: Frege 1892; Russell 1905; Carnap 1947; Chesterman 1991; Krifka et al. 1995; Lyons 1999.

Referential opacity, referential transparency

A use of a REFERRING EXPRESSION is **referentially opaque** within a PROPOSITION if the substitution of a CO-REFERENTIAL expression changes the proposition's TRUTH VALUE. For example, *Superman* is referentially opaque in *Lois believes that Superman invented diet cola*, because if we substitute *Clark Kent* for *Superman*, then the truth of the statement is no longer assured, since Lois may not believe that Clark Kent invented diet cola, even though *Superman* and *Clark Kent* **refer** to the same person. PROPOSITIONAL ATTITUDE statements like this example provide **opaque contexts** for referring expressions.

The opposite of *referential opacity* is **referential transparency**. In *Superman lives in Metropolis*, *Superman* is referentially transparent because if this sentence is true, then it is always also true that *Clark Kent lives in Metropolis*.

Referring expression

A **referring expression** is an expression that REFERS in a context to an individual or set of individuals. In natural language, this would usually be expressed as a NOUN phrase, but not all uses of noun phrases refer. For example, in *Noam Chomsky is a linguist*, *Noam Chomsky* refers to a particular individual, but *a linguist* does not refer to any particular linguist, but rather describes the PROPERTY of being a linguist.

Relative (property)

See ABSOLUTE.

Relative clause

See RESTRICTIVE/NON-RESTRICTIVE.

Representational approach

See DENOTATIONAL/REPRESENTATIONAL APPROACH.

Restrictive/non-restrictive

The use of noun modifiers may, in some cases, be ᴀᴍʙɪɢᴜᴏᴜs between **restrictive** interpretations, which limit the denotation of the noun phrase, and **non-restrictive** ones, which add additional descriptive information. For example, consider *lazy* in the following sentence:

The lazy children think money grows on trees.

Lazy here can be interpreted as restrictively limiting the set of children who think that money grows on trees:

'only the children who are lazy (but not the industrious ones) think that money grows on trees'

Or it can be read with a non-restrictive meaning, to describe children in general:

'all children are lazy and think money grows on trees'

The same difference is evident in English relative clauses, although punctuation can be used to differentiate them:

The children who are lazy think the rest of the world revolves around them. (restrictive)
The children, who are lazy, think the rest of the world revolves around them. (non-restrictive)

In traditional (prescriptive) grammar, this difference is also indicated in inanimate noun phrases by *that* (restrictive) versus *which* (non-restrictive). *That* always forces a restrictive meaning, but most English speakers now use *which* for either type of relative clause.

Reversive

See ᴀɴᴛᴏɴʏᴍ, ɴᴇɢᴀᴛɪᴏɴ.

Rigid designation, rigid designator

In the approach to PROPER NAMES and NATURAL KIND terms proposed by SAUL KRIPKE, names are **rigid** in what they can REFER to – that is, they always refer to the same individual in every POSSIBLE WORLD. Such **rigid designation** is established through an act of **dubbing**, in which it is decided and established that an entity E will have the name N. This establishes a CAUSAL CHAIN of acts of reference to E using N, which can all be traced back to the original act of dubbing. In other words, in this approach names do not have descriptive SENSES, and referential use of a name is tied to a number of social acts that establish its CONVENTIONAL reference.

Salience

Salience generally refers to the prominence of some entity in relation to other entities in our perception and conceptualization. Salient entities therefore attract attention. In linguistics, the notion of salience has been used in various ways: it has, for instance, been used to account for the notions of TOPIC and FOCUS, REFERENCE assignment and the use of DEFINITE referring expressions (e.g. the referent of *the dog* in *The dog has chewed up my slippers* will be assumed to be salient in the discourse). Particularly within COGNITIVE LINGUISTIC approaches, it is argued that linguistic structure reflects the varying salience of different aspects of conceptualization, including FIGURE/GROUND asymmetries.

See also CONSTRUAL.

Salva veritate

Salva veritate is a Latin expression used particularly in philosophy of language to mean 'while preserving the TRUTH VALUE' of an expression. For example, substitution of one phrase for another *salva veritate* results in PARAPHRASE.

Scale, scalar meaning

GRADABLE meanings, such as the meaning of an adjective like *long*, require flexibility in their denotation, since, for instance, what counts as a *long road* differs from what counts as a *long snake*. The use of *long* in the COMPARATIVE requires further flexibility, since, for example, a snake that is *longer* than a short snake is not necessarily *a long snake*. Many semantic approaches treat the underlying representations of such meanings as one-dimensional **scales** and the meanings of adjectives like *long* as inherently comparative with reference to points on that scale. So, for instance, the interpretation of *long* in *Royal Road is long* (R in the scale below) is with reference to some standard, typical length for roads (N for 'neutral').

short 0——L——N——R——> *long*

On this scale, anything that is to the right of its comparison point is *long* and anything in the other direction with reference to a comparison point is *short*. So, Royal Road is *long*, but Lover's Lane (L in the scale above) is *short*. Still, we can describe the short Lover's Lane as *200 metres long* because in this case the comparison is made with the beginning of the scale (0) and L is in the 'long' direction with reference to that.

See also ADJECTIVE, ABSOLUTE.

Key texts: Bierwisch and Lang 1989; Kennedy 1999.

Scope

The **scope** of a LOGICAL OPERATOR (or its natural language equivalent), such as NEGATION or QUANTIFICATION, is the extent of its operation upon the parts of a sentence. For instance, in *It seems like Dora is not happy*, the negative *not* has scope over the *Dora . . . happy* clause, but not over the *It seems like* clause. Scopal AMBIGUITIES arise where the placement of a natural language operator allows for more than one interpretation of its scope, and one of the advantages of using LOGIC as a METALANGUAGE is the ability to represent operator scope unambiguously. An example of a scopal ambiguity occurs in *Someone saw every play on Broadway*. In one interpretation, the *some* in *someone* has the wider scope – that is, in a logical representation of the sentence, the existential quantifier would come before the universal quantifier, and affect a larger part of the proposition than the universal quantifier would:

$\exists x \, (Ox \wedge \forall y \, (Py \rightarrow Sxy))$
'There is some x such that x is a person (symbolized as 'O' here) and for all y, if y is a play, then x saw y.'

In this case, there is one individual who has seen every play. But if *every* has the wider scope, then it is interpreted as 'Every play on Broadway is such that some person has seen it':

$\forall y \, (Py \rightarrow \exists x \, (Ox \wedge Sxy))$
'For all y, if y is a play then there is an x such that x is a person and x saw the play.'

'There is some x such that x is a person (symbolized as 'O' here) and for all y, if y is a play, then x saw y.'

Script

The notion of **script** refers to a dynamic representation of background knowledge, which can be used as a basis for making INFERENCES. A script provides a general, stereotypical description of the sequence of events involved in some activity such as visiting a restaurant, having a birthday party or getting married. The restaurant script, for instance, specifies that a visit to a restaurant involves the steps of entering the restaurant, ordering the food, eating and paying the bill. On the basis of such background information, one can fill in information that is not mentioned explicitly, including, for instance, that Margaret probably paid for her meal in the example below:

Margaret went to a small Italian restaurant by the station. She ordered a risotto. After eating, she caught the last train home.

The notions of FRAME and IDEALIZED COGNITIVE MODEL are related to and can be viewed as subsuming the notion of scripts.

Key text: Schank and Abelson 1977.

Selectional restriction

Selectional (or **selection**) **restrictions** are constraints that determine which co-occurrences of words or meanings of words are semantically well-formed, rather than ANOMALOUS or abnormal. Selectional restrictions are generally considered to be separate from grammatical constraints such as that transitive verbs must take noun phrases as their objects. Thus a sentence such as *The carrots drank the chair* is odd, but not because it does not conform with the expected grammatical structure of an English sentence, but because it violates the selectional restrictions of the verb *drink*, which requires that its subject argument is animate and its object argument refers to a liquid.

In some approaches, including early COMPONENTIAL approaches, selectional restrictions are assumed to be specified semantically, in the lexical entries of words. For example, the entry for the adjective *pregnant* would state that it may only modify nouns that have the features [+ANIMATE, +FEMALE]. However, identifying selectional restrictions is not always straightforward. One problem is determining what counts as normal and what anomalous. FIGURATIVE language is often assumed to violate selectional restrictions, but many figurative uses are quite normal and acceptable – consider, for example, *The plants drank several litres of water on a hot day*. Even if one assumes that acceptable but figurative uses can be demarcated from literal uses, the acceptability of expressions can depend on the CONTEXT and it is usually possible to imagine some contexts where an anomalous expression is acceptable. For example, *My brother is pregnant* might be acceptable if the brother is a female-to-male transsexual.

Semantic change

Semantic change concerns changes to the meanings of words over time. Words may develop new SENSES, the denotations of existing senses may shift or old senses become obsolete. New senses always develop as extensions of established ones, leading to POLYSEMY as the newer and older senses co-exist. Sometimes the senses of a polysemous lexeme shift in their prominence, so that the earliest sense is no longer perceived to be the main or 'core' sense of the word. For example, the earliest sense of *to express* is 'squeeze or press something out', but the verb is more commonly used today to mean 'to state something in words'. Older senses can also become obsolete – for example, *meticulous* has lost its original sense 'fearful, timid'.

A number of different types of semantic change can be identified. In META-PHORICAL changes, a word comes to be used to refer to something it does not denote literally, but that has some kind of resemblance to the literal meaning, as in *head* 'body part above the neck' > 'a person in charge of an organization'. METONYMIC changes involve a word being used to refer to something that is associated with its literal denotation, as in *anorak* 'a hooded jacket' > 'a nerdy person, stereotypically viewed as wearing an anorak'. In **broadening** (or **generalization**) a word gains a sense that is more INCLUSIVE than one of its established senses, as in the case of *to ship* 'send something by ship' > 'send something by any transport'. **Narrowing** (or **specialization**) involves the opposite change: *liquor* 'any fluid' > 'an alcoholic beverage, a spirit'. Also opposite in their effects are **amelioration** and **pejoration**: in the former a word gains a more positive meaning (e.g. *meticulous* 'fearful, timid' > 'scrupulous, precise') while in the latter its meaning becomes more negative (*mistress* 'a woman in a position of power' > 'a sexual partner of a man, other than his wife'). Semantic **bleaching** involves the weakening of meaning, typically through overuse – consider, for instance, expressions that are used to mean something is very good, such as *brilliant, fantastic* or *to die for*. Semantic bleaching can also refer to the loss of lexical meaning that occurs in the process of GRAMMATICALIZATION, when a lexical item comes to be used for a grammatical function.

The denotation of a word can also change due to changes in the external environment, including technological advancement – consider, for example, how the things we call computers have changed since the mid-twentieth century.

See also ETYMOLOGY.

Key texts: Stern 1931; Ullmann 1957; Blank 1999.

Semantic field

Semantic field has two meanings. Descriptively, a **semantic field** is a set of related concepts, typically lexicalized concepts in PARADIGMATIC RELATION to one another. So, we can say that *promise* and *complain* belong to the semantic field of speech act verbs.

Semantic field can also refer to a theoretical representation of a set of related vocabulary. Semantic, or lexical, field theory concerns the relation of a conceptual, semantic field to a language's vocabulary, and ways in which these constrain each other. FRAME SEMANTICS can be seen as a development from field theory.

Key text: Lehrer 1974.

Semantic relation

Generally, **semantic relation** can refer to any relation of meaning between any two or more meaningful things, including the PROPOSITIONAL RELATIONS of ENTAILMENT, PARAPHRASE and CONTRADICTION. *Semantic relation* is also often used as a synonym for LEXICAL RELATION, including the relations of ANTONYMY, HYPONYMY and SYNONYMY.

Semantic role

Semantic roles (sometimes, particularly in GENERATIVE GRAMMAR, also called **thematic roles** or **theta roles**) are the roles played by participants in some situation. For example, in *Mary broke the egg*, Mary initiates and carries out the action of breaking and the egg is the object affected by Mary's breaking action. We could then say that Mary and the egg have the semantic roles of BREAKER and BREAKEE, respectively, but such very specific semantic roles that only apply to the verb *break* would not capture general similarities between the roles of participants in different situations. Therefore, accounts of semantic roles generally assume more general descriptions of roles. There is much debate over the set of roles and their definitions, but some that are often recognized are given below:

- AGENT: volitional initiator of an action – **Mary** *broke the egg*; **Natalie** *sent Pauline a birthday card.*
- PATIENT: the entity that undergoes and is affected by the event – *Mary broke* **the egg**; **The egg** *broke.*
- THEME: the entity that has a state or position or is characterized as changing that state or position – **The bananas** *are ripe*; *Jessica pushed* **the chair** *against the door.*
- EXPERIENCER: an animate being that is aware of some situation or is affected inwardly by it, but is not in control of it – **Mary** *loves eggs*; **I**'*m hungry*; **Vernon** *heard the doorbell* (compare *Vernon listened to the doorbell*, where Vernon has voluntary control over the situation and can therefore be viewed as an Agent).
- STIMULUS: a mental or physical sensory input that the EXPERIENCER is affected by – *Mary loves* **eggs**; *Vernon heard* **the doorbell**; **Butterflies** *fascinate me.*

- INSTRUMENT: the means by which the action is performed – *Mary broke the egg with **a teaspoon**; **The arrow** pierced the curtain*.
- BENEFICIARY: the entity for whose benefit the action is performed – *Mary boiled **me** some eggs; Mary boiled some eggs for **me***.
- LOCATION: the place where the situation takes place – *We met in **Paris**; The handkerchief is under **the pillow***.
- SOURCE: the location from which something moves – *I finally made it back from **the airport***.
- GOAL: the location towards which something moves – *I travelled to **Copenhagen***.
- RECIPIENT: in events describing exchanges of possession, the entity that receives another entity – *Natalie sent **Pauline** a birthday card*. In some classifications GOAL also covers RECIPIENT, to the extent that the recipient can be viewed as a kind of figurative goal.

Semantic roles are used to characterize the relationship between semantics and syntax. In some approaches it is assumed that lexical entries for verbs specify the semantic roles of their ARGUMENTS. This then provides an interface for mapping those arguments onto the syntactic roles of subject and object. Many authors have sought to make generalizations about the kinds of roles that are preferred in the subject position cross-linguistically. Fillmore (1968), for example, proposes the following subject hierarchy: AGENT > INSTRUMENT > PATIENT. This makes the generalization that if a verb assigns an AGENT role to one of its arguments, that argument will be realized in the subject position. If no AGENT is present, the next highest role in the hierarchy will occur as the subject. This can then explain the pattern we find with *break* and other similar verbs, such as *burst* and *split*:

Mary broke the egg. (subject is AGENT, object is PATIENT)
The teaspoon broke the egg. (subject is INSTRUMENT, object is PATIENT)
The egg broke. (subject is PATIENT)

Alternations in the syntactic realization of semantic roles are also effected through grammatical VOICES.

Semantic roles are, however, not without their problems. There is a significant lack of consensus among theorists over the number of roles and their definitions. At one extreme are approaches that subsume several roles under two very general roles of Proto-Agent and Proto-Patient (see Dowty 1991). In contrast, work in **Frame Semantics** assumes very fine-grained roles such as buyer, seller and goods that apply to a small set of verbs related to commercial transactions.

See also **predicate, valency, case**.

Key texts: Fillmore 1968; Givón 1984; Jackendoff 1990; Dowty 1991.

Semiotic triangle

See **sign**.

Semiotics

Semiotics is the general study of **signs** and the processes by which meaning is created. This includes the study of linguistic signs (such as words), but also any other kinds of signifiers of meaning, including gestures and facial expressions, traffic lights and various cultural constructs such as music, clothing, architecture and myths. **Ferdinand de Saussure**, who is considered the father of modern linguistics, was also highly influential in defining the field of semiotics: he provided a definition of the sign as a pairing of a **signifier** and a **signified** (a form and a meaning) and argued that linguistics should be considered a branch of a general science of signs. Saussurean **structural** linguistics also influenced many European semioticists, while the American branch of semiotics was more influenced by the work of the philosophers C. S. Peirce and Charles Morris.

Further reading: Chandler 2007.

Sense

The term **sense** is one of two aspects of meaning, the other being **reference**, a distinction first made by the philosopher **Gottlob Frege**. While reference is what an expression points to in the world, sense is the semantic aspect of meaning – the definitional properties that determine which things are referred to when an expression is used.

Sense can also refer to a DEFINITION in a dictionary.

See also INTENSION, POLYSEMY, SIGN.

Key texts: Frege 1892.

Sentence

The term **sentence** refers to the largest structural unit that is constructed according to the grammatical rules of a language (units larger than sentences, such as paragraphs, are not constructed according to any particular grammatical rules). **Sentence types** include **declarative**, **interrogative** and **imperative** sentences:

> I've brought a camera. (declarative)
> Did you bring a camera? (interrogative)
> Bring a camera! (imperative)

The sentence is the object of study for theories of syntax. In semantics, the notion of the sentence is important for making the distinction between three levels of structure and meaning: sentences, UTTERANCES and PROPOSITIONS. Sentences are abstract grammatical structures, which is to say that the same sentence may be instantiated by any number of specific utterances. If I say *The sunset is beautiful* and you also say *The sunset is beautiful*, our two utterances are instances of one sentence. The meaning of a sentence is determined COMPOSITIONALLY by the meanings of the individual words and the grammatical structure that relates them, whereas utterance meaning is dependent on the CONTEXT. The notion of proposition, on the other hand, represents a level of abstraction over sentences in that different sentences can be used to express the same proposition.

Sign

A **sign** is an entity that stands for another entity. WORDS are therefore signs, in that their forms stand for their meanings, but so are any other kinds of forms (be they auditory, visual, tactile or olfactory), as long as they are invested with some meaning. The general study of signs is called SEMIOTICS.

There are two main ways of viewing the structure of signs. **Ferdinand de Saussure** defined a sign as consisting of two parts, a **signifier** (form) and a **signified** (a concept). The triadic view of the sign, on the other hand, distinguishes between the form of the sign, its meaning (a sense or a concept) and its referent, the entity referred to in the world. These three parts of the sign are often depicted as a **semiotic triangle** (or **triangle of signification**), as shown in Figure 9.

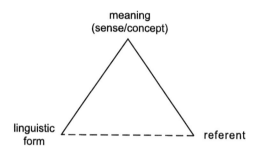

Figure 9 Semiotic triangle

This triangle shows that the relationship between a linguistic expression's form and its referent in the world is indirect and mediated through a concept or the expression's sense. The notion of the semiotic triangle is commonly attributed to Ogden and Richards (1923), but similar conceptions of the structure of the sign are found in the works of many other thinkers, including **Aristotle** and the philosopher C. S. Peirce.

Peirce also famously distinguished between different types of signs. In **symbolic signs**, the relationship between the form and the meaning is arbitrary and has to be learnt as a cultural convention. Most linguistic signs are therefore symbols, but so are the meanings of the different colours of traffic lights or the meaning of the Western custom of wearing black during a period of mourning. **Iconic signs** involve a resemblance between the form and the meaning while in indexical **signs** there is a non-arbitrary, causal connection between the form and the meaning. Thus a weathercock is indexical for the direction of the wind and a medical symptom is indexical for some illness.

Key texts: Saussure 1916; Peirce 1931–1958.

Signified, signifier

See SIGN.

Simile

A **simile** is a FIGURE OF SPEECH that makes an explicit comparison between two dissimilar entities or situations. The following are examples of similes:

(1) Her eyes were like deep mountain pools.
(2) Angus ran like the wind.
(3) Emily was as quiet as a mouse.
(4) Life is like riding a bicycle.

While both similes and METAPHORS highlight a resemblance between two things (e.g. eyes and mountain pools), similes express a comparison between two distinct things through the use of use of expressions like *like* or *as*. Metaphors, on the other hand, can be viewed as figuratively representing the two things as equivalent: *Her eyes were deep mountain pools*. It is not uncommon for similes to spell out the common properties between the two things being compared – for example, quietness in (3). In cases like (4), where the basis of the comparison would otherwise be very open-ended, speakers often continue with an explanation, as in this quote from Albert Einstein: *Life is like riding a bicycle. To keep your balance you must keep moving.*

Not all *X is like Y* statements are similes. Some are not figurative and simply state a similarity between two things: *Tahini is like peanut butter; You're like my dad*. These are not similes because the comparison is not figurative – converting them into metaphors (by removing the *like*) would completely change the meaning: *Tahini is peanut butter; You're my dad*.

Key texts: Glucksberg 2001.

Singular

See NUMBER, REFERENCE.

Situation

In SITUATION SEMANTICS, a **situation** is a partial representation of reality (or a possible reality) that serves as a model by which a proposition can be interpreted.

Situation is also used more loosely and theory-neutrally to refer to the type of thing that a PROPOSITION denotes. It can be seen in this way as a cover term for EVENTS and STATES.

Situation semantics

Situation semantics is a theory of propositional meaning that was devised as an alternative to POSSIBLE WORLD semantics. Instead of positing that models of whole worlds are necessary to arrive at truth values for proposition, situation theory relies on models of partial worlds, or SITUATIONS. This, it is claimed, is more in keeping with the way people, with their partial knowledge of the world, determine the truth or falsity of a proposition. The nature of the situations themselves is subject to some dispute, but situation-based approaches have been particularly successful in accounting for problems in QUANTIFICATION, ANAPHORA and TENSE, among other topics.

Key text: Barwise and Perry 1983.

Social meaning

Social meaning is information about the speaker and/or their relation to the speaking context (including the addressee) that is conveyed through linguistic choices. For instance, if I say *hi* rather than *hello* or *how do you do?*, I may be indicating that I think that my relation to the addressee is intimate and that the situation is relatively casual. If I say *howzit*, I display a South African identity. AFFECT can be considered to be a type of social meaning, and social meaning is sometimes included in broader definitions of CONNOTATION.

See also DENOTATION.

Source

In CONCEPTUAL METAPHOR THEORY, **source** is used to refer to the DOMAIN whose structure is projected or mapped metaphorically to a TARGET domain. The corresponding term in traditional descriptions of METAPHOR is VEHICLE.

See SEMANTIC ROLE for a description of **source** as a semantic/thematic role.

Specialization

See SEMANTIC CHANGE.

Specific reference

See REFERENCE.

State, stative

A sentence such as *Lily resembles her father* denotes a **state** (as opposed to an EVENT), in that resembling is something that just is, rather than something that happens. A verb like *resemble* is thus a **stative** verb – that is, one that indicates a state. The opposite of *stative* is DYNAMIC. Stative expressions contrast with dynamic expressions in their interactions with morphological ASPECT. For instance, statives are usually anomalous in the progressive (#*Lily is resembling her father*) or with certain types of time expression (#*Lily resembled her father in an hour*).

See also AKTIONSART, VENDLER CLASSES.

Stimulus

See SEMANTIC ROLE.

Structural semantics

The term **structural semantics** can be used to refer to a number of approaches to meaning that focus on the relations among LEXEMES. Such approaches have their roots in FERDINAND DE SAUSSURE's conception of meaning as emerging from associations between lexicalized meanings. Such approaches vary in the levels at which they hold that these relations operate, which relations are most relevant, and the extent to which relations are responsible for determining meaning. One example of a structural approach is SEMANTIC FIELD **theory**.

Key texts: Saussure 1916; Lyons 1963; Coseriu and Geckeler 1981.

Subjunctive

See MOOD.

Subordinate, superordinate

In a more general sense, a **superordinate** category (or term) is one that includes another category (or the meaning of another term), its **subordinate**. Thus we can say that ARMCHAIR is subordinate to CHAIR or that *chair* is the superordinate of *armchair* (see INCLUSION and HYPONYMY).

The terms **superordinate-level category** and **subordinate-level category** are used more specifically in relation to (and contrast with) the BASIC LEVEL of categorization. Superordinate-level categories are categories that are more inclusive or general than categories at the basic level, while subordinate-level categories are less inclusive or more specific than basic-level categories. CHAIR is a basic-level category, and therefore FURNITURE is a superordinate-level category while ARM CHAIR is a subordinate-level category. Superordinate-level categories are often designated by uncountable nouns, such as *furniture* or *cutlery* (see COUNTABILITY) whereas labels for subordinate-level categories are often compound nouns, such as *armchair* or *soup spoon*.

See also TAXONOMY.

Syllepsis

See ZEUGMA.

Symbol, symbolic sign

See SIGN.

Synecdoche

Synecdoche is a kind of FIGURE OF SPEECH in which a part of an entity stands for the whole entity or vice versa or a CATEGORY stands for a SUBORDINATE category or vice versa. For example, in *John's got a new motor*, *motor* stands for the whole car, whereas in *Daisy has got a temperature*, *temperature* is used to refer to the more specific 'high temperature (as a sign of illness)'. Synecdoche is traditionally distinguished from METONYMY, but many accounts, including most COGNITIVE LINGUISTIC approaches, see synecdoche as a type of metonymy.

Synonym, synonymous, synonymy

Synonymy is the relation of sameness of meaning. Generally, it is used to refer to sameness of lexical meaning; however, it is also sometimes used as a synonym for PARAPHRASE. Sameness of meaning can be diagnosed by a **substitution test**; that is, if two expressions can be substituted for one another in a sentence without changing its meaning, then they are said to be **synonyms**. However, absolute substitutability is rare, and whether two lexemes are synonyms or not depends on whether synonymy is defined solely with regard to the lexemes' DENOTATION or not. Different types of synonym can be distinguished on the basis of what aspects of the words are similar and the extent to which they are similar. **Sense synonyms** are those that are substitutable in at least one of their SENSES, but not necessarily all of them. For example, *sugar* and *sucrose* are substitutable in contexts in which *sugar* refers to table sugar, but not when *sugar* is used as a term of endearment. **Cognitive** (also called **logical**) synonyms share their DENOTATIONAL meaning, but not necessarily their CONNOTATIONS or SOCIAL MEANING. **Near-synonyms** have overlapping or very similar (but not the same) meanings (see PLESIONYM).

See also LEXICAL RELATION, PARADIGMATIC.

Key texts: Cruse 1986; Murphy 2003.

Syntagmatic, syntagmatic relation

A **syntagmatic relation** is a type of LEXICAL RELATION in which two or more words are related by typically co-occurring with one another in phrases.

For instance, *cat* is in syntagmatic relations with the noun *food* (as its modifier), the verb *miaow* (as a typical subject) and the adjective *black* (which often modifies it).

See also PARADIGMATIC.

Synthetic

As opposed to an ANALYTIC PROPOSITION, a **synthetic** proposition is one whose truth or falsity must be judged with reference to something outside of the proposition itself. For example, in order to know whether *This book is 200 pages long* is true or not, one would have to examine the book.

Target

In CONCEPTUAL METAPHOR THEORY, **target** refers to the DOMAIN to which structure from the SOURCE domain is projected or mapped. The corresponding term in traditional descriptions of METAPHOR is TENOR. Particularly in COGNITIVE LINGUISTIC literature, the term *target* is also used to designate the entity that is referred to METONYMICALLY, via some other, associated entity (which is called the VEHICLE). For example, in *Downing Street refused to comment*, the vehicle 'Downing Street' refers metonymically to the target 'the British Prime Minister'.

Tautology

A **tautology** is a SENTENCE (or PROPOSITION) that can never be false. For example, *Unicorns either exist or do not exist* is a tautology because it is true both in the case that unicorns exist and in the case that unicorns do not exist. No other possible relations of unicorns and existence are possible.

See also CONTRADICTION, ANALYTIC.

Taxonomy

A **taxonomy** is the organization of a set of things (such as meanings) into proper INCLUSION relations and is typically represented in tree structure. See ONTOLOGY for an illustration.

See also BASIC LEVEL, SUBORDINATE, SUPERORDINATE, HYPONYM, TAXONYM.

Taxonym, taxonymy

Taxonymy is a subtype of HYPONYMY where the relationship between the hyponym and the hyperonym can be expressed in the frame *X is **a kind of** Y* or *X is **a type of** Y*. Hyperonym–hyponym pairs whose relationship is not taxonymic sound odd in such frames, although they can occur in the more general *X is a Y* frame. Thus while *spaniel* and *bitch* are both hyponyms of *dog*, only *spaniel* is a **taxonym** (a taxonymic hyponym) of *dog*, whereas *bitch* is a simple hyponym of *dog*:

> A spaniel is a kind of/type of dog.
> ?A bitch is a kind of/type of dog.
> A bitch is a dog.

The notion of taxonymy as a subtype of hyponymy comes from the work of Alan Cruse, who proposes that taxonymy is the inclusion relationship upon which well-formed TAXONOMIES are founded. Thus *spaniel*, *Alsatian* and *poodle* are good taxonyms of *dog* because they subdivide the species of dog into distinctive and internally coherent categories. The category labelled by *bitch*, on the other hand, is not as distinctive or internally coherent, in that it can include any dog as long as it is female.

Key texts: Cruse 1986, 2002.

Telic, telicity

The term **telic** is derived from the Greek *telos* 'end' and refers to the property of EVENTS (or descriptions of those events, typically by verbs) having a state of completion. Having a 'state of completion' has a couple of consequences: (a) if an event potentially described by a telic verb is stopped partway through, then the telic verb does not apply to the situation, and (b) if the event proceeds beyond the point of completion, then it is a new instance of that event type. So, *somersault* is telic because if Ursula starts to somersault, but falls onto her side before getting her body all the way around, then she cannot be said to *have somersaulted*. If Vern completes a full somersault and *keeps somersaulting*, we must understand the continuous action of somersaulting as referring to a number of discrete somersaults.

Atelic events, on the other hand, are situations that could go on without a conclusion. In this case, starting an atelic action is the same as doing that action. So, for example, if Wilma started to slide down a slide but stopped halfway down, it could be truthfully said that *Wilma slid*. And if Wilma started sliding and never stopped, it would still be true that *Wilma slid*.

In GENERATIVE LEXICON theory, **telic** refers to one of the QUALIA roles. This use is unrelated to the aspectual meaning.

See also VENDLER CLASSES.

Tenor

The term **tenor** (sometimes also called **topic**) is used in descriptions of the structure of METAPHOR; it refers to the entity that is being compared figuratively to another entity (the VEHICLE). Thus in *He is at a cross-roads in his life*, the tenor is 'life', and it is being described in terms of the vehicle 'a journey'. In CONCEPTUAL METAPHOR THEORY, the tenor is instead called the TARGET.

Tense

Tense is a grammatical category that describes the temporal location of a situation. That is, tense answers the question *When?*. Insofar as tense locates the situation in relation to the time of speaking, it is a DEICTIC category. The temporal location of a situation can be expressed lexically, through expressions such as *now*, *tomorrow*, *five minutes ago*, *on 23 July* and *last year*, but tense refers specifically to the GRAMMATICALIZED marking of location in time. This typically takes the form of verbal inflections, as in *Liam live**s** in Liverpool* and *Liam live**d** in Liverpool*. There are languages that lack grammaticalized tense: Chinese, for example, relies on temporal adverbs to locate situations in time.

The distinctions in temporal location that are made through tense are more limited than can be made via lexical means: no language has a tense that means 'exactly five minutes ago'. Instead, languages grammaticalize a small number of different tenses, distinguishing, for example, between 'now', 'before now' and 'after now'. Some languages distinguish up to six or seven tenses: the native American language Kiksht, for example, has different tenses for 'remote past', 'from one to ten years ago', 'from a week to a year ago', 'last week', 'yesterday or in the last couple of days' and 'earlier today' (Comrie 1985). English has two morphological tenses, past tense (*lived*, *went*) and present tense (*lives*, *goes*). The future is not marked inflectionally in English;

reference to future time is instead expressed via the modal auxiliary verb *will*, the *be going to* construction or present tense forms:

> Liam **will** leave for Liverpool tomorrow.
> Liam **is going to** leave for Liverpool tomorrow.
> Liam **is** leaving for Liverpool tomorrow.
> Liam leave**s** for Liverpool tomorrow.

Because present tense forms, such as those in the last two examples, are also used to refer to the future, the English present tense is often called **non-past**. Note also that English simple present tense forms of DYNAMIC verbs in fact very rarely refer to 'now' – a sentence such as *Nina knits knee-high socks* does not mean she is knitting right now, but rather that she customarily does so (see HABITUAL). This illustrates how tense is inevitably bound up with ASPECT – both are categories that relate to time and both are marked on the verb string.

Present tense forms can also be used to describe events that happened before 'now', as in the **historical present**:

> Yesterday, I**'m** walking home when I **notice** that they**'ve** cut down the tree outside my house!

Past tense forms also have uses that do not refer to events that took place before now, including in COUNTERFACTUALS and to mark politeness:

> If I **won** the lottery, I'd start a charity for poor linguists.
> I just **wanted** to ask if you could lend me some money until pay day.

See also ASPECT, PERFECT, PERFECTIVE.

Key text: Comrie 1985.

Thematic role, theta role

See SEMANTIC ROLE.

Theme

See SEMANTIC ROLE.

'Theory' Theory

The so-called **'Theory' Theory** is a theory of CONCEPTS that assumes that concepts are defined against a conceptual base of non-expert, folk '**theories**'. Such theories provide an explanation for why a particular entity is a member of a CATEGORY and of the relations that exist between the various properties of their instances. A bird, for example, is not just a miscellaneous collection of birdy features, such as feathers, wings, beak and eyes and the ability to fly and lay eggs. The features are also related in various ways: the eyes are located above the beak and there is a causal relation between having wings and being able to fly. Unlike the CLASSICAL THEORY OF CONCEPTUALIZATION and many approaches to the PROTOTYPE THEORY, 'Theory' Theory stresses that such relations must be part of conceptual representations.

'Theory' Theory also aims to account for the coherence and boundaries of categories. One of the problems with the Prototype Theory is that it entails that we might categorize a dog as a marginal member of the category BIRD, given that dogs share some features with prototypical birds, such as having eyes and legs. However, according to the 'Theory' Theory, categorization is not simply based on easily accessible perceptual attributes and similarity to a prototype. Instead, the folk theories that concepts are understood against provide an explanation of the underlying properties that define categories. Thus the concept BIRD is understood against a basic theory of biological kinds that explains that a bird is a bird because it has a certain kind of genetic makeup that derives from its parents. Physical properties, such as feathers and wings and the ability to fly and lay eggs are then manifestations of this underlying genetic makeup. The theory need not explain perfectly what the genetic makeup consists of because it is a folk theory, rather than a scientific one.

Work in 'Theory' Theory is focused on issues such as characterizing the differences between NATURAL KIND concepts (such as BIRD) and artefact concepts (e.g. CUP, HAMMER) and explaining children's acquisition of concepts and the development of the conceptual system. 'Theory' Theory has, however, been criticized for the lack of consensus among its proponents about what counts as a theory and how the theories should be represented.

Key texts: Murphy and Medin 1985; Keil 1989; Gopnik and Meltzoff 1997.

Topic

The **topic** of a sentence is the part that expresses what the sentence as a whole is about. So, for example, in the sentence *Abby's dog has fleas* the topic is *Abby's dog* and the rest of the sentence tells you something about Abby's dog. That is, *has fleas* is a **comment** on the topic of Abby's dog. Another way of expressing this is that *Abby's dog* is **given** information – we are already expected to be aware of Abby's owning of a dog when this sentence is uttered, whereas the information about the fleas is **new** information. Sometimes languages structure information with particular marking of the topic and comment roles. For instance, in *This soup I can eat all day*, the phrase *this soup* is in a special position at the start of the sentence in order to emphasize that it is the topic.

Topic is also used as a synonym for TENOR in descriptions of the structure of METAPHOR.

See also FOCUS.

Trajector

See FIGURE/GROUND.

Transitivity

See VALENCY.

Triangle of signification

See SIGN.

Truth condition, truth-conditional semantics

Truth conditions are the conditions that a world must meet in order for a PROPOSITION to be true. For example, if you were to utter *I am wearing a hat*, it would only be true if at the moment that you uttered it, you were wearing at least one hat. The truth conditions for that sentence include the condition in which you are wearing a beret, the condition in which you are wearing a fedora, the condition in which you are wearing two hats and the one in which you have a hat on a string around your neck – since these scenarios are logically consistent with the claim *I am wearing a hat*.

Truth-conditional semantics refers to any theory of the meaning of declarative sentences in which meaning consists of the truth conditions of the sentence. It thus excludes any aspects of meaning that are beyond the DENOTATIONAL realm, including CONNOTATION and INFERENCES that are PRAGMATIC in nature. FORMAL SEMANTIC theories tend to be truth-conditional.

See also POSSIBLE WORLD, MONTAGUE GRAMMAR.

Key text: Davidson 1967.

Truth function

A **truth function** is formal function that maps TRUTH VALUES to other truth values. LOGICAL OPERATORS represent truth functions. For example, the NEGATION operator ¬ maps 'true' values to 'false' values and vice versa. In other words, if a true PROPOSITION is negated, the resulting proposition is false, and if a false proposition is negated, the resulting proposition is true.

Truth value

A PROPOSITION's **truth value** is whether it is true or false with respect to a particular MODEL.

Underspecification, underspecified

See VAGUENESS.

Universal quantifier

See QUANTIFICATION.

Universe (of discourse)

In FORMAL approaches to semantics, the **universe of discourse** (also **domain of discourse**) is the set of individuals over which the QUANTIFIERS quantify. In MODEL-THEORETIC semantics, this refers to the set of entities that are included in the MODEL.

Univocal, univocality

See VAGUENESS.

Unbounded

See BOUNDEDNESS.

Unmarked

See MARKEDNESS.

Utterance

An **utterance** is a specific, concrete instance of language use. This can be taken to include both spoken and written language use, but in some uses *utterance* refers more specifically to complete instances of spoken language that are typically bounded by pauses. Utterances often instantiate SENTENCES, although not necessarily: in the following dialogue Ben's utterance corresponds to an incomplete or elliptical sentence:

Anna: What was the meal you had at that restaurant like?
Ben: Wonderful.

The meaning of an utterance is dependent on the CONTEXT: factors such as the time and place where it is uttered and who the speaker and hearer are. The speaker's intonation can also affect the meaning of an utterance – in the example above, Ben could, for instance, employ an intonation that signals that he means the opposite of 'wonderful'. Utterance meaning is the object of study for PRAGMATICS.

See also PROPOSITION.

Vague, vagueness

The term *vagueness* has many different meanings and there are also a number of alternative terms that have been used by different authors to cover the different kinds of phenomena that can be referred to as vagueness.

One meaning of **vagueness** refers to the underspecification or generality of SENSE. For example, the word *cousin* can refer to either a male or a female, or an infant or a pensioner and it therefore has a sense that is vague or underspecified with respect to gender and age. This meaning of *vagueness* contrasts with AMBIGUITY, where a linguistic form has multiple distinct senses (e.g. *light* 'not dark'; 'not heavy' or *bug* 'an insect'; 'a listening device'). Other terms for vagueness in this sense include **univocality**, **underspecification**, **generality**, **indeterminacy** and **monosemy**.

Various criteria have been proposed to determine whether particular uses of a linguistic form are instances of the same vague sense or different ambiguous senses. According to the definitional criterion, for example, two different interpretations should be considered instances of the same vague sense if it is possible to unite them under a general DEFINITION. Thus *cousin* is vague with respect to the readings 'male cousin' and 'female cousin', as it is possible to unite these readings under the definition 'an offspring of a parent's sibling'. In contrast, the 'insect' and 'listening device' readings of *bug* are distinct senses as it is impossible to construct a definition that includes both insects and listening devices, while still excluding things that are not called bugs. Another ambiguity criterion relies on the fact that only distinct senses may give rise to a ZEUGMA. However, no consensus exists over the applicability of ambiguity criteria such as these and different theoretical approaches make very different assumptions about the distinction between ambiguity and vagueness.

In addition to the meaning described above, **vagueness** can also refer to cases where the entities that words refer to lack definite boundaries. For example, there is no clear cut-off point where the ankle stops and the calf begins. A third use of *vagueness* is in reference to the FUZZINESS of category boundaries: for example, the boundaries of the category SPORT are not clear-cut (does chess count as a sport?). Similarly, the meanings of GRADABLE ADJECTIVES such as *tall* have also been described as being vague insofar as there

is no clear cut-off point between being tall and being not tall. The term
indeterminacy has also been applied to these kinds of vagueness.

Key texts: Geeraerts 1993; Devos 2003.

Valency

Valency refers to the number of ARGUMENTS a VERB requires in order to express
a complete PROPOSITION. Verbs can therefore be classified according to their
valency, as in the following examples, where the arguments are enclosed
in square brackets:

> It is **thundering**. (valency-zero/**avalent**)
> [Valerie] **grinned**. (valency-one/**monovalent**)
> [Thomas] **caught** [a fish]. (valency-two/**divalent** [or **bivalent**])
> [Kyle] **gave** [his aunt] [some flowers]. (valency-three/**trivalent**)

Valency corresponds to the classification of PREDICATES into **one-**, **two-** and
three-place predicates. There is also a relationship between semantic valency
and the **transitivity** of verbs. Transitivity relates to the number of objects a
verb requires, ignoring its subject, whereas valency also includes the subject
argument. Thus a valency-one verb like *grin* has one argument, the subject
and no objects, which means it is intransitive. A valency-two verb like *catch*
is transitive and requires one object, while a valency-three verb like *give* is
ditransitive and takes two objects.

Note, however, that there is not always a one-to-one correspondence between
the semantic arguments of a verb and the syntactic roles of subject and
object. The *it* subject of a valency-zero or avalent verb such as *thunder* (or
other weather verbs, such as *rain*, *hail*, *sleet* or *snow*) is not an argument in
that it does not refer to anything and it would not make sense to ask 'What
thundered?' The *it* subject of weather verbs is instead generally considered
to be a 'dummy' that is only required because in English all sentences must
have overt subjects.

Variable

In LOGIC and in some other semantic METALANGUAGES, a **variable** represents
an individual whose identity is not fixed. In logic, variables are typically

represented by small letters from the end of the alphabet and must be anchored by QUANTIFIERS, so that if P means 'is a pigeon', then ∀x Px means that 'everything (i.e. any value that could be assigned to x) is a pigeon'.

Vehicle

The term **vehicle** is commonly used in descriptions of the structure of METAPHOR. The vehicle is the entity to which something else is compared figuratively. In *The New Age movement has its roots in the 1960s*, the New Age movement is described in terms of or compared to a plant. 'A plant' is therefore the vehicle, while 'the New Age movement' is the TENOR. In CONCEPTUAL METAPHOR THEORY, the vehicle is instead called the SOURCE.

Vehicle is sometimes also used to refer to the entity (or expression) that is being used to refer to another entity in METONYMY; for example, in *Downing Street refused to comment*, 'Downing Street' is the vehicle that is used to refer metonymically to the British Prime Minister.

Vendler classes

The philosopher Zeno Vendler described types of verbs based on their inherent ASPECTUAL differences. The classes he distinguished can be broken down COMPONENTIALLY according to three dichotomies, as shown in the table below. Vendler's classification remains one of the most popular in describing types of SITUATIONS.

Situation types	STATIC/DYNAMIC	PUNCTUAL/DURATIVE	TELIC/ATELIC
State Avery seems pleasant. Everybody knows Becca.	static	(durative)	n/a
Activity Claude sang. Dean thinks a lot.	dynamic	durative	atelic
Accomplishment Ella transferred her bank account. Fred sang three songs.	dynamic	durative	telic
Achievement Gia appeared. Helen blinked.	dynamic	punctual	telic

While Vendler intended his categories as categories of verb meanings, it has since been noted that TELICITY in particular is sensitive to the ARGUMENTS of the verb. For example, in the table the predicate *sing* is classified as an activity, but when it is joined with a BOUNDED noun phrase like *three songs*, it is an achievement, since the singing of three songs has a conclusion – at the end of the third song.

See also AKTIONSART.

Key text: Vendler 1957.

Verb

Verb is a grammatical class of words that typically express an action, event or state and can serve as the PREDICATE of a sentence and thus occur with one or more noun phrases expressing ARGUMENTS. Unlike some other parts of speech (including adjectives), verbs are found universally in the languages of the world. In many languages, verbs are inflected for TENSE and may also be marked morphologically for ASPECT, MODALITY and VOICE and for NUMBER, PERSON and GENDER AGREEMENT with other parts of the sentence. The words in bold below are verbs:

> Eva **danced**.
> Louisa **is knitting** a scarf.
> Kate **should have recognized** me.

Verbs can be classified into subclasses in various different ways. One distinction that is particularly significant in English is that between **auxiliary** and **lexical verbs**. While lexical verbs are OPEN-CLASS items that express the situation that the sentence is about (e.g. *danced*, *knitting* and *recognize* in the examples above), auxiliary verbs (including **modal verbs**) are CLOSED-CLASS items that occur with lexical verbs as part of a complex verb string (e.g. *should have* recognized) and are used to mark the grammatical properties of tense, aspect and modality.

Verbs can also be classified on a number of different semantic dimensions. One involves the type of situation the verb expresses – for example, whether it is an EVENT or a STATE. It is also possible to classify verbs according to more specific types of situations, for instance, as verbs of motion (e.g. *run*, *slide*, *go*) or cooking verbs (*boil*, *fry*, *sauté*). Another dimension along which verbs may be subcategorized is the number and type of **ARGUMENTS** they occur with (see **VALENCY**, **SEMANTIC ROLES**). Verbs may also be classified according to how the situations they express take place in relation to time – for example, whether they are instantaneous (e.g. *recognize*) or take place over a longer period of time (*dance*, *knit*). Such categories of lexical **ASPECT** are called by the German term **AKTIONSART** (see also **VENDLER CLASSES**).

Key texts: Schachter 1985; Leech 2004.

Voice

Voice refers to the grammatical marking of the relationship between the participants in a situation (**ARGUMENTS**) and the grammatical roles of subject and object. In the **active voice**, which is usually the most **UNMARKED** voice, the subject is an entity that performs the action expressed by the verb while the object is the entity that undergoes the action, as in the example below. The roles of the participants in the situation are often described in terms of **SEMANTIC ROLES** such as AGENT and PATIENT:

Otto	cleaned the gutters.
Subject	Object
AGENT	PATIENT

In the **passive voice**, the participant that occurs as the object of the active sentence occurs in the subject position, while the subject argument of the active sentence may be expressed optionally. The verb is also marked morphologically for the passive voice (in English, the past participle form of the verb occurs with the auxiliary *be*):

The gutters	were cleaned (by Otto).
Subject	Optional adjunct
PATIENT	AGENT

The passive voice therefore has the effect of promoting the object argument and demoting the subject argument.

Some languages also have a further grammatical category of **middle voice**. Middle voice typically serves to emphasize that the argument that occurs in the subject position is affected by the event expressed by the verb. In English, middle voice occurs in a very limited class of examples such as the ones below:

> These oranges peel very easily.
> The tickets aren't selling that well.

Like passives, these examples involve the promotion of a non-AGENT partici-pant into the subject position, but English does not have any special morphological marking of middle voice. In other languages, such as the West African language of Fula, middle voice is morphologically distinct from active and passive and may be used to express meanings such as reflexivity (the subject acts on him/her/itself).

Well-formed formula

A **well-formed formula** (or **WFF**) in a FORMAL semantic METALANGUAGE is a formal expression in which all of the requirements of the grammar of the metalanguage are met. For example, PREDICATE CALCULUS requires that all VARIABLES are bound by a QUANTIFIER, so if x is a variable, then $\exists y(Qxy)$ is not a well-formed formula because nothing BINDS the x variable. On the other hand, $\exists x \exists y(Qxy)$ is well-formed.

See also LOGIC.

Word

Defining **word** as a linguistic phenomenon is notoriously difficult to do. Outside linguistic study, words are usually defined in orthographic terms, as a series of written characters that is not interrupted by a blank space. This definition is not terribly useful in linguistics, since (a) it only works for languages that have a writing system that marks word boundaries, and (b) it is circular, in that the orthographic marking of word boundaries requires a prior intuition of where words begin and end. Semantic definitions of *word* that require that a word stands for a single CONCEPT are undone by the fact that there are plenty of concepts that require phrases in order to be expressed (see CONCEPT). The most successful linguistic definitions of word are thus grammatical in nature, to do with morphological marking and behaviour as a single unit in syntactic structures. Nevertheless, the term is used loosely in semantics and LEXICOLOGY to mean LEXEME.

Zeugma

In semantics, a **zeugma** (or **syllepsis**) is a linguistic construction where a single constituent is related to two different semantic interpretations, in a way that gives rise to a semantic ANOMALY. For instance, in the sentence below, *put out* is used to mean both 'extinguish' and 'let go outside':

> #Millie put out her cigarette and her cat.

For the zeugmatic, anomalous reading to arise, the two interpretations that are evoked simultaneously need to be semantically distinct. Therefore, the possibility of constructing a zeugmatic sentence provides a way of testing whether particular readings of a linguistic form are AMBIGUOUS (POLYSEMOUS or HOMONYMOUS) or just VAGUE. In the first sentence below, *head* refers simultaneously to the topmost part of the human body and to the end of a bed. The resulting sentence is anomalous, which suggests that these readings of *head* are distinct, ambiguous senses.

> #Alison bumped her head against that of the bed.
> Alison bumped her head against that of her brother.

In contrast, the second sentence does not give rise to a zeugmatic reading because *head* is used in the same 'body-part' sense in reference to both Alison and her brother.

Key Thinkers in Semantics

Aristotle (384 BCE–322 BCE)

Aristotle was born in Macedonia, the son of the physician to Amyntas II, the king of Macedonia. He joined Plato's Academy in Athens at the age of 17, and remained there for 20 years until Plato's death in 347 BCE. Aristotle then left Athens, and during his years away tutored the teenage boy who would become Alexander the Great. In 335 BCE Aristotle returned to Athens, and founded his own school of philosophy, Lyceum. After the death of Alexander the Great in 323 BCE, Aristotle no longer felt safe in Athens due to the upsurge in anti-Macedonian sentiments, and he escaped Athens to retire on the island of Euboea, where he died one year later.

Aristotle's surviving body of work concerns a range of disciplines, from logic, metaphysics, physics and other natural sciences to politics, poetics and rhetoric. Although he was not primarily interested in studying language for its own sake, some of his thinking has had a crucial and lasting influence on the study of language and meaning: many important concepts that still form part of current theories can be traced back to Aristotle.

In his work we see an early statement of the semiotic triangle (see SIGN) and the beginnings of the notion of meanings as mental entities. In *De Intepretatione*, Aristotle distinguishes between the forms of words, the thoughts they stand for and the actual things in the world, a distinction paralleling that between word form, sense and referent. He also establishes that the relationship between the forms and meanings of words is ARBITRARY, given that the spoken and written forms of words can be different for different people and languages, while the mental states and entities in the world remain constant. The relationship between mental states and things in the world, however, is natural, based on resemblance. Words therefore have meaning because they are symbols for mental states that resemble things out there in the real world – a view which proved very influential in the philosophy of language.

Equally important was Aristotle's theory of truth and the idea that sentences (or thoughts) can be either true or false. In *Metaphysics*, he defines truth as stating something is the case in the real world when it is the case (or stating that something is not the case, when it is indeed not the case), while falsity is the opposite: saying that something is the case when it is not (or that it is not the case when it is). This suggests that Aristotle viewed truth as a matter of correspondence with reality; a view that was further developed by many philosophers of language, including BERTRAND RUSSELL and LUDWIG WITTGENSTEIN. Aristotle lays the foundations of classical LOGIC in his discussion of negation, universal and particular statements and modality. In Aristotle's work we also see the division of PROPOSITIONS into a subject and a predicate, which describes a PROPERTY that applies to the subject. A proposition must have a TRUTH VALUE, and thus Aristotle distinguishes sentences that express propositions by making an assertion that may be either true or false from sentences that do not make such assertions, such as wishes or prayers. Declarative statements and their truth conditions were to remain the focus of philosophers of language until the twentieth century when scholars such as J. L. Austin began to consider the meaning of other types of speech acts.

Aristotle also argued that things in the world can be defined in terms of their essences, which are distinct from their accidental properties. Although for Aristotle DEFINITIONS concerned things in the world, rather than the meanings of the words that referred to them, his notion of definitions as statements of essences proved to be highly influential for lexical semantics and lexicography. In his work on rhetoric, Aristotle also provides a definition of METAPHOR. Although his use of *metaphor* also covers METONYMIES and SYNECDOCHES, he is often credited with establishing that metaphors are based on a similarity between two different things.

It is difficult to overstate Aristotle's lasting importance for semantics, given the influence he had on later scholars and the number of concepts that he discussed or defined that are still assumed in some form in current semantic theories.

Further reading

Ackrill, John Lloyd (1981) *Aristotle the philosopher*. Oxford: Oxford University Press.

Allan, Keith (2004) 'Aristotle's footprints in the linguist's garden.' *Language Sciences* 26, 317–342.

Charles, David (2000) *Aristotle on meaning and essence*. Oxford: Oxford University Press.

Modrak, Deborah (2001) *Aristotle's theory of language and meaning*. Cambridge: Cambridge University Press.

Seuren, Pieter A. M. (1998) *Western linguistics: an historical introduction*. Oxford: Blackwell.

Rudolf Carnap (1891–1970)

Rudolf Carnap was a German-born philosopher of science, mathematics, language and epistemology. Born in Ronsdorf, he studied mathematics, physics and philosophy at the University of Jena. His progress was undermined by service in the First World War and his catholic interests – his initial thesis in physics was rejected as too philosophical, while the philosophers considered it 'pure physics'. After completing a revised philosophical thesis on the theory of space, he joined the philosophy faculty at the University of Vienna in 1926 and taught briefly at the University of Prague in 1931. The rise of the Third Reich in Germany created an intolerable situation for Carnap, a socialist and pacifist. He emigrated to the United States in 1935 and in 1941 became a citizen. He held professorships at the University of Chicago (1936–1952) and the University of California at Los Angeles (1954–1970), with visiting positions at Harvard and Princeton along the way.

In his early career, Carnap studied with **Gottlob Frege** and corresponded heavily with **Bertrand Russell**, which established his interest in logic and semantics. In *The logical syntax of language* (1937), he argued that any philosophical issue that cannot be construed in terms of questions about language is meaningless.

In 1930, he met Alfred Tarski, the founder of **model-theoretic** semantics of logical languages, and from that point Carnap's work on the philosophy of language takes off. In 'Testability and meaning' (1936–1937), he introduced the notion of **analytic** and **synthetic** statements. Carnap's most famous thesis in the philosophy of language is *Meaning and necessity* (1947). There he presents a formal interpretation of Frege's **sense** and **reference**, reinterpreted as **intension** and **extension**, respectively. An intension in his approach is a function between a model and an extension. A name's intension is an individual concept, a predicate's is a **property** and a sentence's is a **proposition**.

W. V. O. Quine, in particular, argued against many of Carnap's positions on language, including the use of abstract categories such as 'property' and 'proposition' and the analytic/synthetic distinction. Carnap responded to many of these objections in 'Empiricism, semantics and ontology' (1950) and 'Meaning postulates' (1952) (see **meaning postulate**). In doing so, Carnap appealed to the possibility of translation between languages, which led Quine (and later **DONALD DAVIDSON**) to respond with his famous arguments on the indeterminacy of translation.

Carnap continued to work throughout his life, making major contributions to logic and the philosophy of science as well as the philosophy of language. At the time of his death, he was working on a logic of induction.

Further reading

Schilpp, Paul (ed.) (1963) *The philosophy of Rudolf Carnap*. LaSalle, IL: Open Court.

Noam Chomsky (b. 1928)

Noam Chomsky is not a semanticist, yet his influence on modern linguistics is so strong that it would be neglectful to omit him from a list of key thinkers. Born in Philadelphia, Chomsky studied philosophy and linguistics at the University of Pennsylvania, earning the Bachelor's degree in 1949 and the doctorate in 1955. That year, he was appointed to the faculty at the Massachusetts Institute of Technology (MIT), and was made full professor in 1961.

Chomsky began his studies at a time when the so-called American Structuralism of Leonard Bloomfield was the main force in American linguistics. This school of linguistic thought removed meaning entirely from the agenda for linguistics, leaving it to psychologists and philosophers. Instead it was concerned with the classification of linguistic constructs and description of their distribution in the language. During his studies under the supervision of Zellig Harris, Chomsky was struck by the unsuitability of structuralism to account for the infinite potential of human grammars, as well as for certain grammatical examples. For example, a simple structural description cannot account for why John is the pleaser in *John is eager to please* but not in *John is easy to please.*

Chomsky's reaction, starting in his thesis, revised and published as *Syntactic structures* (1957), was to redefine the field. Rather than just describing and classifying linguistic structures, the aim of linguistics should be to explain how people become competent speakers of their languages. Thus a theory should be able to predict an infinite number of possible sentences in a language, rule out any sentences that would not be grammatical in that language and describe the relations among elements of the sentence in order to account for ambiguities and structural variations. The grammatical theory he developed included a context-free phrase structure grammar (with rules such as S → NP VP, that is, a sentence can be composed of [just] a noun phrase and a verb phrase) and a set of transformational rules for deriving different 'surface' sentence types (such as declaratives and questions, actives and passives) from the same 'deep' structure created by the phrase structure grammar. This approach is called GENERATIVE GRAMMAR. He further developed his approach in *Aspects of the theory of syntax* (1965), and continued to revise it, so that the 'standard theory' of 1965 was regularly replaced by different versions with different constraints on transformational rules. The current Chomskyan theory is called *The Minimalist Program* (1995).

The mechanics of the grammatical system are only a small part of the 'Chomsky revolution' in linguistics. Chomsky was responsible for redefining linguistics as a branch of cognitive psychology – and a rationalist brand of cognitive psychology at that. His review (1959) of B. F. Skinner's *Verbal behavior* makes the case that a theory that holds that language is learnt through experience alone is doomed to fail, since it cannot account for the universality, speed and creativity of children's language acquisition. Instead, he argues that some **innate** knowledge of language and how to acquire it must be present in humans. He also claims that knowledge of language is of a different type from other types of knowledge and that there must be a **modular** language faculty in the mind that operates on its own principles. Within the language faculty, Chomsky also proposes submodules, so that the syntactic, phonological and semantic aspects of language are processed separately, and interact only in restricted way. The semantic module, called Logical Form, interacts with the outputs of the syntactic module in order to interpret them, thus it is an **interpretive semantics** (see GENERATIVE GRAMMAR).

In the late 1960s and early 1970s, proponents of GENERATIVE SEMANTICS aimed to make generative linguistics more semantically driven, but Chomsky considered this approach to be misguided. In *Language and responsibility* (1977: 139), he claims that the study of meaning 'should be excluded from the field of linguistics', but that a grammatical theory and its constructs 'must be chosen so as to provide the best possible explanation of semantic phenomena, as well as others'.

Challenges to the Chomskyan paradigm – particularly non-transformational syntactic theories and COGNITIVE LINGUISTICS – have been gaining support since the 1980s, although they cannot be said to have overcome the influence of Chomskyan theory. Outside linguistics, Chomsky is now best known for his left-wing political views and activism, particularly with reference to American foreign policy. Although retired from university duties, he continues to write and speak on political and linguistic matters.

Further reading

Barsky, Robert F. (1997) *Noam Chomsky: a life of dissent*. Cambridge, MA: MIT Press.

Harris, Randy Allen (1993) *The linguistics wars*. Oxford: Oxford University Press.

Searle, John R. (1972) 'Chomsky's revolution in linguistics.' *The New York Review of Books* 29 June 1972. Available at http://www.chomsky.info/onchomsky/19720629.htm

Donald Davidson (1917–2003)

Donald Davidson's contributions to the philosophy of language were wide-ranging and influential. Born in 1917 in Massachusetts, Davidson studied English literature and later classics and philosophy at Harvard University, receiving the Bachelor's degree in 1939. After naval service during the Second World War, he received the doctorate in Philosophy in 1949 for a thesis on Plato's 'Philebus', also at Harvard. From his classicist roots, his interests took an increasingly analytic turn, influenced by his mentor, **W. V. O. Quine**.

A few of Davidson's essays from the 1960s and 1970s stand out for their lasting contributions to the philosophy of language. 'Truth and meaning' (1967) argues that sentence meaning in natural language can be analysed in terms of the sentence's truth. Here, he follows the 1944 work of mathematician Alfred Tarski, who developed a theory of truth for application to formal languages. In Tarski's account, truth conditions are expressed as statements, called T-sentences, which take the form 'S is true if and only if p', where S is a sentence and p is a proposition that states the conditions under which S is true. A complete theory of truth for a language, then, consists of a complete collection of T-sentences that cover all of the possible sentences of that language. In trying to apply this account of truth to natural language, we run into the problem that there is no complete set of sentences in a language – new sentences can always be created and acquiring a language does not amount to acquiring all of its sentences. Davidson also pointed out that the logical BICONDITIONAL represented by 'if and only if' is not sufficient for stating truth conditions, since a T-sentence would be true even if the S and the p were only coincidentally both true, if S were *Snow is white* and p were 'water is wet'. In response to these problems, Davidson argued that meaning must be understood to be COMPOSITIONAL. Compositionality is achieved through the introduction of axioms that determine the conditions on the use of expressions in the language. In the case of *Snow is white*, the axioms needed are as follows:

An axiom of reference for the referring expression: *Snow* refers to snow.
An axiom of satisfaction for the predicate *white*: *White* is satisfied by white things.
An axiom of connection, to combine the predicate and argument: *a is b* is true if and only if what *a* refers to satisfies *b*.

These combine to give us the T-sentence.

Snow is white is true if and only if snow is white.

In order to understand that this is not a tautology, we must be aware that the second 'snow is white' is a METALANGUAGE statement, which could be stated instead in other terms and that can be applied to other natural languages. So, a T-sentence for German could be as follows:

Schnee ist weiss is true if and only if snow is white.

In order to demonstrate that a theory of truth could be adapted to be a theory of natural language meaning, Davidson wrote a number of essays exploring some potentially problematic uses of language, such as quotation, modification and non-declarative utterances. In 'On saying that' (1968), he argues that statements of indirect speech (e.g. *John said that snow is white*) should be treated as composed of an expression that refers to the speaker (*John*), a two-place predicate (*said*) and (most innovatively) a demonstrative (*that*) that refers to the utterance of the indirectly quoted material (*snow is white*). In order for such a sentence to be true, it is not necessary that the speaker actually said the sentence that follows *that*, but rather that he must have uttered something that 'samesays' what the indirectly quoted material said.

Davidson is also known for his development of Quine's ideas on 'radical translation' – that is, translation with no prior knowledge of the translated language or its culture, into a theory of 'radical interpretation' (1973). Davidson proposed that in such situations, a 'Principle of Charity' (sometimes also called 'radical accommodation') is invoked, by which one accepts the interpretation of an utterance that is in the most agreement with one's own set of beliefs.

Davidson's work extended to other areas of philosophical inquiry, including philosophy of mind, epistemology and ethics. During his career, he held positions at a number of universities. His longest associations were with Stanford (1951–1967) and the University of California at Berkeley (1981–2003). He worked actively until his sudden death at the age of 86.

Further reading

LePore, Ernest and Kirk Ludwig (2007) *Donald Davidson's truth-theoretic semantics*. Oxford: Clarendon Press.

Morris, Michael (2007) *An introduction to the philosophy of language* (chapters 9 and 10). Cambridge: Cambridge University Press.

Ramberg, Bjørn T. (1989) *Donald Davidson's philosophy of language: an introduction*. Oxford: Blackwell.

Charles J. Fillmore (b. 1929)

Charles Fillmore received his doctorate in Linguistics in 1961 at the University of Michigan. He taught at the Ohio State University until 1971, when he moved to the University of California at Berkeley, where he is now Professor Emeritus of Linguistics.

Fillmore's work is characterized by its focus on the interface between syntax and semantics. His early work on the Case Grammar theory had an important role in bringing the notion of SEMANTIC ROLES to modern linguistics. In his 1968 paper 'The case for case', Fillmore proposed that verbs were associated with deep-structure cases, such as Agentive, Instrumental or Objective (which later came to be called 'Patient'). How these deep cases were mapped onto surface syntax was then determined by a subject hierarchy, which stated that 'if there is an A[gentive], it becomes the subject; otherwise, if there is an I[instrumental], it becomes the subject; otherwise, the subject is the O[bjective]' (Fillmore 1968: 33). The significance of this approach lies in the description it provides of the relationship between syntactic VALENCY and the ARGUMENT structure of a verb.

However, Fillmore came to view general semantic roles as insufficient for a full characterization of the semantic structure of verbs. This led him to develop the notion of FRAMES as abstract scenarios against which the meanings of related words are understood. He first applied frames to the description of groups of related verbs, such as *buy*, *sell*, *cost* and *pay*, which he argued to evoke the same general scenario of commercial transactions, although the different verbs focused on different participant roles in the event (Fillmore 1977). In his later publications on **FRAME SEMANTICS** (e.g. 1982, 1985), Fillmore developed the notion of frames to encompass cognitive structures that represent various kinds of schematizations of experience, including knowledge of cultural institutions, practices and expectations, and argued that such complexes of encyclopaedic knowledge are essential for understanding the meanings of words. This work was an important influence on other COGNITIVE LINGUISTIC theories of meaning, including the DOMAIN-based theory of meaning in Ronald Langacker's COGNITIVE GRAMMAR and **G**EORGE **L**AKOFF's notion of IDEALIZED COGNITIVE MODELS.

Fillmore is also one of the early designers and proponents of CONSTRUCTION GRAMMAR. In their 1988 paper 'Regularity and idiomaticity in grammatical constructions: the case of *let alone*', Fillmore and his co-authors Paul Kay and Mary Catherine O'Connor proposed a model of grammar where linguistic forms (including both lexical forms and syntactic configurations) are linked directly with their semantic and pragmatic properties. The formalism of Construction Grammar was developed further in the 1999 paper by Kay and Fillmore, which examined the idiomatic construction that underlies expressions such as *What's this fly doing in my soup?*. Fillmore's work on constructions influenced the work of many other authors, including Adele Goldberg.

Fillmore's most recent work has focused on the FrameNet project at Berkeley. This project is a development of Fillmore's Frame Semantics and aims to provide a corpus-based, on-line lexical database of the semantic and syntactic properties of English words in terms of the frames that underlie their meanings. Fillmore has also published on Japanese linguistics, corpus-based approaches to POLYSEMY (e.g. Fillmore and Atkins 1992) and DEIXIS (Fillmore 1997).

Further reading

The FrameNet project: http://framenet.icsi.berkeley.edu/

Jerry A. Fodor (b. 1935)

Jerry Fodor is a philosopher whose work on the nature of the mind and of language is notable for its engagement with mainstream linguistic ideas and his collaboration with linguists and psychologists. Born in New York City in 1935, Fodor received a Bachelor's degree from Columbia in 1956 and completed the doctorate in Philosophy at Princeton under Hillary Putnam in 1960. His first academic appointment, which he held until 1986, was at MIT, where he engaged with the ideas of **NOAM CHOMSKY** and his contemporaries there. As well as publishing many monographs and articles in philosophy and cognitive science outlets, he has published several important articles in linguistics journals. His writing is often marked by an irreverent tone.

Fodor has developed a number of philosophical positions associated with Chomskyan linguistics, particularly the modularity of mind (in the 1983 book of that name) and arguments for the existence of innate types of knowledge. However, some of his positions cannot be considered to be mainstream within modern linguistics, and he has critiqued the approaches of others (e.g. Steven Pinker in *The mind doesn't work that way*, 2000) who appear at first glance to have taken the same positions as him.

Fodor endorses a computational theory of mind – that is, that thought can be represented as the processing of a symbolic system. Much of his work (e.g. 1975, 1994, 2008) has argued for an innate Language of Thought (LOT) or 'mentalese', that is, a grammar and vocabulary for mental processes that Fodor claims is realized neurologically. He argues that the LOT must be prior to language, since in order to link linguistic forms to meanings, those meanings (or the building blocks for them) must already exist in the mind. This position is in direct opposition to psychological behaviourism and its premise that prior to experience the mind is a blank slate. His work has repeatedly returned to the questions of whether (and to what extent) thought and meaning are externalistic (i.e. with reference to the world outside the mind) or internalistic (solipsistic) – and his thoughts on this matter have changed over the years. He has argued for various versions of an 'asymmetrical causal dependency theory' of meaning, by which laws determine that things that are dogs are causally linked to the symbol *dog*. Yet not every instance of use of the symbol *dog* is caused by a dog – for instance, I might see a calf from a distance and mistakenly call it a *dog*. It is only possible to refer to a calf as a *dog* because of the extant causal law that dogs cause *dog* and the absence of a symmetric law that *dog* causes dogs.

Fodor is also still known for his early work with Jᴇʀʀᴏʟᴅ Kᴀᴛᴢ, attempting a ᴅᴇᴄᴏᴍᴘᴏsɪᴛɪᴏɴᴀʟ approach to meaning as a complement to the then-new field of generative syntax. Their 'The structure of a semantic theory' (1963) stands as a classic example of a componential approach to meaning. (For further discussion, see Jᴇʀʀᴏʟᴅ Kᴀᴛᴢ.) In the 1970s, Fodor collaborated with linguists and psycholinguists, including Janet Dean Fodor, Thomas Bever and Merrill Garrett, looking for processing evidence for decomposed meaning – and found none. This can be seen to have inspired his subsequent view that lexical meanings cannot be broken down compositionally into meaningful parts (see Fodor 1998) – a position that contrasts with his vehement arguments against semantic ʜᴏʟɪsᴍ at the sentential level (see Fodor and Lepore 1992). His views on lexicalized concepts are at odds with most common assumptions in linguistic semantics, in which componential lexical semantics is a thriving enterprise. Nevertheless, he holds that compositionality of meaning ends at the level of single concepts and from there 'meaning' must be described in terms of causal relations between symbols and the things they symbolize.

Fodor has been Professor of Philosophy at Rutgers University (New Jersey) since 1988 and continues to publish prolifically.

Further reading

Semantics: an interview with Jerry Fodor. *Revista Virtual de Estudos da Linguagem* (*ReVEL*). 5 March 2007. Available at http://internalism. googlegroups.com/web/Fodor%20-%20Semantics%20(interview).pdf

Gottlob Frege (1848–1925)

Gottlob Frege was a German mathematician and logician who is counted as a (if not *the*) father of modern logic and analytic philosophy and whose contributions to the philosophy of language have shaped nearly all that has come since. After undergraduate studies at the University of Jena, he received the doctorate in Mathematics from the University of Göttingen in 1873. After this, he returned to Jena where he lectured in mathematics until his retirement in 1918. From there he published a number of groundbreaking works in arithmetic and logic.

It was in preparing his major mathematical treatise (his *Begriffschrift*, 1879) that he realized that natural language was unfit for the purpose of precisely describing mathematical truths. He set about arguing that arithmetic could be described in purely logical terms, without recourse to empirical fact. In doing so, he developed a logical language that incorporated mathematical notions of functions, arguments and variables, with quantification over those variables. In other words, Frege developed the first PREDICATE LOGIC.

The development of such sophisticated logical systems gave rise to his consideration of some problems of meaning and the philosophy of language. His most influential work in this regard is *Uber Sinn und Bedeutung* 'On sense and reference' (1892), which is attributed as having the earliest cogent arguments for the separation of SENSE and REFERENCE in discussions of meaning (developing ideas from the earlier paper *Funktion und Begriff* 'Function and concept', 1891). The first paradox that he presented is now referred to as 'Frege's problem' or 'Frege's puzzle'; he noted that a statement of identity like *The morning star is the morning star* is synonymous with another statement, *The morning star is the evening star*, since the two so-named stars are in reality both the planet Venus. Frege argued that the perceived difference in the meaning of these two sentences is due to the differences in the 'modes of presentation' of the expressions that refer to Venus and that these differences indicate that the 'true meaning' of the sentences is to be found in the sense rather than the reference of the sentences. Similarly, he pointed out the problem of substituting referentially synonymous expressions in PROPOSITIONAL ATTITUDE contexts – for example, *John believes that the morning star is bright* is not synonymous with *John believes that the evening star is bright*. Again, this lack of synonymy can be accounted for if one considers the meaning of the embedded proposition to be its sense, rather than its reference. In the case of propositions, Frege held that the reference was the truth value of the statement.

Frege is also attributed with the principle of semantic COMPOSITIONALITY – which is sometimes referred to as 'Frege's principle'. That is, the meaning of a whole is a function of the meaning of its parts. This is sometimes taken to be in conflict with his equally influential 'Context Principle', by which the meaning of a word cannot be known without reference to the meaning of the proposition that contains it.

The importance of Frege's work was only truly appreciated after his death, and much of his renown is due to **BERTRAND RUSSELL**'s attention. Frege's influence can be seen in the work of Russell, **W. V. O. QUINE**, **LUDWIG WITTGENSTEIN** and **RICHARD MONTAGUE**. Translations of his works are collected in *Philosophical writings* (1952).

Further reading

Kenny, Anthony (1995) *Frege: an introduction to the founder of modern analytic philosophy*. Oxford: Blackwell.

Morris, Michael (2007) *An introduction to the philosophy of language* (chapter 2). Cambridge: Cambridge University Press.

Noonan, Harold W. (2001) *Frege: a critical introduction*. Cambridge: Polity.

Ray Jackendoff (b. 1945)

Ray Jackendoff is an American linguist and cognitive scientist. Born in Chicago, his undergraduate studies at Swarthmore College (Pennsylvania) concentrated on Mathematics. He studied Linguistics at MIT under **Noam Chomsky**, receiving the doctorate in 1969 for his thesis *Some rules of semantic interpretation for English*. Jackendoff has been one of the key theorists in the integration of semantics and **generative grammar**, and the theory that he has developed, **Conceptual Semantics**, can be seen as straddling the divide between the generative tradition and **cognitive linguistics**.

From the start of his career, Jackendoff was concerned with problems of semantic representation in generative linguistic theory. He was a key architect of the 1970s versions of the Chomskyan programme, the Extended Standard Theory (particularly in *Semantic interpretation in generative grammar*, 1972) and the Revised Extended Standard theory (*X-bar syntax*, 1977). As such, he was a key participant in the 'Linguistics Wars' of the late 1960s and early 1970s, which pitted proponents of **generative semantics** (such as **George Lakoff**) against the Chomskyan theoreticians of **interpretive semantics**. While the generative semanticists argued for semantic representation at deep structure, Jackendoff highlighted the role of surface structure relations in semantic interpretation.

In later work, Jackendoff takes a parallel route to the Chomskyan core, abandoning its 'syntacto-centric' viewpoint in favour of a more lexical and semantically driven view. This has culminated in his CS approach. In common with cognitive linguistic theories, CS treats the business of linguistic semantics as co-extensive with the representation of human thought and conceptualization. In other words, (a) there is no distinction between the representation of the meanings of linguistic expressions and of other kinds of thinkable thoughts, and (b) there is no direct relation between language and 'reality' – that relation (if it is possible) must be mediated through the mental representation of 'reality'. At the same time, Jackendoff remains committed to basic generative principles: particularly, the goals of accounting for the acquisition and creativity of language by positing some innate knowledge and mental architecture for language.

Jackendoff laid the groundwork for CS in his 1976 paper 'Toward an explana-tory semantic representation', in which he defines an explanatory semantic analysis as 'when certain linguistically significant generalizations are inherent in the choice of formalism, when the theory claims that the language could not be any other way' (p. 91). The approach was properly developed through two monographs, *Semantics and cognition* (1983) and *Semantic structures* (1990). Semantic structures are typed according to a number of basic ONTOLOGICAL CATEGORIES, such as THING and EVENT, and the ontological type of a meaning constrains its possible structure. These structures typically involve (possibly recursive) predicate-argument relations, composed of semantic COMPONENTS, which, at some level, should be decomposable into semantic PRIMITIVES. The result is a semantic representation that is relatively formal, but more like natural language than a logical language in the number of categories that it admits.

A key element of Jackendoff's approach is a tripartite parallel architecture for linguistic representation (see *The architecture of the language faculty*, 1997 and *Foundations of language*, 2002), consisting of a phonological system, a syntactic system and a conceptual system. The conceptual system is not a specifically *linguistic* system – and so in representing the conceptual system, Jackendoff aims to provide a 'grammar of thought'. **Lexical concepts**, that is, concepts that are represented by words, are linked to phonological and (/or) syntactic information, as illustrated by the lexical representation of *tree* in Figure 10.

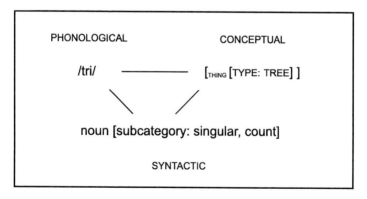

Figure 10 Lexical representation of *tree*

An effect of the tripartite architecture is that syntactic structures can be linked to conceptual structures without necessarily having a phonological form specified. For example, the structure [$_{VP}$V NP Adj] as in [$_{VP}$ [$_V$ *hammer*] [$_{NP}$ *the metal*] [$_A$ *flat*]] or [$_{VP}$ [$_V$ *dye*] [$_{NP}$ *her hair*] [$_A$ *red*]] is linked to a resultative meaning ('do an action that results in something having a new property'). In other words, the abstract [V NP Adj] construction is associated with a concept, ACTION-CAUSES-PROPERTY. This flexibility of CS in what counts as a meaningful unit of language has led to productive interactions with Construction Grammar (e.g. Goldberg and Jackendoff 2004).

Since 1971, Jackendoff has been on the faculty at Brandeis University (Massachusetts), now as Professor Emeritus, having been appointed to the Seth Merrin Chair in Humanities at Tufts University (Massachusetts) in 2005. He continues to publish prolifically on semantics as well as on consciousness, evolution of language and generative approaches to music – an intersection with his 'other life' as a classical clarinettist.

Further reading

The December 2007 issue of *The Linguistic Review* (vol. 24, no. 4) includes a number of articles responding to Jackendoff's work.

Jerrold J. Katz (1932–2002)

Jerrold Katz was an American philosopher who engaged directly with linguistic theory, grappling with the problem of how to incorporate a theory of meaning in generative grammar and the nature of the philosophical underpinning of linguistic theory. As such, he might be thought of as much as a 'linguistic philosopher' as a 'philosopher of language'.

Katz was born in Washington in 1932 and took his Bachelor's degree at George Washington University. After a period in the Army Counterintelligence Corps, he completed the doctorate in Philosophy in 1960 at Princeton University. From there, he went to MIT, first as a research associate, but attaining a full professorship by 1969. In 1975 he was appointed Distinguished Professor of Philosophy at the City University of New York Graduate Center, where he served for the rest of his career.

At MIT he became one of the key architects of the interpretive semantics of early GENERATIVE GRAMMAR. With JERRY FODOR, he published 'The structure of a semantic theory' (1963), which stands as a classic example of a mentalistic componential approach to meaning. Katz and Fodor's semantic representations of SENSES combined **semantic markers**, the components of meaning that are responsible for the semantic relation of a word to other words in the language, and **distinguishers**, which determine the properties that differentiate the defined term from others in its semantic class. In the example below, the markers are represented in parentheses and the distinguishers in square brackets.

Bachelor (Human) (Male) [has never been married]

In order to integrate the lexical meaning with phrasal meaning, they introduced the notion of **projection rules**, by which the semantic components of a lexeme project up the phrasal tree to give the meanings of phrases and, eventually, the whole sentence. In order to explain semantic ANOMALIES, they introduced the notion of SELECTIONAL RESTRICTIONS. These ideas were incorporated into the Standard Theory (Chomsky 1965), the prevalent and most influential linguistic theory of the time.

Katz continued to develop this approach into the 1970s (Katz and Postal 1964; Katz 1972), but in later work he rejected the Chomskyan view of language. Instead, he adopted the Platonic Realist position of language as an abstract object that should be studied without reference to human minds.

Katz also forcefully rejected **Gottlob Frege**'s view of sense and reference that had earlier motivated work such as his *Semantic theory* (1972). He replaced the Fregean notions with 'The new intensionalism' (1992). In a series of publications from the 1980s, culminating in *The metaphysics of meaning* (1990) and *Sense, reference and philosophy* (2004), he argued that sense does not determine reference, but instead that it 'mediates' reference, and that such a 'thin' relationship between sense and reference is necessary in order to account for many of the long-standing problems in philosophy of language, such as the analytic–synthetic distinction, the semantics of proper names and of natural kind terms. Rather than using predicate logic to represent senses and propositional relations, Katz (2004) proposed a 'mereological' theory of sense, in which senses are defined relationally in terms of other senses for which they are parts or wholes.

Further reading

Langendoen, D. Terence (2005) 'Katz, Jerrold J. (1932–2002).' In Keith Brown (ed.), *Encyclopedia of Language and Linguistics*, 2nd edn. Amsterdam: Elsevier.

Saul Kripke (b. 1940)

Saul Kripke has been called a philosophical Wunderkind. Born on Long Island, New York and raised in Nebraska, Kripke began publishing articles on MODAL LOGIC while in his teens. He studied mathematics at Harvard University, and began teaching logic while still an undergraduate. After receiving the Bachelor's degree in 1962, he was appointed a Fellow at Harvard and received a Fulbright Fellowship before taking on faculty positions at Harvard, Rockefeller University (New York) and Princeton University. Much of Kripke's influential work has been delivered as lectures and published some time after the ideas were first discussed.

In his earliest published works, including 'Semantical considerations on modal logic' (1963), Kripke developed a semantics for modal logic that is now usually called *Kripke semantics*, and which remains the standard semantics for such logics.

From logic, Kripke's interests spread to questions of the philosophy of language. His best-known work is *Naming and necessity* (1980, after a series of lectures in 1970). There he argued against the descriptivist approach to names associated with GOTTLOB FREGE and BERTRAND RUSSELL, and proposed instead a 'causal' theory of names and natural kind terms in which names are RIGID DESIGNATORS that achieve reference through causal chains. In 'A puzzle about belief' (1979), Kripke further argues that a descriptive approach to names does not solve one of the problems it is supposed to solve: that is, two names that refer to the same thing can behave differently in expressions of PROPOSITIONAL ATTITUDE.

Other much-discussed works by Kripke include 'Outline of a theory of truth' (1975) and *Wittgenstein on rules and private language* (1982). In 'Outline', Kripke argues against the Tarskian position that a language cannot contain its own truth predicates, and thus not all sentences that seem to present a 'Liar's paradox' have indeterminable truth status. In this work, Kripke argues that the truth of such sentences can be determined if their truth can be 'grounded' on sentences that do not contain the truth predicate. On that assumption sentence (1) has a truth value, but sentence (2) does not, because it is **ungrounded**.

(1) The sentence *'Snow is white' is true* is true.

(2) This sentence is false.

Kripke is credited with bringing **Ludwig Wittgenstein**'s *Philosophical investi-gations* back to the philosophical fore in the 1980s in *Wittgenstein on rules and private language* (1982). However, it is almost universally accepted that Kripke attributes notions to Wittgenstein that are not in keeping with the text of *Philosophical investigations*. For that reason, the positions attributed to Wittgenstein in Kripke's book have come to be referred to as *Kripkenstein*. Kripkenstein has taken on a life of its own in the philosophical literature as the presentation of and argument against a form of 'meaning scepticism' in which it is impossible to tell whether someone following a rule in their use of a symbol (such as the rule that the symbol + refers to a particular mathe-matical function) is following the same rule as they followed when they used that symbol on another occasion. The solution is a 'communitarian view' of language in which meaning lies not in the individual but in a community of speakers using conventionalized form-meaning associations.

Further reading

Ahmed, Arif (2007) *Saul Kripke*. London: Continuum.

Fitch, G. W. (2005) *Saul Kripke*. Teddington, UK: Acumen.

Preti, Consuelo (2002) *On Kripke*. Toronto: Wadsworth.

George Lakoff (b. 1941)

George Lakoff is an American linguist and cognitive scientist. Born in New Jersey, he gained his doctorate in Linguistics at Indiana University in 1966. Following appointments at Harvard, University of Michigan and Stanford University, he has been Professor of Linguistics at the University of California at Berkeley since 1972.

Lakoff is best known today as one of the founders of COGNITIVE LINGUISTICS. But in the late 1960s and early 1970s, Lakoff was one of the leading figures of GENERATIVE SEMANTICS, together with James McCawley, John Robert Ross and Paul Postal. Generative Semanticists essentially saw syntax as being determined by semantics. They argued that underlying surface syntax is a level of deep structure that expresses full propositions. This underlying semantic representation is then transformed into syntax by transformational rules. However, the Generative Semantics movement faced fierce opposition from followers of NOAM CHOMSKY (such as RAY JACKENDOFF), who criticized the theory for its highly complex deep structures and lack of constraints on transformational rules. Although Lakoff's later work abandoned transformational analysis and the view that semantics may be modelled through formal (logical) representations, he has argued that some of his cognitive linguistic work is an 'updated version' of Generative Semantics, insofar as it also stresses that the function of language is to convey meaning and that syntactic form is determined by and reflects semantics (Lakoff 1987: 583).

Lakoff's importance for current semantic theory lies particularly in his work on CONCEPTUAL METAPHOR. The year 1980 saw the publication of *Metaphors we live by*, in which Lakoff and his co-author Mark Johnson argue that metaphor is fundamentally conceptual and that many conventional metaphorical expressions are reflections of systematic conceptual metaphors that map structure from one conceptual DOMAIN to another. This serves the purpose of understanding more abstract notions such as LIFE, EMOTION, TIME or QUANTITY in terms of more concrete, physical notions such as MOTION, HEAT, VERTICALITY, and so on. Importantly, Lakoff and Johnson's view of metaphor also entails that the human conceptual system is EMBODIED, that is, grounded in bodily experiences.

His other publications have developed the view of embodied cognition further, particularly *Women, fire and dangerous things* (1987) and the 1999 book co-authored with Johnson, *Philosophy in the flesh*. He has also refined or revised some of the earlier ideas about conceptual metaphor, for example, by expanding on the constraints on metaphorical mappings or projections and on the role of IMAGE SCHEMAS in metaphor (e.g. Lakoff 1993). However, in response to criticisms of earlier versions of the theory, Lakoff's more recent work has rethought the way experiential correlations motivate different types of metaphors and also focused on describing the neural basis of metaphor (see Lakoff and Johnson 1999, the Afterword to the 2003 edition of *Metaphors we live by* and also Gallese and Lakoff 2005).

Lakoff 's work on conceptual metaphor remains influential, and conceptual metaphor analysis has been applied to a range of different fields, including religion, law, economics, education and literature and poetry (see Lakoff and Turner 1989). Lakoff has also applied conceptual metaphor analysis and the notion of alternative framings to social and political issues (e.g. Lakoff 2002). In the *Where mathematics comes from* (2000, co-authored with Rafael E. Núñez), Lakoff argues that our understanding of mathematics, too, is metaphorical and fundamentally grounded in human sensorimotor experience. Conceptual Metaphor Theory has also played a role in inspiring other cognitive linguistic theories of meaning and metaphor, including CONCEPTUAL BLENDING THEORY.

His other significant contributions to semantics include his work on categorization in *Women, fire and dangerous things*. The same volume also presents an early CONSTRUCTION GRAMMAR analysis as well as an analysis of the POLYSEMY of the preposition *over* in terms of a radial category of senses centred on a prototypical, or central, sense. This analysis, which was a reworking of a study by Lakoff's student Claudia Brugman has spawned a number of other polysemy analyses of spatial particles.

Further reading

Brockman, John (1999) '"Philosophy in the flesh": a talk with George Lakoff.' *Edge: Third Culture*. Available at http://www.edge.org/3rd_culture/lakoff/lakoff_p2.html

Pires De Oliveira, Roberta (2001) 'Language and ideology: an interview with George Lakoff.' In René Dirven, Bruce Hawkins and Esra Sandikcioglu (eds), *Language and ideology*. Amsterdam: Benjamins.

David Lewis (1941–2001)

David Lewis was born in a college town in Ohio, where his parents taught. He started his undergraduate studies at Swarthmore College (Pennsylvania) intending to study chemistry, but a year abroad at Oxford inspired his interest in philosophy. At Oxford he attended lectures by the metaphysicist Gilbert Ryle and language philosophers J. L. Austin, P. F. Strawson and H. P. Grice (all key figures in the development of linguistic PRAGMATICS). He finished his Bachelor's degree in philosophy in 1964 and went on to Harvard, where he studied with **W. V. O. QUINE**. He earned the doctorate in 1967 for his thesis on convention. After six years teaching at the University of California at Los Angeles, he was appointed Professor at Princeton University in 1973.

His reworked thesis was published as *Convention: a philosophical study* in 1969, and won the Matchette Prize in Philosophy, marking it as the year's best book by a young philosopher. He defines CONVENTIONS as 'regularity in behavior' (p. 51) and illustrates his discussion in part with discussions of language as conventional behaviour. He develops this further in 'Languages and language' (1975; reprinted in *Philosophical papers*, vol. 1), where he looks for the interface between language as a truth-functional system and as a set of social practices.

Perhaps his most influential work in the philosophy of language was *Counterfactuals* (1973), in which he develops the use of POSSIBLE WORLDS in the interpretation of COUNTERFACTUAL CONDITIONALS, that is, those that rely on a premise that is counter to reality. Lewis proposed that a similarity relation between possible worlds and the actual world is necessary to determine the truth or falsity of propositions like the following:

> If the America had lost the War of Independence, it would belong to the British Commonwealth today.

That proposition is true if there is a world in which America lost the war and belongs to the British Commonwealth and that world is more like the actual world than any world in which America did not lose the war and belongs to the Commonwealth.

Lewis developed a more radical view of possible worlds than most. In *On the plurality of worlds* (1986) and elsewhere he took a 'modal realist' view, in that he held that all possible worlds are as real as the actual world – in contrast with most thinkers in possible world semantics who hold that possible worlds are sets of propositions, rather than real worlds.

Lewis suffered from diabetes for most of his life and died suddenly from complications of the disease at the age of 60.

Further reading

Nolan, Daniel (2005) *David Lewis*. Chesham: Acumen.

Richard Montague (1930–1971)

Richard Montague was a logician, mathematician and philosopher of language whose system of formal representation, now known as **Montague grammar** (or **Montague semantics**), was a breakthrough in integrating formal logic with a serious attempt to describe natural language.

Montague was born in Stockton, California. He pursued his studies at the University of California at Berkeley, first as an undergraduate with interests in philosophy, mathematics and languages, then as a postgraduate studying under 'the father of modern logic', Alfred Tarski. He received his doctorate in 1957, after he had already been on the faculty in Philosophy at the University of California at Los Angeles for two years. He was appointed Professor of Philosophy in 1963.

Montague grammar is a truth-conditional and model-theoretic approach – that is, the meaning of a sentence is conceived as conditions under which the sentence would be true in some model (or set of models – that is, **possible worlds**). While other such approaches have been proposed, Montague's has received the most attention and development. His system is mathematical in nature, and not to be taken as a mentalistic account of how meaning is represented in the mind.

In a series of papers, notably 'English as a formal language' (1970a) and ' Universal grammar' (1970b), Montague set out to demonstrate that the relation between syntax and semantics in a natural language like English could be represented in the same way as the syntax-semantics relation for a formal logic. He held that the structure of a sentence determines a corresponding semantic structure, based on the principle of **compositionality**. He further demonstrated the mechanics of the theory in 'The proper treatment of quantification in ordinary English' (1973 – popularly abbreviated *PTQ*), which came to be the main text for Montague grammar in the linguistic tradition. The grammar itself is an **intensional logic** based on **modal logic** and set and type theories from mathematics. In PTQ, Montague introduces **lambda** abstraction as a means to account for the reference of quantified noun phrases.

Montague was murdered at the age of 40, leaving a body of work, some of it published posthumously, that propelled the development of formal semantics within linguistics. His work was further developed and popularized by a number of theorists, notably David Dowty and Barbara Partee.

Further reading

Dowty, David (1979) *Word meaning and Montague grammar*. Dordrecht: Reidel.

Dowty, David R., Robert E. Wall and Stanley Peters (1981) *Introduction to Montague semantics*. Dordrecht: Reidel.

Partee, Barbara H. (1975) 'Montague grammar and transformational grammar'. *Linguistic Inquiry* 6, 203–300.

Willard Van Orman Quine (1908–2000)

Willard Van Orman (usually referred to as 'W. V.' or 'W. V. O.') Quine was an influential logician and philosopher of language who was responsible for problematizing some commonly held positions in analytic philosophy. He was born in Ohio and graduated from its Oberlin College in 1930 with a Bachelor's degree in Mathematics. Two years later, he completed the doctorate at Harvard, and subsequently began his life-long teaching career there.

Quine's views were empiricist – that is, he believed that we can only know what we have experienced. In terms of language, this meant that he doubted any theory of meaning that involved aspects that could not be acquired through the experience of linguistic behaviour. His 'Two dogmas of empiricism' (1951) argued against two commonly held positions among empiricists (or 'logical positivists') of the time: that statements are meaningful either because they are true or false based on their own properties (i.e. ANALYTIC) or because their truth value can be judged on the basis of immediate experience. Quine argued that analyticity cannot be satisfactorily explained. His argument depended in part on the position that analyticity must ultimately be defined in terms of PARADIGMATIC SEMANTIC RELATIONS and that those relations must ultimately be defined in terms of analyticity. As for the relation of statements to experience, Quine argued that the truth of a statement cannot be judged without reference to our entire body of beliefs – a theory of the world. This leads him to a variety of semantic HOLISM, known as **confirmation holism** or **epistemological holism**.

In *Word and object* (1960) and further in *Ontological relativity* (1968), Quine argues for the **indeterminacy of translation** and hence the indeterminacy of meaning. He imagines a situation in which a field linguist is in a foreign culture. A native points to a rabbit scurrying by and says *Gavagai*! While it might be natural to assume that *gavagai* means 'rabbit', it might also mean any number of other things like 'lunch' or 'scurrying' or 'fluffy tail' or 'white' – the field linguist cannot know, except to observe the behaviour of the native with respect to the word and object. That is, there is no such thing as meaning divorced from a context of use. The same indeterminacy of meaning can apply to one's own language. When you use the word *rabbit*, others can only assume what you mean by *rabbit* by basing it on their experience and your behaviour in using the term. An expression can only be said to be

'meaningful' insofar as it can be said to be a synonym of another expression –
but synonymy itself is not a definable term on Quine's reckoning.

An assumption of psychological behaviourism is inherent in Quine's views on
language. Since the tenets of behaviourism were forcefully argued against
by **NOAM CHOMSKY**, his views are less influential in the linguistic tradition than
they have been in the philosophy of language.

Quine's influence in the philosophy of language continues through further
consideration of his works and through the work of his students, who have
included **DONALD DAVIDSON** and **DAVID LEWIS**. His autobiography, *The time of
my life* was published in 1985.

Further reading

Orenstein, Alex (2002) *W. V. Quine*. Princeton, NJ: Princeton University Press.
Quine, W. V. (1985) *The time of my life: an autobiography*. Cambridge, MA:
    MIT Press.

Bertrand Russell (1872–1970)

Bertrand Russell was one of the most noted intellectuals of the twentieth century. A philosopher, mathematician, social theorist and pacifist, Russell's significant contributions to the development of mathematical logic and his status as a founding father of analytical philosophy have meant that his influence permeates modern philosophy of language.

Russell was born into an aristocratic and very progressive family in Wales. His parents both died while he was a young child, leaving him to be raised in his paternal grandparents' home, where he was privately educated before being granted a scholarship to study mathematics at Trinity College, Cambridge University in 1890. After his Bachelor's degree in mathematics (1893), he was elected to a fellowship in philosophy there.

Russell is responsible for the invention of the first type theory for mathematics and logic, as explicated in his 1903 *The principles of mathematics* and later, with Alfred North Whitehead, in *Principia Mathematica*. His type theory presents a hierarchy of proposition types: those that are about individuals, those that are about sets of individuals, those that are about sets of sets of individuals, and so forth. The establishment of types allows for a solution to 'Russell's paradox' in the naïve set theory of **Gottlob Frege**. Fregean set theory carries the assumption that for any criterion there can be a set that contains all and only the objects that fulfil that criterion. Russell pointed out that this assumption leads to a paradox, since it allows for a set of all sets that do not contain themselves. In Russell's type theory, every item is assigned a type, and items belonging to the 'higher' types can only be composed of items belonging to the 'lower' types. This prevents the self-contradictory loop present in Frege's theory. The development of type theory has made possible many formal approaches to semantics, including **Montague grammar**.

Russell is also particularly noted for his approaches to description and reference, which he set out in 'On denoting' (1905). Using **first-order logic**, Russell demonstrated how various types of denoting expressions (noun phrases in natural language) could be represented using logic. The paper contained one of the most famous examples in the semantic literature: *The present king of France is bald*. Since there was no king of France at the time of writing, the sentence is paradoxical, and thus one might claim that it has no truth value.

On Russell's treatment, the use of the definite description *the present king of France* asserts (a) the existence of a present king of France, and (b) the uniqueness of the referent of *the present king of France*. Russell thus paraphrases the entire sentence as: 'There is an x such that x is a present king of France, there is nothing other than x that is a present king of France, and x is bald.' Since the first of the propositions conjoined in this paraphrase is false, the sentence as a whole is false. This approach set the stage for what superseded it: the notion (due to P. F. Strawson) that definite descriptions PRESUPPOSE unique reference.

Russell's views on PROPER NAMES are often cited, as he particularly argued against the Fregean position that definite descriptions (*the X*) can be treated as proper names. Instead, he holds that names directly refer to their referents (but do not describe them), while definite descriptions describe (sets of) things in order that something can be said about them. In this way, a name that does not refer to anything is meaningless, while a definite description like *the present king of France* that describes nothing that exists is nevertheless meaningful.

Russell's career was severely affected by his refusal to fight in the First World War. For this, he lost his position at Cambridge and was imprisoned for six months. After the Second World War, he taught at the University of Chicago and later the University of California at Los Angeles, but his appointment to a professorship at City College of New York was annulled after protests that his social views made him 'morally unfit' to teach. He returned to Great Britain in 1944 and rejoined the faculty at Trinity College. He continued to publish on a varied range of subjects and was politically active and vocal throughout his life.

Further reading

Irvine, Andrew (ed.) (1999) *Bertrand Russell: critical assessment*, 4 vols. London: Routledge.

Russell, Bertrand (1967–1969) *The autobiography of Bertrand Russell*, 3 vols. London: Allen & Unwin.

Ferdinand de Saussure (1857–1913)

Saussure was a Swiss linguist who is commonly considered the father of modern linguistics. His most significant contributions lie in his definition of language as a system of ARBITRARY SIGNS and the various distinctions he drew: between *langue* and *parole*, between synchronic and diachronic linguistics and between SYNTAGMATIC and PARADIGMATIC relations.

Saussure was born in Geneva in 1857. He first enrolled at the University of Geneva to study physics and chemistry, but after one year he transferred to the University of Leipzig, where he studied Indo-European languages. His teachers included many so-called Neogrammarians, the prominent historical linguists of his day. Saussure received his doctorate at Leipzig in 1880. After a period of teaching in Paris, he took up a professorship at the University of Geneva in 1891, which he held until his death in 1913. His groundbreaking ideas on language were only published posthumously in 1916. The publication, *Cours de linguistique générale*, was a reconstruction of Saussure's ideas by his colleagues on the basis of lecture notes from the courses Saussure gave at Geneva. He had, however, mentioned that he had been working on a manuscript of a book on the science of language, and in 1996 that manuscript was found in Saussure's family home. It was published in 2002 as *Écrites de linguistique générale*, and in an English translation in 2006.

Saussure was particularly concerned with establishing what kind of entity language is and defining the scope and focus of linguistics. In this regard, he made a distinction between *langue* as the underlying system of language and *parole* as the actual realization of language. (*Langue* and *parole* are sometimes translated into English as *language* and *speech*, respectively, but it is common to use the original French terms.) While *parole* is an observable, physical phenomenon, *langue* is an abstract entity, a set of conventions for language use within a speech community. Representations of *langue* exist in individual brains, but *langue* is ultimately a social product, it 'is never complete in any single individual, but exists perfectly only in the collectivity' (Saussure 1916/1983: 13). For Saussure, the study of *langue* should be the priority of the linguist and in this respect the distinction between *langue* and *parole* correlates largely with the distinction **NOAM CHOMSKY** later made between linguistic **competence** and **performance**. Saussure also emphasized that to study *langue*, one needs to focus on the synchronic state of language at a given point in time, as opposed to considering language diachronically, in terms of the historical changes it has undergone, as was the main focus of linguistic analysis at the time.

Saussure stressed the systematic nature of *langue*. He famously defines language as a system of arbitrary signs (and consequently envisions linguistics as a part of the larger field of SEMIOTICS, or *semiology*, as he called it). A linguistic sign is arbitrary in that there is no motivated reason for why a particular signified (concept) should be designated by a particular signifier (an acoustic image) but also because signs make arbitrary divisions in the realms of sounds and concepts. Saussure argued that both the phonological and the conceptual substance are inherently shapeless; what gives them structure is the combination of the signifier and the signified in a linguistic sign. The sign systems of different languages may thus make different, arbitrary divisions: for example, the concepts designated by the forms *connaître* and *savoir* in French are covered by the single English form *know*. An important aspect of Saussure's view is that both the sound and meaning units of language are essentially defined by the contrasts they have with other units in the language system. In describing the relations that make up *langue*, Saussure makes a distinction between syntagmatic and associative (later called *paradigmatic*) relations. His characterization of language as system of contrasts and relations between units laid the foundations of structural linguistics, including the Prague School (see MARKEDNESS) and the American tradition associated particularly with Leonard Bloomfield (see also STRUCTURAL SEMANTICS).

Further reading

Culler, Jonathan (1986) *Ferdinand de Saussure*. Revised edition. Ithaca, NY: Cornell University Press.

Harris, Roy (2001) *Saussure and his interpreters*. Edinburgh: Edinburgh University Press.

Sanders, Carol (ed.) (2004) *Cambridge companion to Saussure*. Cambridge: Cambridge University Press.

Leonard Talmy (b. 1942)

Leonard Talmy is an American linguist and cognitive scientist, known for his work on COGNITIVE SEMANTICS. Talmy carried out undergraduate studies in mathematics at the University of Chicago and in linguistics at the University of California at Berkeley, where he gained his Bachelor's degree in Linguistics in 1963. He received his doctorate in Linguistics at Berkeley in 1972. He is Professor Emeritus of Linguistics at the State University of New York at Buffalo and has continued to give talks and publish since his retirement in 2005. Most of Talmy's work until 2000, originally published in articles and book chapters, is reprinted, sometimes in an extensively revised and updated form, in the two-volume book *Toward a cognitive semantics* (2000).

Talmy's doctoral thesis, *Semantic structures in English and Atsugewi*, was the starting point for his work on EVENT structure, his typology of motion event LEXICALIZATION patterns being particularly well-known and influential. Talmy (1985, 2000) analyses a motion event as having four components: 'Motion', 'Figure' (the entity that moves), 'Ground' (the entity relative to which the movement occurs) and 'Path' (the direction/path of the movement). A motion event may also be associated with another event that expresses the 'Manner' or 'Cause' of the motion. Languages can be classified according to how they typically express these different elements in motion verbs, so that English motion verbs such as *run* or *creep* conflate the 'Motion' and 'Manner' elements, while Spanish motion verbs, such as *entrar* 'go in' and *salir* 'go out', conflate 'Motion' and 'Path'. Languages such as Spanish, French, Korean, Tamil and Turkish are called **verb-framing** languages because they typically express the path of the figure's motion within the verb. Languages such as English, German, Finnish, Chinese and Ojibwa, on the other hand, are **satellite-framing** because they typically express the path in a so-called satellite – a verb particle or verbal affix, such as *out* in *Bertie ran **out** of the house* (Talmy 1991, 2000). Although other authors before Talmy had observed that languages such as English and French lexicalize motion and information about the path differently, Talmy's contribution lies in the detailed description of the structure of motion events and the typological distinctions he makes regarding the verb and satellite lexicalization patterns.

Talmy has also focused more generally on the question of how formal linguistic structure reflects conceptual structure and on the shared conceptual structure between language and other non-linguistic cognitive systems, including visual perception, kinaesthetic perception, attention, reasoning and motor control. For example, attention is reflected in FIGURE/GROUND asymmetry (which explains, for example, the oddity of ?*Elvis resembles my brother* versus *My brother resembles Elvis*) and in the windowing of attention on certain parts of a situation (compare *The book fell out of my bag*, which highlights the initial portion of the path, versus *The book fell on the floor* where the focus is on the final portion) (Talmy 1996). Kinaesthetic perception relates to the force dynamics system, which expresses our experience of how entities interact with respect to force, including the exertion of force, resistance to force and the removal of restraint. Force dynamics is reflected in grammar, for example, in the meanings of modal verbs such as *can*, *should* and *must*, which particularly expresses the interaction of sentient entities with psychosocial force (Talmy 1988a, 2000).

Talmy argues that while OPEN-CLASS elements in language relate to the conceptual content system, CLOSED-CLASS elements specify notions that relate to the conceptual structuring system, which includes systems such as attention and force dynamics. Talmy therefore provides a detailed description of the semantics of grammar, linking it systematically to general aspects of cognition (Talmy 1988b, 2000). Talmy's work on the relationship between language and cognition contributed greatly to the development of COGNITIVE LINGUISTICS, and Talmy has been named one of the founding fathers of this approach to the study of language, along with GEORGE LAKOFF, CHARLES FILLMORE and Ronald Langacker.

Further reading

Iberretxe Antuñano, Iraide (2005) 'Leonard Talmy: a windowing to conceptual structure and language: Part 1, Lexicalisation and typology.' *Annual Review of Cognitive Linguistics* 3, 325–347.

Iberretxe Antuñano, Iraide (2006) 'Leonard Talmy: a windowing to conceptual structure and language. Part 2, Language and cognition, past and future.' *Annual Review of Cognitive Linguistics* 4, 253–268.

Anna Wierzbicka (b. 1938)

Anna Wierzbicka is the inventor of NATURAL SEMANTIC METALANGUAGE theory, which she has applied to a wide range of meaning- and culture-related issues in her prodigious published output. Born in Poland, Wierzbicka studied Polish language and literature at the University of Warsaw and later received the doctorate at the Polish Academy of Sciences for her thesis on Polish Renaissance prose.

In 'The double life of a bilingual' (1997), Wierzbicka credits a lecture by Warsaw University linguist Andrzej Bogusławski in 1965 as the inspiration for the direction of her research. Bogusławski discussed Gottfried Leibniz's search for 'the alphabet of human thoughts' and argued the world's languages provide the best possible source of insight into the building blocks of thinking. Thus linguists might succeed where philosophers had failed. Wierzbicka's decision to dedicate her working life to the pursuit of this goal was only strengthened by a post-doctoral year at the MIT, where she found the dominant generative, syntacto-centric approach of the time, as personified by NOAM CHOMSKY, 'sterile and uninspiring'. By 1969 she had published her first book (*Dociekania semantyczne* 'Semantic explorations') on her approach to the discovery of the 'alphabet of human thought', which has come to be known as the Natural Semantic Metalanguage (NSM).

NSM is a COMPONENTIAL approach to meaning in the mind. It assumes that all complex meanings can be represented in terms of a core vocabulary of semantic primes (PRIMITIVES) that are combined using a core grammar. All of the primes should have reflexes in the vocabularies of all languages.

The year 1972 saw Wierzbicka's translation of *Dociekania semantyczne* into English, as *Semantic primitives*, and her move to Australia, where she has been associated with Australian National University in Canberra ever since. There she found a vibrant test ground for her approach, given the available range of languages and experts on those languages. The 14 primitives of *Semantic primitives* have expanded to more than 60 (see *Semantics: primes and universals*, 1996). Through the 1970s and 1980s, Wierzbicka applied her methods to a broad range of linguistic phenomena, including CASE relations, COUNTABILITY and word classes. In contrast to the predominant views at the time that the relation between grammatical categories and word meaning is

ARBITRARY, Wierzbicka took on questions such as why one can *have a drink* but not *have an eat* or why *oats* is countable but *wheat* is non-countable and argued for semantic motivations for grammatical structures and classifications. Several of these works were collected in *The semantics of grammar* (1988).

Linked with her arguments for the iconicity of grammatical categories is Wierzbicka's position that linguistic form reflects cultural patterns and values – and thus cross-linguistic semantic research is 'ethnopsychology'. On this theme, Wierzbicka has published a body of work in cross-linguistic/cross-cultural semantics – exploring, for instance, the differences in emotion terms and terms of address in *Semantics, culture and cognition* (1992) and in words for 'friend', 'freedom' and other value-laden vocabulary in *Understanding cultures through their key words* (1997). Following in the tradition of Wilhelm von Humboldt, Wierzbicka holds that few lexicalized concepts can be expected to be exact translations of one another, since they reflect the cultures in which they are used. Nevertheless, the subtle differences in meaning among words must be explicable in terms of the primes of the NSM.

Wierzbicka's own experiences as a bilingual and an immigrant have inspired much of her cross-linguistic work, which has led (starting with the first edition of *Cross-cultural pragmatics* in 1991 – revised in 2003) to a theory of **cultural scripts**: culture-specific conventions of discourse, which again are paraphrased in the vocabulary and grammar of NSM.

NSM has garnered more and more of a following in the past decade, and Wierzbicka, often with her colleague Cliff Goddard at the University of New England (Australia), continue to expand both the metalanguage itself and its applications.

Further reading

Goddard, Cliff (1998) *Semantic analysis: a practical introduction.* Oxford: Oxford University Press.
Wierzbicka, Anna (1997) 'The double life of a bilingual: a cross-cultural perspective.' In Michael Bond (ed.), *Working at the interface of culture: eighteen lives in social science.* London: Routledge.

Ludwig Wittgenstein (1889–1951)

Ludwig Wittgenstein is considered by many to be one of the greatest philosophers of the twentieth century. His work focused on logic, mathematics and the relationship between language, thought and the world. Because he later rejected many of the ideas he had held in his earlier work, it is common to distinguish between the 'early' and 'late' stages of Wittgenstein's thought.

Wittgenstein was born in Vienna in 1889, the son of a wealthy entrepreneur in the steel industry. He initially set out to study physics and mechanics, and in 1908 came to Britain to study aeronautical engineering at the University of Manchester. During this time his interests turned to the philosophical foundations of mathematics. This led him to contact **Gottlob Frege** and, on Frege's advice, **Bertrand Russell**, who became a mentor and key influence on Wittgenstein's early thinking. Wittgenstein studied with Russell in Cambridge from 1911 to 1913, but at the outbreak of the First World War in 1914 he returned to Austria and signed up for the Austrian army. During the war, some of which he spent in an Italian prisoner of war camp, Wittgenstein formulated the *Tractatus logico-philosophicus* (*TLP*) (1921/1922), which was to be the only philosophical work published during his lifetime.

In *TLP*, Wittgenstein proposes a 'picture theory' of meaning, according to which our thoughts and the propositions expressed in sentences are meaningful insofar as they are pictures of reality. Reality consists of facts, which are states of affairs in the world and take the form of configurations of objects and their relations. A picture of reality must have the same logical structure as reality: every element and relation in the picture is isomorphic with objects and relations in reality. The close interdependence of the propositions expressed in sentences and facts means not only that sentences are meaningful only when they relate to existing (or possible) states of affairs but also that what is not expressible in language is not a fact. Thus, 'The limits of my language mean the limits of my world' (*TLP* 5.6).

In the years after the publication of *TLP* Wittgenstein withdrew from philosophy and spent time as a gardener, schoolteacher and architect. But in 1929 he returned to Cambridge, where *TLP* was submitted and accepted as a doctoral thesis. He set out to develop a new philosophy that eventually came to reject many of the ideas in the earlier work.

Wittgenstein's later work is best represented in *Philosophical investigations* (*PI*), which was published posthumously in 1953. It sees Wittgenstein move away from logic and the description of language as a representation of reality to considering the properties of ordinary language. Wittgenstein's later view of language and meaning can be summarized as 'meaning is use': the meanings of words do not lie in their reference to objects in reality, but rather in the uses to which they are put. There are a multitude of different uses of language or 'language-games': reporting an event, making a joke, issuing an order, translating, greeting, thanking, and so on. This focus on the everyday uses of language marks Wittgenstein as a precursor of the so-called ordinary language philosophers, such as J. L. Austin, although he did not directly influence their work.

In discussing the notion of 'language-games' Wittgenstein argues that like different kinds of games (chess, poker, noughts-and-crosses, etc.), the different uses of language (or different uses of particular words) are not definable by a common shared essence, but are instead related by FAMILY RESEMBLANCES. This argument against definitions based on necessary and sufficient conditions was a direct influence on Eleanor Rosch and PROTOTYPE THEORY.

Wittgenstein considered the rules of language-games, which determine the appropriate use of language, to be a matter of public agreement, of social convention. He posits that there can be no private language whose rules are only known to one individual and which can be used to describe only one's own inner experiences. This 'private language argument' became the source of tension between scholars who stressed the social nature of language and those who describe language as a mental entity of an individual, including NOAM CHOMSKY.

In 1939 Wittgenstein was appointed Professor of Philosophy at Cambridge and became a British citizen. During the Second World War, he worked in hospitals in London and Newcastle, before returning to Cambridge in 1944. He gave up his professorship only three years later, and was diagnosed with cancer in 1949. He died in Cambridge in 1951.

Further reading

Anscombe, G. E. M. (1959) *An introduction to Wittgenstein's Tractatus*. London: Hutchinson.

Baker, G. P. and P. M. S. Hacker (1980–1996) *An analytical commentary on the Philosophical investigations*. 4 vols. Oxford: Blackwell.

Monk, Ray (1990) *Ludwig Wittgenstein: the duty of genius*. London: J. Cape.

Sluga, Hans and David G. Stern (eds) (1996) *The Cambridge companion to Wittgenstein*. Cambridge: Cambridge University Press.

Key Texts in Semantics

Abbott, Barbara (2002) 'Definiteness and proper names: some bad news for the description theory.' *Journal of Semantics* 19, 191–201.

Allwood, Jens, Lars-Gunnar Andersson and Östen Dahl (1977) *Logic in linguistics*. Cambridge: Cambridge University Press.

Aristotle (1984) *The complete works of Aristotle*, 2 vols. Ed. Jonathan Barnes. Princeton, NJ: Princeton University Press.

Barlow, Michael and Suzanne Kemmer (eds) (2000) *Usage-based models of language*. Stanford: CSLI.

Barsalou, Lawrence W. (1993) 'Flexibility, structure, and linguistic vagary in concepts: manifestations of a compositional system of perceptual symbols.' In Alan F. Collins, Susan E. Gathercole, Martin A. Conway and Peter E. Morris (eds), *Theories of memory*. London: Erlbaum.

Barwise, Jon and John Perry (1983) *Situations and attitudes*. Cambridge, MA: MIT Press.

Barwise, Jon and Robin Cooper (1981) 'Generalized quantifiers and natural language.' *Linguistics and Philosophy* 4, 159–219. Reprinted in Portner and Partee (2002).

Bejoint, Henri (2000) *Modern lexicography: an introduction*. Oxford: Oxford University Press.

Berlin, Brent, Dennis E. Breedlove and Peter H. Raven (1973) 'General principles of classification and nomenclature in folk biology.' *American Anthropologist* 7, 214–242.

Bierwisch, Manfred and Ewald Lang (eds) (1989) *Dimensional adjectives: grammatical structure and conceptual interpretation*. Berlin: Springer.

Blake, Barry J. (2001) *Case*. Cambridge: Cambridge University Press.

Blank, Andreas (1999) 'Why do new meanings occur? A cognitive typology of the motivations for lexical semantic change.' In Andreas Blank and Peter Koch (eds), *Historical semantics and cognition*. Berlin: Mouton de Gruyter.

Bloomfield, Leonard (1933) *Language*. New York: Holt, Rinehart and Winston.

Carnap, Rudolf (1936–1937) 'Testability and meaning.' *Philosophy of Science* 3, 419–471 and 4, 1–40.

Carnap, Rudolf (1937) *The logical syntax of language*. Trans. Amethe Smeaton. London: Routledge.

Carnap, Rudolf (1947) *Meaning and necessity*. Chicago: University of Chicago Press. Second edition, 1956.

Carnap, Rudolf (1950) 'Empiricism, semantics and ontology.' *Revue Internationale de Philosophie* 4, 20–40.

Carnap, Rudolf (1952) 'Meaning postulates.' *Philosophical Studies* 3, 65–73. Reprinted in *Meaning and necessity*, 2nd edn (1956). Chicago: University of Chicago Press.

Chandler, Daniel (2007) *Semiotics: the basics*, 2nd edn. London: Routledge.

Chesterman, Andrew (1991) *On definiteness*. Cambridge: Cambridge University Press.

Chierchia, Gennaro and Sally McConnell-Ginet (1990) *Meaning and grammar: an introduction to semantics*. Cambridge, MA: MIT Press.

Chomsky, Noam (1957) *Syntactic structures*. The Hague: Mouton.

Chomsky, Noam (1959) 'Review of Skinner's *Verbal behavior*.' *Language* 35, 26–58.

Chomsky, Noam (1965) *Aspects of the theory of syntax*. Cambridge, MA: MIT Press.

Chomsky, Noam (1977) *Language and responsibility*. New York: Pantheon Books.

Chomsky, Noam (1986) *Knowledge of language: its nature, origin, and use*. New York: Praeger.

Chomsky, Noam (1995) *The minimalist program*. Cambridge, MA: MIT Press.

Comrie, Bernard (1976) *Aspect*. Cambridge: Cambridge University Press.

Comrie, Bernard (1985) *Tense*. Cambridge: Cambridge University Press.

Corbett, Greville (1991) *Gender*. Cambridge: Cambridge University Press.

Coseriu, Eugenio and Horst Geckeler (1981) *Trends in structural semantics*. Tübingen: Narr.

Croft, William (2001) *Radical construction grammar*. Oxford: Oxford University Press.

Croft, William and D. Alan Cruse (2004) *Cognitive linguistics*. Cambridge: Cambridge University Press.

Cruse, D. A. (1986) *Lexical semantics*. Cambridge: Cambridge University Press.

Cruse, D. Alan (2002) 'Hyponymy and its varieties.' In Rebecca Green, Carol A. Bean and Sung Hyon Myaeng (eds), *The semantics of relationships: an interdisciplinary perspective*. London: Kluwer.

Davidson, Donald (1967) 'Truth and meaning.' *Synthese* 17, 304–323. Reprinted in Davidson (2001) and Martinich (2005).

Davidson, Donald (1968) 'On saying that.' *Synthese* 19, 130–146. Reprinted in Davidson (2001).

Davidson, Donald (1973) 'Radical interpretation.' *Dialectica* 27, 314–328. Reprinted in Davidson (2001).

Davidson, Donald (1979) 'Moods and performances.' In A. Margalit (ed.), *Meaning and use*. Dordrecht: Reidel. Reprinted in Davidson (2001).

Davidson, Donald (2001) *Inquiries into truth and interpretation*, 2nd edn. Oxford: Clarendon Press.

Davis, Stephen (ed.) (1991) *Pragmatics: a reader*. Oxford: Oxford University Press.

Devos, Filip (2003) 'Semantic vagueness and lexical polyvalence.' *Studia Linguistica* 57, 121–141.

Dixon, Robert M. W. (1982) *Where have all the adjectives gone?: and other essays in semantics and syntax*. The Hague: Mouton.

Dowty, David (1979) *Word meaning and Montague grammar*. Dordrecht: Reidel.

Dowty, David (1991) 'Thematic proto-roles and argument selection.' *Language* 67, 574–619.

Dowty, David R., Robert E. Wall and Stanley Peters (1981) *Introduction to Montague semantics*. Dordrecht: Reidel.

Evans, Gareth (1973) 'The causal theory of names.' *Aristotelian Society* suppl. vol. 47, 187–208. Reprinted in Martinich (2005).

Evans, Vyvyan and Melanie Green (2006) *Cognitive linguistics*. Edinburgh: Edinburgh University Press.

Fauconnier, Gilles (1994) *Mental spaces*. Cambridge: Cambridge University Press.

Fauconnier, Gilles (1997) *Mappings in thought and language*. Cambridge: Cambridge University Press.

Fauconnier, Gilles and Mark Turner (1998) 'Conceptual integration networks.' *Cognitive Science* 22, 133–187.

Fauconnier, Gilles and Mark Turner (2002) *The way we think*. New York: Basic Books.

Fillmore, Charles J. (1968) 'The case for case.' In Emmon Bach and Robert T. Harms (eds), *Universals in linguistic theory*. New York: Holt, Rinehart and Winston.

Fillmore, Charles J. (1977) 'Topics in lexical semantics.' In Roger Cole (ed.), *Current issues in linguistic theory*. Bloomington: Indiana University Press.

Fillmore, Charles J. (1982) 'Frame semantics.' In *Linguistics in the morning calm*. Seoul: Hanshin.

Fillmore, Charles J. (1985) 'Frames and the semantics of understanding.' *Quaderni di Semantica* 6, 222–254.

Fillmore, Charles J. (1997) *Lectures on deixis*. Stanford: CSLI. (A reprint of lectures delivered in 1971, first published in 1975 as *Santa Cruz lectures on deixis*, Bloomington: Indiana University Linguistics Club.)

Fillmore, Charles J. and Beryl T. Atkins (1992) 'Towards a frame-based organization of the lexicon: the semantics of RISK and its neighbors.' In Adrienne Lehrer and Eva Feder Kittay (eds), *Frames, fields, and contrast: new essays in semantics and lexical organization*. Hillsdale, NJ: Erlbaum.

Fillmore, Charles J., Paul Kay and Mary Catherine O'Connor (1988) 'Regularity and idiomaticity in grammatical constructions: the case of *let alone*.' *Language* 64, 501–538.

Fodor, Janet Dean, Jerry A. Fodor and Merrill F. Garrett (1975) 'The psychological unreality of semantic representations.' *Linguistic Inquiry* 6, 515–531.

Fodor, Jerry and Ernest Lepore (1992) *Holism: a shopper's guide*. Oxford: Blackwell.

Fodor, Jerry A. (1975) *The language of thought*. Hassocks, Sussex: Harvester.

Fodor, Jerry A. (1983) *The modularity of mind*. Cambridge, MA: MIT Press.

Fodor, Jerry A. (1994) *The elm and the expert: mentalese and its semantics*. Cambridge, MA: MIT Press.

Fodor, Jerry A. (1998) *Concepts: where cognitive science went wrong*. Oxford: Oxford University Press.

Fodor, Jerry A. (2000) *The mind doesn't work that way*. Cambridge, MA: MIT Press.

Fodor, Jerry A. (2008) *LOT 2: The language of thought revisited*. Oxford: Oxford University Press.

Fodor, Jerry A., M. F. Garrett, Edward C. T. Walker and Cornelia H. Parkes (1980) 'Against definitions.' *Cognition* 8, 263–367.

Frege, Gottlob (1892) *Uber Sinn und Bedeutung* (On sense and reference). Translated and reprinted in Frege (1952).

Frege, Gottlob (1952) *Philosophical writings*. Ed. P. T. Geach and Max Black. Oxford: Blackwell.

Gallese, Vittorio and George Lakoff (2005) 'The brain's concepts: the role of the sensory-motor system in reason and language.' *Cognitive Neuropsychology* 22, 455–479.

Geeraerts, Dirk (1993) 'Vagueness's puzzles, polysemy's vagaries.' *Cognitive Linguistics* 4, 223–272.

Gibbs, Raymond W. (1994) *The poetics of mind: figurative thought, language and understanding*. Cambridge: Cambridge University Press.

Givón, Talmy (1984) *Syntax: a functional-typological introduction*. Amsterdam: Benjamins.

Glucksberg, Sam (2001) *Understanding figurative language*. Oxford: Oxford University Press.

Goddard, Cliff (1998) *Semantic analysis*. Oxford: Oxford University Press.

Goldberg, Adele E. (1995) *Constructions: a construction grammar approach to argument structure*. Chicago: University of Chicago Press.

Goldberg, Adele E. and Ray Jackendoff (2004) 'The English resultative as a family of constructions.' *Language* 80, 532–568.

Gopnik, Alison and Andrew N. Meltzoff (1997) *Words, thoughts and theories*. Cambridge, MA: MIT Press.

Grady, Joe, Todd Oakley and Seana Coulson (1999) 'Blending and metaphor.' In Raymond W. Gibbs and Gerard J. Steen (eds), *Metaphor in cognitive linguistics*. Amsterdam: Benjamins.

Grice, H. P. (1975) 'Logic and conversation.' In Peter Cole and Jerry L. Morgan (eds), *Syntax and semantics, 3: speech acts*. New York: Academic. Reprinted in Martinich (2005).

Grice, H. P. (1978) 'Further notes on logic and conversation.' In P. Cole (ed.), *Syntax and semantics, 9: pragmatics*. New York: Academic.

Grimshaw, Jane (1990) *Argument structure*. Cambridge, MA: MIT Press.

Groenendijk, Jeroen and Martin Stokhof (1991) 'Dynamic predicate logic.' *Linguistics and Philosophy* 14, 39–100.

Haiman, John (1980) 'Dictionaries and encyclopedias.' *Lingua* 50, 329–357.

Haiman, John (1983) 'Iconic and economic motivation.' *Language* 59, 781–819.

Hampe, Beate (ed.) (2005) *From perception to meaning: image schemas in cognitive linguistics*. Berlin: Mouton de Gruyter.

Harris, Randy Allen (1993) *The linguistics wars*. Oxford: Oxford University Press.

Haspelmath, Martin (2006) 'Against markedness (and what to replace it with).' *Journal of Linguistics* 42, 25–70.

Hockett, Charles F. (1960) 'The origin of speech.' *Scientific American* 203, 89–96.

Hopper, Paul J. and Elizabeth Closs Traugott (2003) *Grammaticalization*. Cambridge: Cambridge University Press.

Horn, Laurence R. (2001) *A natural history of negation*, 2nd edn. Stanford: CSLI.

Hornstein, Norbert (1995) *Logical form: from GB to Minimalism*. Oxford: Blackwell.

Huang, Yan (2007) *Pragmatics*. Oxford: Oxford University Press.

Hulk, Aafke and Christine Tellier (1999) 'Conflictual agreement in Romance nominals.' In J.-Marc Authier, Barbara Bullock and Lisa Reed (eds), *Formal perspectives on Romance linguistics*. Amsterdam: Benjamins.

Jackendoff, Ray (1972) *Semantic interpretation in generative grammar*. Cambridge, MA: MIT Press.

Jackendoff, Ray (1976) 'Toward an explanatory semantic representation.' *Linguistic Inquiry* 7, 89–150.

Jackendoff, Ray (1977) *X-bar syntax*. Cambridge, MA: MIT Press.

Jackendoff, Ray (1983) *Semantics and cognition*. Cambridge, MA: MIT Press.

Jackendoff, Ray (1990) *Semantic structures*. Cambridge, MA: MIT Press.

Jackendoff, Ray (1991) 'Parts and boundaries.' In Beth Levin and Steven Pinker (eds), *Lexical and conceptual semantics*. Oxford: Blackwell.

Jackendoff, Ray (1997) *The architecture of the language faculty*. Cambridge, MA: MIT Press.

Jackendoff, Ray (2002) *Foundations of language: brain, meaning, grammar, evolution*. Oxford: Oxford University Press.

Jackendoff, Ray (2006) 'On conceptual semantics.' *Intercultural Pragmatics* 3, 353–358.

Jakobson, Roman (1965) 'Quest for the essence of language.' *Diogenes* 51, 21–37.

Johnson, Mark (1987) *The body in the mind: the bodily basis of meaning, imagination, and reason.* Chicago: University of Chicago Press.

Kamp, Hans (1981) 'A theory of truth and semantic representation.' In Jeroen Groenendijk, Theo Janssen and Martin Stokhof (eds), *Formal methods in the study of language.* Amsterdam: Mathematisch Centrum. Reprinted in Portner and Partee (2002).

Karttunen, Lauri (1974) 'Presupposition and linguistic context.' *Theoretical Linguistics* 1, 181–194. Reprinted in Davis (1991).

Katz, Jerrold J. (1972) *Semantic theory.* New York: Harper and Row.

Katz, Jerrold J. (1990) *The metaphysics of meaning.* Cambridge, MA: MIT Press.

Katz, Jerrold J. (1992) 'The new intensionalism.' *Mind* 101, 689–719.

Katz, Jerrold J. (2004) *Sense, reference, and philosophy.* New York: Oxford University Press.

Katz, Jerrold J. and Jerry A. Fodor (1963) 'The structure of a semantic theory.' *Language* 39, 170–210.

Katz, Jerrold J. and Paul M. Postal (1964) *An integrated theory of linguistic descriptions.* Cambridge, MA: MIT Press.

Kay, Paul and Charles J. Fillmore (1999) 'Grammatical constructions and linguistic generalizations: the *What's X doing Y* construction.' *Language* 75, 1–33.

Keenan, Edward L. (ed.) (1975) *Formal semantics of natural language.* Cambridge: Cambridge University Press.

Keil, Frank C. (1989) *Concepts, kinds, and cognitive development.* Cambridge, MA: MIT Press.

Kennedy, Christopher (1999) *Projecting the adjective: the syntax and semantics of gradability and comparison.* New York: Garland.

Kövecses, Zoltán (2002) *Metaphor: a practical introduction.* Oxford: Oxford University Press.

Kratzer, Angelika (1981) 'The notional category of modality.' In H. J. Eikmeyer and H. Rieser (eds), *Words, worlds, and contexts.* Berlin: Mouton de Gruyter. Reprinted in Portner and Partee (2002).

Krifka, Manfred, Francis Jeffry Pelletier, Gregory Carlson, Alice ter Meulen, Godehard Link and Gennaro Chierchia. (1995) 'Genericity: an introduction.'

In Gregory Carlson and Francis Jeffry Pelletier (eds), *The generic book*. Chicago: University of Chicago Press.

Kripke, Saul (1963) 'Semantical considerations on modal logic.' *Acta Philosophica Fennica* 16, 83–94.

Kripke, Saul (1975) 'Outline of a theory of truth.' *Journal of Philosophy* 72, 690–716.

Kripke, Saul (1979) 'A puzzle about belief.' In A. Margalit (ed.), *Meaning and use*. Dordrecht: Reidel.

Kripke, Saul (1980) *Naming and necessity*. Cambridge, MA: Harvard University Press.

Kripke, Saul (1982) *Wittgenstein on rules and private language*. Cambridge, MA: Harvard University Press.

Labov, William (1973) 'The boundaries of words and their meanings.' In Charles-James Bailey and Roger W. Shuy (eds), *New ways of analyzing variation in English*. Washington, DC: Georgetown University Press.

Lakoff, George (1971) 'On generative semantics.' In Danny D. Steinberg and Leon A. Jakobovits (eds), *Semantics: an interdisciplinary reader in philosophy, linguistics and psychology*. Cambridge: Cambridge University Press.

Lakoff, George (1987) *Women, fire and dangerous things*. Chicago: University of Chicago Press.

Lakoff, George (1993) 'The contemporary theory of metaphor.' In Andrew Ortony (ed.), *Metaphor and thought*, 2nd edn. Cambridge: Cambridge University Press.

Lakoff, George (2002) *Moral politics: how liberals and conservatives think*, 2nd edn. Chicago: University of Chicago Press.

Lakoff, George and Mark Johnson (1980) *Metaphors we live by*. Chicago: Chicago University Press. Second edition, 2003.

Lakoff, George and Mark Johnson (1999) *Philosophy in the flesh*. New York: Basic Books.

Lakoff, George and Mark Turner (1989) *More than cool reason*. Chicago: University of Chicago Press.

Lakoff, George and Rafael E. Núñez (2000) *Where mathematics comes from*. New York: Basic Books.

Landau, Sidney I. (2001) *Dictionaries: the art and craft of lexicography*, 2nd edn. Cambridge: Cambridge University Press.

Langacker, Ronald W. (1987–1991) *Foundations of cognitive grammar*, vols 1 and 2. Stanford: Stanford University Press.

Langacker, Ronald W. (2008) *Cognitive grammar: a basic introduction*. Oxford: Oxford University Press.

Leech, Geoffrey N. (2004) *Meaning and the English verb*, 3rd edn. London: Pearson Longman.

Lehrer, Adrienne (1974) *Semantic fields and lexical structure*. Amsterdam: North Holland.

Lehrer, Adrienne (1985) 'Markedness and antonymy.' *Journal of Linguistics* 21, 397–429.

Levin, Beth (1993) *English verb classes and alternations*. Chicago: University of Chicago Press.

Levinson, Stephen C. (1983) *Pragmatics*. Cambridge: Cambridge University Press.

Levinson, Stephen C. (2000) *Presumptive meanings*. Cambridge, MA: MIT Press.

Lewis, David (1969) *Convention: a philosophical study*. Cambridge, MA: Harvard University Press.

Lewis, David (1973) *Counterfactuals*. Cambridge, MA: Harvard University Press.

Lewis, David (1975a) 'Adverbs of quantification.' In Edward L. Keenan (ed.) (1975). Reprinted in Portner and Partee (2002).

Lewis, David (1975b) 'Languages and language.' In Keith Gunderson (ed.), Minnesota studies in the philosophy of science, *vol. VII*. Minneapolis: University of Minnesota Press. Reprinted in Lewis (1983) and Martinich (2005).

Lewis, David (1983–1987) *Philosophical papers*, 2 vols. New York: Oxford University Press.

Lewis, David (1986) *On the plurality of worlds*. Oxford: Basil Blackwell

Lyons, Christopher (1999) *Definiteness*. Cambridge: Cambridge University Press.

Lyons, John (1963) *Structural semantics*. Oxford: Blackwell.

Lyons, John (1977) *Semantics*, 2 vols. Cambridge: Cambridge University Press.

McCawley, James D. (1973) *Grammar and meaning*. Tokyo: Taishukan. Reprinted by Academic Press (New York), 1976.

McCawley, James D. (1981) *Everything that linguists have always wanted to know about logic but were ashamed to ask.* Oxford: Blackwell.

Margolis, Eric and Stephen Laurence (eds) (1999) *Concepts: core readings.* Cambridge, MA: MIT Press.

Martinich, A. P. (ed.) (2005) *The philosophy of language*, 5th edn. Oxford: Oxford University Press.

Mel'čuk Igor (1987) 'A formal lexicon in the meaning-text theory (or How to do lexica with words).' *Computational Linguistics* 13, 261–276.

Montague, Richard (1970a) 'English as a formal language.' In Bruno Visentini et al. (eds), *Linguaggi nella società e nella tecnica.* Milan: Edizioni di Comunità, pp. 189–224. Reprinted in Montague (1974).

Montague, Richard (1970b) 'Universal grammar.' *Theoria* 36, 373–398. Reprinted in Montague (1974).

Montague, Richard (1973) 'The proper treatment of quantification in ordinary English.' In K. J. J. Hintikka, J. M. E. Moravcsik and P. Suppes (eds), *Approaches to natural language: proceedings of the 1970 Stanford workshop on grammar and semantics.* Dordrecht: Reidel. Reprinted in Montague (1974) and Portner and Partee (2002).

Montague, Richard (1974) *Formal philosophy: selected papers of Richard Montague.* Ed. R. H. Thomason. New Haven, CT: Yale University Press.

Moravcsik, Edith (1978) 'Reduplicative constructions.' In Joseph H. Greenberg (ed.), *Universals of human language, vol. 3: word structure.* Stanford: Stanford University Press.

Murphy, Gregory L. and Douglas L. Medin (1985) 'The role of theories in conceptual coherence.' *Psychological Review* 92, 289–316.

Murphy, Gregory L. (2002) *The big book of concepts.* Cambridge, MA: MIT Press.

Murphy, M. Lynne (2003) *Semantic relations and the lexicon.* Cambridge: Cambridge University Press.

Muskens, Reinhard (1996) 'Combining Montague semantics and discourse representation.' *Linguistics and Philosophy* 19, 143–186.

Nerlich, Brigitte, Zazie Todd, Vimala Herman and David D. Clarke (eds) (2003) *Polysemy: flexible patterns of meaning in mind and language.* Berlin: Mouton de Gruyter.

Newmeyer, Frederick J. (1995) *Generative linguistics: a historical perspective.* London: Routledge.

Nunberg, Geoffrey, Ivan A. Sag and Thomas Wasow (1994) 'Idioms.' *Language* 70, 491–538.

Ogden, C. K. and I. A. Richards (1923) *The meaning of meaning*. London: Routledge & Kegan Paul.

Ortony, Andrew (ed.) (1993) *Metaphor and thought*, 2nd edn. Cambridge: Cambridge University Press.

Palmer, Frank R. (2001) *Mood and modality*, 2nd edn. Cambridge: Cambridge University Press.

Paradis, Carita (2001) 'Adjectives and boundedness.' *Cognitive Linguistics* 12, 47–65.

Partee, Barbara H. (1975) 'Montague grammar and transformational grammar.' *Linguistic Inquiry* 6, 203–300.

Peeters, Bert (ed.) (2000) *The lexicon-encyclopedia interface*. Oxford: Elsevier.

Peirce, Charles Sanders (1931–1958) *Collected writings*, 8 vols. Ed. Charles Hartshorne, Paul Weiss and Arthur W. Burks. Cambridge, MA: Harvard University Press.

Portner, Paul and Barbara H. Partee (2002) *Formal semantics: the essential readings*. Oxford: Blackwell.

Pustejovsky, James (1991) 'The syntax of event structure.' *Cognition* 41, 47–81.

Pustejovsky, James (1995) *The generative lexicon*. Cambridge, MA: MIT Press.

Putnam, Hillary (1975) 'The meaning of meaning.' In Keith Gunderson (ed.), *Minnesota studies in the philosophy of science, vol. VII*. Minneapolis: University of Minnesota Press. Reprinted in Martinich (2005).

Quine, W. V. (1951) 'Two dogmas of empiricism.' *The Philosophical Review* 60, 20–43. Reprinted in Quine (1961) and Martinich (2005).

Quine, W. V. (1961) *From a logical point of view*, 2nd edn. Cambridge, MA: Harvard University Press.

Quine, W. V. (1968) *Ontological relativity and other essays*. New York: Columbia University Press.

Quine, Willard Van Orman (1960) *Word and object*. Cambridge, MA: MIT Press.

Radden, Günter and Zoltán Kövecses (1999) 'Towards a theory of metonymy.' In Klaus-Uwe Panther and Günter Radden (eds), *Metonymy in language and thought*. Amsterdam: Benjamins.

Ravin, Yael and Claudia Leacock (eds) (2000) *Polysemy: theoretical and computational approaches*. Oxford: Oxford University Press,

Rosch, Eleanor (1973) 'On the internal structure of perceptual and semantic categories.' In Timothy E. Moore (ed.), *Cognitive development and the acquisition of language*. New York: Academic.

Rosch, Eleanor (1975) 'Cognitive representations of semantic categories.' *Journal of Experimental Psychology: General* 104, 192–233.

Rosch, Eleanor (1978) 'Principles of categorization.' In Eleanor Rosch and Barbara B. Lloyd (eds), *Cognition and categorization*. Hillsdale, NJ: Erlbaum.

Rosch, Eleanor and Carolyn B. Mervis (1975) 'Family resemblances: studies in the internal structure of categories.' *Cognitive Psychology* 7, 573–605.

Rosch, Eleanor, Carolyn B. Mervis, Wayne D. Gray, David M. Johnson and Penny Boyes-Braem (1976) 'Basic objects in natural categories.' *Cognitive Psychology* 8, 382–439.

Russell, Bertrand (1903) *The principles of mathematics.* Cambridge: Cambridge University Press.

Russell, Bertrand (1905) 'On denoting.' *Mind* 14, 479–493. Reprinted in Martinich (2005).

Russell, Bertrand (1919) *Introduction to mathematical philosophy*. London: Allen & Unwin.

Saussure, Ferdinand de (1916) *Cours de linguistique générale*. Ed. Charles Bally and Albert Sechehaye. Lausanne: Payot. English translation, *Course in general linguistics*. Trans. Roy Harris (1983). London: Duckworth.

Saussure, Ferdinand de (2002) *Écrites de linguistique générale*. Ed. Simon Bouquet and Rudolf Engler. Paris: Gallimard. English translation, *Writings in general linguistics*. Trans. Carol Sanders and Matthew Pires (2006). Oxford: Oxford University Press.

Schachter, Paul (1985) 'Part of speech systems.' In Timothy Shopen (ed.), *Language typology and syntactic description, vol. 1: clause structure*. Cambridge: Cambridge University Press.

Schank, Roger C. and Robert P. Abelson (1977) *Scripts, plans, goals and understanding*. Hillsdale, NJ: Erlbaum.

Searle, John (1978) 'Literal meaning.' In *Erkenntnis* 1, 207–224. Reprinted in John Searle (1979) *Expression and meaning: studies in the theory of speech acts*. Cambridge: Cambridge University Press.

Smith, Edward E. and Douglas L. Medin (1981) *Categories and concepts*. Cambridge, MA: Harvard University Press.

Sperber, Dan and Deidre Wilson (1995) *Relevance: communication and cognition*, 2nd edn. Oxford: Blackwell.

Stern, Gustaf (1931) *Meaning and change of meaning with special reference to the English language*. Göteborg: Elander.

Strawson, P. F. (1970) *Meaning and truth*. Oxford: Oxford University Press.

Talmy, Leonard (1985) 'Lexicalization patterns: semantic structure in lexical forms.' In Timothy Shopen (ed.), *Language typology and syntactic description, vol. 3*. Cambridge: Cambridge University Press.

Talmy, Leonard (1988a) 'Force dynamics in language and cognition.' *Cognitive Science* 12, 49–100.

Talmy, Leonard (1988b) 'The relation of grammar to cognition.' In Brygida Rudzka-Ostyn (ed.), *Topics in cognitive linguistics*. Amsterdam: Benjamins.

Talmy, Leonard (1991) 'Path to realization: a typology of event conflation.' In *Proceedings of the 17th Annual Meeting of the Berkeley Linguistics Society*. Berkeley: Berkeley Linguistics Society.

Talmy, Leonard (1996) 'The windowing of attention in language.' In Masayoshi Shibatani and Sandra Thompson (eds), *Grammatical constructions: their form and meaning*. Oxford: Oxford University Press.

Talmy, Leonard (2000) *Toward a cognitive semantics*, 2 vols. Cambridge, MA: MIT Press.

Tarski, Alfred (1944) 'The semantic conception of truth and the foundations of semantics.' *Philosophy and Phenomenological Research* 4, 341–375. Reprinted in Martinich (2005).

Taylor, John R. (2002) *Cognitive grammar*. Oxford: Oxford University Press.

Ullmann, Stephen (1957) *The principles of semantics*. Oxford: Blackwell.

Varela, Francisco J., Evan Thompson and Eleanor Rosch (1991) *The embodied mind*. Cambridge, MA: MIT Press.

Vendler, Zeno (1957) 'Verbs and times.' *Philosophical Review* 66, 143–160.

Verkuyl, H. J. (1993) *A theory of aspectuality: the interaction between temporal and atemporal structure*. Cambridge: Cambridge University Press.

Wanner, Leo (ed.) (1996) *Lexical functions in lexicography and natural language processing*. Amsterdam: Benjamins, pp. 37–102.

Whitehead, Alfred North and Bertrand Russell (1910–1913) *Principia Mathematica*, 3 vols. Cambridge: Cambridge University Press.

Wierzbicka, Anna (1969) *Dociekania semantyczne*. Warsaw: Ossolineum.

Wierzbicka, Anna (1972) *Semantic primitives*. Trans. Anna Wierzbicka and John Besemeres. Frankfurt: Athenäum.

Wierzbicka, Anna (1980) *Lingua mentalis: the semantics of natural language.* Sydney: Academic.

Wierzbicka, Anna (1984) 'Apples are not a "kind of fruit".' *American Ethnologist* 11, 313–328.

Wierzbicka, Anna (1985) 'Oats and wheat.' In John Haiman (ed.), *Iconicity in syntax.* Amsterdam: Benjamins. Reprinted in Wierzbicka 1988.

Wierzbicka, Anna (1988) *The semantics of grammar.* Amsterdam: Benjamins.

Wierzbicka, Anna (1992) *Semantics, culture and cognition: universal human concepts in culture-specific configurations.* New York: Oxford University Press.

Wierzbicka, Anna (1996) *Semantics: primes and universals.* Oxford: Oxford University Press.

Wierzbicka, Anna (1997) *Understanding cultures through their key words.* New York: Oxford University Press.

Wierzbicka, Anna (2003) *Cross-cultural pragmatics: the semantics of human interaction*, 2nd edn. Berlin: Mouton de Gruyter.

Wierzbicka, Anna (2006) *English: meaning and culture.* New York: Oxford University Press.

Wittgenstein, Ludwig (1922/1961) *Tractatus logico-philosophicus.* 1922 edition translated from the German *Logisch-philosphische abhandlung* (1921) by Charles Kay Ogden, London: Routledge & Kegan Paul. 1961 edition is a new English translation by David Francis Pears and Brian McGuinness, London: Routledge.

Wittgenstein, Ludwig (1953) *Philosophical investigations.* Trans. from the German *Philosophische untersuchungen* by G. E. M. Anscombe, ed. by G. E. M. Anscombe and Rush Rhees. Oxford: Blackwell. Second edition, 1958.

Zgusta, Ladislav (1971) *Manual of lexicography.* Prague: Academia and The Hague: Mouton.

Index

*For terms and names with multiple page references, **bold font** indicates the page where the main definition or discussion can be found.*